AN APPROACH TO WITTGENSTEIN'S PHILOSOPHY

AN APPROACH TO WITTGENSTEIN'S PHILOSOPHY

Derek Bolton

First published 1979 by
THE MACMILLAN PRESS LTD
London and Basingstoke
Associated companies in Delhi
Dublin Hong Kong Johannesburg Lagos
Melbourne New York Singapore Tokyo

Printed in Great Britain by
REDWOOD BURN LIMITED
Trowbridge & Esher

British Library Cataloguing in Publication Data

Bolton, Derek
    An approach to Wittgenstein's philosophy
    1. Wittgenstein, Ludwig
    I. Title
    192   B3376.W564

ISBN 0-333-25920-3

To My Parents

Wenn es möglich gewesen wäre, den Turm
von Babel zu erbauen ohne ihn zu erklettern,
es wäre erlaubt worden.

Franz Kafka

Contents

Preface

I .attempt in this commentary to elucidate Wittgenstein's philosophy, by examination of the text, and by use of an historical perspective. The main aim is to show that his early work, the *Tractatus Logico-Philosophicus*, marked an ending of the modern philosophical tradition, i.e. that which dates roughly from the seventeenth century; and further, that in his later work, particularly in the *Philosophical Investigations*, Wittgenstein moved away from the fundamental assumptions of that tradition, towards a philosophy more suited to the present time. This historical perspective is intended to fill a gap in Wittgenstein scholarship to date.

Wittgenstein began his working life as an engineer, but his interest soon turned to philosophy and logic, and at the age of 22, in 1911, he went to Cambridge to study under Russell. He wrote the *Tractatus* largely while on active service in the Austrian army during the First World War. In the Preface he claimed to have solved, on all essential points, the problems of philosophy. In accordance with this belief, he gave up philosophy, and turned to school-teaching, and to architecture. However, Wittgenstein came to doubt what he had earlier written, and once more took up philosophy. He returned to Cambridge in 1929, and worked there almost continuously until his death in 1951. Many works from this 'later period' have been published posthumously, the best known being the *Philosophical Investigations*. In the Preface to this work, Wittgenstein wrote that he had recognised 'grave mistakes' in his *Tractatus*. We may assume that he saw the *Investigations* as correcting those 'mistakes'. Thus Wittgenstein's philosophy falls broadly into two parts; our task is to understand each, and the relation between them.

Whatever view be taken of the relation between the early and later philosophy, it is clear that Wittgenstein's *method* altered drastically. The *Tractatus* is densely written, uses technical vocabulary, contains much apparently dogmatic assertion and generalisation, and is little clarified by examples. The opposite is so in the *Investigations*. The later work appears so different that Russell judged it to be of little philosophical interest (Russell, 5: pp. 216–17). The difficulty is to see the point of Wittgenstein's plain remarks and observations. Thus the two works present the reader with different kinds of problem: the *Tractatus* appears as a particularly difficult piece of abstract philosophy, whereas the *Investigations* is superficially easier to understand, but its philosophical import may well seem elusive.

The difference of style has led me to use different methods of commentary in each case. Concerning the *Tractatus*, I have aimed to make explicit its major doctrines and the connections between them. These doctrines are defined with the aid of a new interpretation of the *Tractatus* numbering system. This system has often been neglected by the commentators, notable exceptions being Stenius and Dietrich. In general I make no piecemeal criticisms of the *Tractatus* doctrines, believing that they are best understood, at least to begin with, as essentially part of a system, not as plausible in their own right. The system rests on certain axioms or assumptions, and it is these that are of special relevance to the main aim of this commentary.

It seems less appropriate, however, to elucidate the meaning of the *Investigations*. For what Wittgenstein meant to say in this work is generally plain; the problem is rather why he said it. Why, for example, did he describe in detail people's use of a simple language on a building site? The question arises whether there are philosophical theses here, comparable to what we are familiar with. And if there are, why are they not explicit? Why did Wittgenstein, master of philosophical theorising, abandon it in his later work? I have approached questions of this kind from an historical point of view. The significance of the *Investigations* lies largely, I suggest, in its overturning certain fundamental ideas characteristic of the modern philosophical tradition. And it is to this tradition that the assumptions of the *Tractatus* system belong.

The relation of the *Tractatus* to previous philosophy is problematic. The book was a formative influence on the logical positivism of the Vienna Circle, and was generally assumed to belong to the empiricist tradition of modern thought. However, Professor Anscombe showed that the concerns of the *Tractatus*—the nature of reference, description, truth and falsity, and so on—are not empiricist ones; they belong rather with Frege's logical philosophy, and are more akin to ancient, than to more modern, philosophy (1: pp. 12ff. and 25ff.). Correct as this assessment was, particularly as a corrective to then prevalent misinterpretations of the *Tractatus*, it does not necessarily exclude there being strong links between the work and seventeenth- and eighteenth-century philosophy. The possibility explored here is that several fundamental doctrines of the *Tractatus* are to be found in the modern tradition. For example, the spatial ontology of the *Tractatus* is closely connected to the conception of nature on which much modern philosophy was based. The question then arises why and how several traditional concepts, such as 'sense-experience', and problems, such as the problem of knowledge, have no place in the *Tractatus*. The answer to this question lies, I suggest, in the fact that *language* is now taken to be the medium of thought or representation. For although the *Tractatus* shares assumptions with previous modern philosophy, it also contains an innovation of great consequence: that the assumptions were made to produce a philosophy of language. The result was the so-called 'picture theory' of language.

In order to define the traditional views with which the *Tractatus* is to be compared and contrasted, I have chosen statements from philosophers such as Descartes, Newton and Locke. I do not attempt a 'history of ideas', nor a full account of a particular philosopher's aim or theory. My concern has been more with the assumptions of seventeenth-century philosophy and the problems they immediately generated, than with major solutions to those problems. In particular there is no detailed discussion of the connections between Wittgenstein's work of either period and the Kantian philosophy, which have been treated by, among others, Stenius, Pears and Hacker.

Part I concerns the *Tractatus*; the first chapter analyses the work, the second assesses its relation to some previous philosophy. These chapters may be read in either order. The reader unfamiliar with the *Tractatus*, but acquainted with the general problems of modern philosophy, may prefer to begin with the second chapter.

It has been increasingly realised that the *Investigations* is not, as Russell and others thought, an abandonment of philosophy. The commentaries by Kenny, Pears and Hacker, among others, have shown that Wittgenstein's later work may be compared with the *Tractatus*, and with positions familiar in the history of thought. The recognition that there is more in common between the early and later work than was previously supposed, has naturally led to the stressing of similarities, as well as of differences, between the two, particularly by Kenny. The view presented here is that the

Investigations makes a radical break from the *Tractatus*; the two works are, I suggest, as different as two works can be, which are still comparable, and written by one man.

Part I helps provide a context for describing the revolution in Wittgenstein's later work. At the beginning of the *Investigations*, Wittgenstein criticises a very general conception of language, one which has the *Tractatus* theory as a special case. The importance of this change is great; for if the *Tractatus* theory of language is rejected, so too is the whole *Tractatus* system, and with it also a major part of the modern philosophical tradition. The *Investigations* is largely (some would say entirely) critical. The objects of criticism are diverse, including some doctrines clearly identifiable with those in the *Tractatus*, but others which are not, such as dualism. The aim of the second chapter, to find what is common between the *Tractatus* and the modern tradition, thus helps to find a connection between the diverse targets of criticism in the *Investigations*, and also a coherence in the positive philosophy which stands opposed to them. The general theme in Part II, chapters 3 to 5, is the replacement of various philosophical theories, some major and some minor. The instrument of change is always the new conception of language, or what underlies it, the central importance of human activity. Comparison is made mainly with seventeenth-century thought, but not entirely. The deeper the rejection of modern assumptions becomes, it appears that the break is in fact away from Greek thought, namely Plato's. Thus in the fourth chapter there is discussion of the relativity of truth, in the light of Plato's critique in the *Theaetetus*. Also, in the third chapter, some essential points of Wittgenstein's new philosophy are compared with Einstein's physics. This comparison is of particular relevance to the aim of this commentary; for just as the *Tractatus* is closely linked to seventeenth-century natural philosophy, so Wittgenstein's later work stands close to the physics of the present time.

In order to relate Wittgenstein's later work to traditional philosophical theories, it must be presented in a like form, the form of a theory. This is not the form of Wittgenstein's writing, and consequently the commentary at times must leave the text. However, this recasting of Wittgenstein's thought serves to clarify the nature of its originality, and also the purpose of its new method.

In pursuing the aim of this commentary, it has not been necessary to touch on every aspect of Wittgenstein's work. I do not discuss his development, in the pre-*Tractatus* notes, treated for example by

Griffin, and in the so-called 'transitionary works', the *Philosophical Remarks* and the *Philosophical Grammar*, discussed by Kenny. Also omitted from discussion is the influence of Frege and Russell, examined particularly by Professor Anscombe and by Kenny. Wittgenstein's later philosophy of mathematics, though relevant to the theme of this commentary, lies outside its scope. Also of direct relevance is Wittgenstein's last work, *On Certainty*, and I hope to devote a second commentary to it.

I should like to express my gratitude to Dr S. W. Blackburn and Dr E. J. Craig, my tutors at Churchill College, Cambridge, for teaching me methods of philosophical analysis. My thanks go also to Professor G. E. M. Anscombe and Dr C. Lewy who supervised my doctoral work with patience and encouragement; and to Dr J. E. J. Altham and Dr J. Griffin who made useful criticisms as my examiners. I am also indebted to Dr P. Williams of Westfield College, University of London, for his help with the discussion of Newtonian and Relativity mechanics. The views expressed in this work do not, of course, necessarily coincide with theirs. I am grateful to my friend, Dr J. D. Adler, for many helpful suggestions in the preparation of the final version. The doctoral dissertation which formed the basis of this work was written while I was in receipt of a grant from the Department of Education and Science, and the book was completed with the aid of a generous award from the Leverhulme Trust.

Both the publishers and myself wish to thank the Literary Executors of Wittgenstein, Routledge & Kegan Paul Ltd, and Basil Blackwell, Publisher, for permission to quote from *Tractatus Logico-Philosophicus* and *Philosophical Investigations*.

London, 1978   *D. E. B.*

References and Abbreviations

Commentaries referred to in the Preface are to be found under the authors' names in the Bibliographical References. References are made in the text when possible, otherwise in the Notes. Wittgenstein's works are referred to by name, with the following abbreviations: *Notebooks* for *Notebooks 1914–16*, *Tractatus* for *Tractatus Logico-Philosophicus*, *Investigations* for *Philosophical Investigations*. References to works by other authors are made by the author's name, together with a number in brackets, and are given in full in the Bibliographical References. Several works by the same author are numbered chronologically by date of publication. References to parts of works are made following the number of the work, either in standard mode (chapter, section, etc.), or by page number to the particular edition cited in the Bibliographical References.

Part I
The Early Philosophy

1 The *Tractatus*: Main Themes

1 THE STRUCTURE OF THE *TRACTATUS*

The structure of the *Tractatus* is marked by its system of numbering; this system indicates assumptions, definitions, summaries, consequences, each of various kinds. Some grasp of the structure of the *Tractatus* is useful for several reasons. It can help the reader to avoid becoming lost in details before he has seen the general philosophical point which the details are meant to be clarifying. Secondly, what the *Tractatus* says about one subject is often significant because it has been deduced from elsewhere, rather than because of superficial plausibility, so that unless the connections between the various claims of the book are seen, those claims are likely to appear disjointed, aphoristic, and obscure. And thirdly, the structure of the *Tractatus* is important for philosophical method, because it makes clear what are the major axioms and theorems of the metaphysics, and hence where attention should be directed, should we need to reject any or all of that metaphysics.

Going by Wittgenstein's explanation of his numbering system (a footnote to the first number), it would seem that the fewer decimals a number has, the greater the logical importance of the proposition or propositions that it marks. In this case, there are seven most important propositions, numbered 1 to 7:

1. The world is all that is the case.
2. What is the case—a fact—is the existence of states of affairs.
3. A logical picture of facts is a thought.
4. A thought is a proposition with a sense.
5. A proposition is a truth-function of elementary propositions. (An elementary proposition is a truth-function of itself.)
6. The general form of a truth-function is $(\bar{p}.\bar{\xi}, N(\bar{\xi}))$. This is the general form of a proposition.

7. What we cannot speak about we must pass over in silence.

The dominant theme through these propositions is the nature of the world, and its representation in thought and language. This theme is brought to completion by proposition 6, which defines the essence of language, and by implication also the essence of the world. It can be seen that the main propositions form a progression in that the meaning of each of them, necessarily except the first, depends partly on a concept which has been introduced and defined in the previous proposition. This is clear up to proposition 6, but applies also to proposition 7. For the general form of proposition which is defined in proposition 6, comprises all that can be said, and so determines also what *cannot* be said, which is what the last proposition instructs us to pass over in silence.

The seven main propositions also form a deduction, though this has to be shown. The most important steps in the deduction from one main proposition to the next are generally marked by propositions with a single decimal place. In general, up to proposition 6, a proposition $n.1$ introduces a theme, the basis of which is proposition n, which is pursued through the remaining $n.m$'s, culminating in a definition, proposition $(n+1)$. The $n.0$'s, especially up to those of proposition 4, draw out the consequences for what has been defined in proposition n, going by what has been used in the definition; they are distinguished from the $n.m$'s in that they do not follow through to a summary in the next whole-numbered proposition. The $n.00$'s draw out consequences of proposition n of a similar kind, but less central than those in the $n.0$'s. The finer structure of the book, marked by numbers of two or more decimal places, is generally similar to the gross structure, but is still more difficult to summarise, since it varies with the particular argument in progress. As noted above, the main deduction of the *Tractatus* is complete by proposition 6, with the definition of the general propositional form. There follow five sections, relatively independent from one another, the 6.1's to the 6.5's, each devoted to something which cannot be expressed (said) in propositions, respectively: logic, mathematics, *a priori* features of natural science, value and the mystical, philosophy.

To show the location of the main themes of the *Tractatus* in its overall structure, the book may be divided into seven sections, the nth section being of the form '$n-1.1-(n.1)$', the brackets indicating that $n.1$ does not belong to the section. The advantages of this scheme (there is at least one other possible of a similar kind) is that the unique status of the first proposition is brought out, and the themes which begin at n.1, which culminate in proposition $n + 1$, and which are commented on in the $n + 1$.0's and the $n + 1$.00's, are presented as self-contained. Each of the seven sections may be given a title, as follows:

In the exposition of the *Tractatus* in this chapter, sections 2 to 5 correspond to the first five sections of the book given above, I and II being treated together in section 2. Section 9 corresponds to VI and VII. The sixth section of the chapter, on reason and necessity, concerns aspects of the 5.1's and 4.46's, drawing straightforwardly on the theory of proposition as truth-function. The seventh and eighth sections discuss the theories of knowledge and subject respectively, neither of which, significantly, have their own place in the general plan of the *Tractatus* suggested above. Where possible I have indicated in brackets following the title of a particular section or sub-section, those parts of the *Tractatus* to which what follows is meant to be relevant. Aspects of the *Tractatus* philosophy which are not raised in this chapter, or not in any detail, include particularly the relation of logic to physics (in the 6.3's), which will be a major theme in the next chapter, and also a variety of topics relating to philosophical logic, symbolic logic, mathematics, probability theory, and so forth. Most of these topics are discussed thoroughly by Professor Anscombe in her commentary (1).

2 ONTOLOGY (cf. 1–2.1)

(i) The beginning

The *Tractatus* begins with the proposition: *The world is all that is the case*. We shall see that this proposition has a unique place in the *Tractatus*, being a postulated truth that serves as an axiom for the whole philosophy. The world is what exists; it is being. The world is a totality, a fact which assumes great significance as the *Tractatus* system unfolds. It appears also later that the world is represented by propositions of language. A proposition truly or falsely represents what is the case. And the world, therefore, is all that is truly represented by propositions.

Following the first proposition is a description of the composition of the world. A later part of this description, in the 2.02's, is deduced from the premise that the world is represented by propositions. In the exposition which follows, however, I shall depart from Wittgenstein's own method by presenting some of the earlier statements about the world also as deductions from that premise.

The investigation of the nature of the world and of propositions is *a priori*, in that it does not presuppose acquaintance with the facts, nor knowledge that particular propositions are true rather than false, or false rather than true. The *a priori* study of the world and its representation by signs is called *logic*. (The term 'logic' is used in the *Tractatus* in a number of connected senses, only one of which corresponds to the definition given here. I shall keep to this definition in what follows, unless otherwise noted.)

(ii) Facts (cf. 1.1–2)

The world is not one thing. For there are many distinct propositions, whose truth-values (either true or false) are independent of one another. The world is the totality of the discrete units, called facts, which are described by each true proposition. The world is thus constituted by the facts, and by their being *all* the facts. The world is divisible into these discrete units, which are independent of one another, as distinct propositions are.

(iii) States of affairs (cf. 2)

Since a proposition can be false, a fact may not exist. It is the existence of facts which makes propositions true, and their non-existence which makes propositions false. Following customary usage, however, we do not speak of 'non-existent facts', but instead employ the concept of what may or may not exist, and which, if it does exist, is a fact. This concept is 'state of affairs'. A fact is the existence of a state of affairs.

(iv) Objects and relations (cf. 2.01)

A state of affairs is not one thing. If a state of affairs were one thing, then if it did not exist, the proposition which asserted falsely that it did exist, would bear no relation to anything in the world. But in this case, the proposition would be no *sign* at all. Because a proposition can be false, we must say that the state of affairs it represents need not exist. But because a false proposition is still meaningful, we must say that it does nevertheless bear a relation to something (existing) in the world. For within this logic, it is presupposed that signs have meaning because they are in some way correlated with the world. And so the false proposition is a source of seeming paradox. The paradox arises if we make the natural assumption that what a proposition represents in the world is the same as what it is correlated with. This assumption is what must be denied. And if the state of affairs which the proposition represents is not the same as what the proposition stands for in order to be meaningful, then it follows that a state of affairs is not one thing.

By the same argument, it cannot be two things either, nor any number of things. The general point is that a state of affairs cannot be just a matter of things. If a state of affairs were only things, then a proposition could say only that those things existed; but then, if the proposition were false, if the things did not exist, there would be nothing left for the proposition to represent, i.e. the proposition would no longer be a proposition. If a proposition stood for just two things, say, how could it be false if they did exist, and how could it be meaningful if they did not?

A proposition must be allowed to be false, without severing its ties with the (existing) world. A state of affairs may or may not exist, and yet whether it does or not must be independent of the existence of any objects involved, for these will have to exist anyway.

The concept which we require at this point is that of *combination*, or *relation*. So clear is the requirement, moreover, that the concept of relation may be defined as what satisfies it. Given the existence of a number of objects, either a certain relation exists between them, or it does not. States of affairs, therefore, are combinations of objects. We can now say: as a whole, a proposition asserts that given objects stand in a certain relation, and is true or false according as they do or do not so stand; *parts* of the proposition stand for the objects involved, and in so doing, those parts, and the proposition they make up, are meaningful. In this way, then, we can account for the fact that a false proposition makes sense.

This argument that states of affairs are combinations of objects, and that all propositions are relational, takes for granted that there are true-or-false signs (i.e. propositions), that the world they represent includes objects, and that correlation of sign with object is the origin of meaning. Given these plausible pre-suppositions, the argument proceeds.

(v) Logical space (cf. 1.13)

Relations require a space for their existence; this belongs to the definition of 'space'. Since the facts of the world are relational, they exist in a space. The precise nature of this space (or of the relations and objects in it) is not given *a priori*, but only its existence as a dimension or dimensions in which relations co-exist. This much alone is required by logic, and therefore the space may be called 'logical space'. The facts in logical space are the world.

(There are several spaces which might be plausible examples of the space whose existence is given *a priori*. They include geometrical space, 'auditory space', 'colour space' and 'time space'. On these possibilities see 2.0131 and 2.0251. Geometrical space is perhaps the most natural example, bearing in mind that there might be these other forms, and it is then natural also to think of 'objects' as massy atoms. In the next chapter I shall argue that logical space is best conceived as geometrical, for a mixture of logical and historical reasons.)

(vi) Objects are simple (cf. 2.02–2.0212)

Suppose that objects were not simple, i.e. were composed of simpler things. Then objects would themselves be states of affairs, that is to say, combinations of things. To suppose that *everything* were complex would be to suppose that states of affairs fitted inside one another in an unending series of Chinese boxes. Just because this series has no end, however, there are no objects at the end, whose configuration did produce all the complex objects; but this means that there would be no states of affairs, and no world. But there is a world, therefore there are simple objects. And it is natural to call only the simple objects 'objects', since all else is configuration of them, i.e. is the existence of states of affairs.

The logic of the argument is simple. When we argued that states of affairs are combinations of objects, it was implicit that the concept *object* is not the same as the concept *combination of objects* (i.e. it was not the concept of a complex object), for otherwise there begins an infinite regress with nothing at the end because there *is* no end. Since we need the concept 'combination of objects', or 'complex object', then we must have the concept 'simple object' too.

The argument may be expressed in terms of propositions, when it is marginally more complicated; this is the form of Wittgenstein's argument. Suppose that the objects which a proposition represents in a certain relation are complex. These complex objects can each be represented by further propositions. Thus we have in the case of propositions, what corresponds to states of affairs fitting inside one another, namely, that the original proposition about complexes can be resolved into those propositions which describe the complexes (i.e. assert their existence), plus another proposition representing the alleged relation of those complexes (cf. 2.0201). Now a regress threatens, similar to the one already noted. We cannot suppose that propositions are *infinitely* resolvable in that way; eventually we must arrive at propositions which are not about complexes, but simples. It can be put also in this way: the sense of a proposition about complexes depends on the existence of those complex objects. Or, its sense depends on the truth of each of those propositions which assert the existence of those complexes. (And its truth depends further on the truth of that single proposition about the relation of the complexes.) If the objects involved in those latter propositions are again complex, it follows that the sense of those propositions depends in turn on the truth of further sets of propositions, which assert the existence of those complexes. Thus another aspect of the regress is seen, in which the sense of every proposition would require the truth of another, which must itself have sense; and so on. If there were no end to this dependence, there would be no meaningful propositions, no true or false representations of the world. But there are; and hence there must be propositions whose meaning does not depend upon the truth of any other propositions. They are about objects, but not complex ones. So, there must be simple objects.

(vii) Objects as substance (cf. 2.02's)

Unless the material of the world existed permanently, through change, the reference and therefore the meaning of signs would be continually changing, passing in and out of existence. The meaning of a statement about the world would depend always on the truth of other statements, which said that the objects which the first was about, were (still) there. Simple objects are the substance of the world; change is all re-arrangement of them. What changes and is unstable is the configuration of objects, the facts in the world, but the objects themselves persist.

3 THOUGHT (cf. mainly 2.1–3.1)

(i) Pictures (cf. 2.1–3; also 4.0's)

We turn now to the logical status of the sign which truly or falsely represents a state of affairs. If we call this sign the 'proposition', our problem is: what is the nature of the proposition?

(A note on terminology is necessary here. The term 'proposition' as defined above corresponds to the term *Gedanke* in the *Tractatus*, which is translated as 'thought'. Wittgenstein used the word *Satz*, usually translated as 'proposition', to mean a particular kind of *Gedanke*, as we shall see in the next section. We shall see also that the difference between *Gedanke* and *Satz* is of little or no interest to logic; the essential point is that both are signs of some kind, which represent the world truly or falsely. I use the term 'proposition' in this section, rather than 'thought', only to emphasise that the problem is concerned with *signs*.)

How does a proposition represent a situation in the world? The logic which poses this problem also suggests how to answer it. The connection between signs and the world seems to be clear in the case of naming: a sign is correlated with the object which it names, and this correlation constitutes the meaning of the sign. So the first reaction to our problem would be to say that a proposition names or stands for a state of affairs. Now we are faced, however, with a whole battery of proofs that a proposition cannot be a name, proofs which draw only on commonly acknowledged features of propositions.

The first proof begins with the fact that a proposition can be false, while remaining meaningful. If a proposition is false, the state of affairs it represents does not exist, so there is nothing for it to name. So if a proposition is a name, then a false proposition, since it cannot be a name, is not a proposition and is senseless. But a false proposition is still a proposition, and it does have sense, therefore a proposition is not a name.

The assumption of this argument is the same as that used in the previous section to establish the ontological conclusion that a state of affairs could not be one thing, a conclusion which is companion to the present one that a proposition cannot be a name. And just as the earlier argument showed further that a state of affairs cannot be only a matter of things, so the present argument shows not only that a proposition cannot be a name, but also that it cannot be a mere collection of names.

The solution to the ontological problem was to invoke the concept of relation, and to conclude that a state of affairs was a combination of objects. This solution was not postulated as a possible one among others; rather, the concept of relation may be so *defined* that a relation between objects is what can exist or not, given in either case that the objects themselves do exist.

This line of thought suggests an analogous account of the proposition as being a relation holding between names. It turns out that this account is right, but the logic behind it is not fully clear yet. Particularly it has to be shown that a proposition *must* be a spatial distribution of names, that there is no other way to account for the fact that a proposition can be true or false. To see the reasons behind this account of the proposition, we must examine further arguments which show that a proposition cannot be a name, or a mere jumble of names. These arguments draw on features of propositions other than that they are meaningful when false.

One feature of propositions, we assume, is that they can be understood before their meaning has been explained. Or: we can understand *new* propositions. But this means that we can know what state of affairs a proposition represents without knowing any arbitrary correlation between the two. Consequently, insofar as naming is an arbitrary correlation, a proposition does not name its state of affairs.

Suppose that a proposition consists solely of names, say, of objects and relations. Then what does the collection of names *say*? How does it say, for example, that the objects named stand in the relation named? How can it manage without what might be called the 'propositional bond'? I think no answer can be given; we could at

best ignore the issue, saying something like: 'they are just understood to be making that assertion'. There are reasons, however, why
the problem cannot be dismissed like that, reasons highlighted by
the next argument.

The relation of naming, as it is understood here, is a conventional
relation: a sign is correlated with something, and the correlation has
nothing to do with the nature of the sign or of the object. But then if
all the meaningful features of a proposition were names, it would be
a matter of convention whether the proposition represented
anything or not. Whether a proposition represents anything or not,
however, is the issue of its truth or falsity. Thus, if a proposition were
only a collection of names, its truth or falsity would be a matter of
convention, that is, dependent only on ourselves, independent of the
signs and, in particular, independent of the states of affairs. But this
consequence contradicts the axiom of the metaphysics being here
explored: it is *the world* which settles the issue of truth or falsity, so it is
not us and our conventions.

And the criticism can be made still stronger, for it is not clear how
there could be any distinction at all between truth and falsity of
propositions, any more than there is between right and wrong
names of things, assuming that names are only arbitrarily related to
their objects.

An attempt to avoid the argument would look like this: 'Certainly
we arbitrarily determine what the constituents of the proposition
represent, such as objects and a relation; but whether the objects
stand in that relation or not, is not dependent on those arbitrary
correlations, but upon how things stand in the world'. And that is
right; but *that* the objects do stand in the relation named is precisely
what the proposition does *not* say, if it consists only of names. That
was the objection just made.

The concept of naming, the arbitrary correlation of signs with the
world, cannot explain how the world is represented by propositions.
The propositional sign cannot be meaningful because it has been
arbitrarily assigned to a state of affairs: because there may be no
state of affairs, if the proposition is false; because the proposition
might be unfamiliar and therefore could not have been so
correlated; and finally, because whether or not the proposition does
represent an (existing) state of affairs depends on the world, not on
arbitrary determinations.

Most philosophers seem to have stopped at this point, con-
founded by the arguments. The arguments have even been resisted.

For example, it may be denied that a false proposition (or description) corresponds to nothing, so that even non-being in some sense is, and falsity is in some sense truth; or again, it may be denied that truth is any more than a convention of language.

The only way to avoid these difficulties and to give a proper account of the proposition is to acknowledge a means of representation which is, at least in part, *unconventional*. And this solution leads towards the picture theory of the proposition, for the only non-conventional relation possible between proposition and state of affairs is an *identity*. That is to say, the proposition must reproduce the state of affairs it represents; this is what 're-presenting' amounts to.

So we can explain immediately why truth is not arbitrary, since whether the world is or is not as the proposition shows, depends upon the world. Also it becomes clear how we can understand a new proposition, for we can see what it means just by looking at it.

Consideration of the false proposition shows that a proposition cannot be only names. By similar reasoning, a state of affairs cannot be just a matter of objects. Therefore what is reproduced in the proposition is not simply objects, but also their combination into a state of affairs, and the proposition cannot be simply names of objects, but must also reproduce a relation. Thus a proposition is a combination of names. The proposition must contain a relation as well as names, for in this way alone the meaning of the proposition, ensured by correlation between its names and objects, is independent of whether the proposition as a whole represents anything existing.

In the picture-proposition, elements of the picture represent objects. The relation in the picture does not reproduce the relation of those objects in the sense that it copies that relation, for then there would be only pictures of what is in fact the case, and no proposition would be false. Rather, the relation of elements of the picture (whatever it may be) shows that the objects named stand in the *same* relation. The picture-proposition represents a possible situation in logical space, that is, a possible relation of objects. That this relation is possible in logical space is shown by its existence in the picture itself. The representation is the sense of the proposition. The proposition is true if the objects represented stand as shown in the picture, and it is false if they do not. The true-false sign is a picture; this may be deduced using only acknowledged features of that sign.[1]

(ii) Form (cf. 2.01–2.04, 2.1–2.2, also 3.315)

The foregoing arguments, which lead to the picture theory of the proposition, lead also to the closely connected doctrines of *form* in the *Tractatus*.

We take up the argument at the negative conclusion that the representation by a proposition is not wholly conventional. This result can be expressed in two ways: that the method of representation must be *logical* (given *a priori*), and in that sense not conventional; and that the method is *natural*, and in that sense not conventional. That these two ways of denying arbitrariness come to the same, finds expression in the *Tractatus* doctrine of the identity of logical form and the form of reality. The subsequent positive conclusion that the relation between proposition and state of affairs, insofar as it is representational, must be that of identity, is expressed in turn by the doctrine that pictorial form is the same as the form of reality. Let us consider these doctrines of form in more detail.

If we subtract from a proposition all the elements which represent the world in a conventional way, there must be, by the arguments above, something left. Its existence is given *a priori*, ensured by the existence of a proposition with a sense, independent of whether the proposition is true, and so independent of whether it is known to be true. It is called the *logical form* of the proposition. The logical form of a proposition is what is essential to its representation of reality, whether true or false.

A state of affairs is a combination of objects. We call the relation which combines objects into a state of affairs the *structure* of the state of affairs. The *form* of a state of affairs is the possibility of its structure. The form of a state of affairs is one form of reality. The *form of reality* is the ways in which objects can be combined into states of affairs.

The form of reality is in objects; objects constitute the form. The possibility of objects occurring in states of affairs is written into them from the beginning; it is given *a priori*. It is essential to objects that they can enter into relations with one another. This possibility is the condition of their representation, hence they cannot be thought devoid of that possibility.

The form of an object is the possibility of its being in relations with other objects. The form of an object depends upon the space it is in. Space, time, and colour (being coloured) are forms of objects. Logical space contains all objects, and all the possibilities of their relations. The possibility of all relations in logical space is the form of reality.

The possible relations in logical space are given *a priori*, independent of whether they do in fact hold between particular objects or not, solely by the existence of propositions with sense. For a proposition represents a state of affairs, that is, a possible combination of objects, and that possible combination is given with the meaningful proposition, no matter whether it is true or false. Thus the form of reality is given with meaningful propositions. But what alone is essential to a meaningful proposition is its logical form. To a logical form corresponds a form of reality, and logical form in general is identical with the form of reality.

That is the result which follows from the negative point that the representing done by a proposition is non-arbitrary. The non-arbitrary *logical* feature of a proposition must be identical with a *natural*, non-arbitrary, feature of the objects represented, i.e. a form of those objects. The further point, leading to the picture theory, is that the non-arbitrary relation between proposition and state of affairs is an identity. And this may be expressed as follows: the non-arbitrary feature of a proposition, its logical form, *is* the relation represented in the proposition.

But that is not exactly right: the logical form of a proposition is not just a relation, for it is not just the relation in a proposition which is essential to its representation of a state of affairs. What is essential is that the objects named can stand in the relation shown. It is this possibility which is the logical form of the proposition; this is what is identical to the form of the objects represented. This possibility is *shown by* the relation in the proposition itself. That the elements in a proposition stand in a given relation shows that that relation is a possible one in logical space. The proposition shows the existence of a logical form, and at the same time, the existence of a form of reality.

We call the determinate way in which the elements of a picture are related, the *structure* of the picture. A picture shares its structure with a possible state of affairs, which may or may not exist. That is why it has sense. This may be expressed alternatively by saying that a picture shares something with the objects which it represents, namely, the possibility of having the structure shown in the picture. This possibility is called the *pictorial form* of the picture. The form of a picture depends upon the form of its elements, and that in turn upon the space they are in. All pictorial form, of whatever kind, is

logical form. For this is what any picture must have in common with
reality in order to be able to represent it, correctly or incorrectly.
Pictures whose pictorial form is logical form (which is all pictures)
are called *logical pictures*. Logical pictures, and only logical pictures,
can represent the world, truly or falsely. Thus the nature of the true-
false sign, which we have been calling the proposition, is now clear:
it is a logical picture of facts.

4 LANGUAGE (cf. 3.1–4.1)

(i) Proposition (cf. 3.1's and 4.00's)

Logical pictures represent facts. In the *Tractatus* these pictures are
called 'thoughts' (*Gedanken*). That thought is a logical picture is all
that logic, the *a priori* study of the world and its representation, has
to say about it. Logic is not concerned, for example, with the nature
of the elements employed in thinking. They are themselves part of
the world, objects and complexes of objects, but logic can deduce
nothing more about them.

Nevertheless, there are distinctions which may be made *a
posteriori*; in particular, we may distinguish between thoughts which
are expressed in signs which are perceptible to the senses, and
thoughts which are expressed by non-perceptible signs (e.g. in the
mind). The former Wittgenstein calls 'propositions' (*Sätze*).

(In the remainder of this section I follow Wittgenstein's own
terminology, using 'thought' for the generic concept of what
represents a state of affairs, which was investigated in the last
section, and 'proposition' for those thoughts which find expression
that can be perceived by the senses.)

The actual configuration of perceptible signs is called a 'propositional sign'. When a propositional sign is used as a picture of a
possible situation, i.e. when its signs are correlated with objects, it is
thereby a proposition, and so also a thought.

The totality of propositions is language. Language is thought
expressed in perceptible signs.

(ii) The proposition as class (cf. 3.3's)

Logic is not concerned with the particular perceptible signs (e.g.
written or spoken words) which are used to express propositions.

The signs used are arbitrary, and their nature is not essential to the expression of sense. What is essential is the structure of the signs, which exhibits a logical form.

Thus two propositions may have the same sense, i.e. represent the same situation, even though the signs they contain are different. Two propositions with the same sense must have something in common, namely, what each individually must have in order to express that sense, namely, a particular logical form, shown by a particular structure. The signs which mark out this structure can be different, but the structure and the logical form it exhibits must be the same.

So we can say that what is essential to a proposition is what it shares with all other propositions which have the same sense. What is common to such a class of propositions is a particular structure and form. There would be some point in calling this common element the 'real proposition', since it is what expresses sense independently of any arbitrary means of representation. But this would be incorrect, because the so-called real proposition is not yet a proposition at all, for it does not name any objects, and therefore it represents no state of affairs, and has no sense. Sense is expressed when the blanks of the structure are filled in with names of objects. In this way the means of representation does become partly conventional, precisely because we are introducing *signs*. Depending upon the signs employed, we obtain a whole class of propositions, each with the same sense.

Wittgenstein calls any part of a proposition which characterises its sense, a *symbol*. Then some of the results above may be expressed as follows:

A symbol marks a structure (a content) and a form. A symbol is the common characteristic mark of a class of propositions.

A symbol has meaning (expresses a sense) only in a proposition. It presupposes the forms of all the propositions in which it can occur.

A symbol is presented by a variable (called a propositional variable) which is obtained from a proposition by replacing its arbitrary signs by variables. This variable shows what is essential to the proposition. Alternatively, the symbol may be located by its association with that class of propositions which contain the symbol; and this is the class of propositions which are values of the propositional variable.

These two presentations of a symbol in fact come to the same thing, since a propositional variable may be defined as the class of its values. This definition is not simply economy, for it expresses the priority mentioned above of the proposition over the bare content and form of a proposition, represented by a propositional variable. The values of the variable (the associated class of propositions) are arbitrarily stipulated; the nature of the signs chosen as names does not matter, and is independent of what they are chosen to signify.

A name has a symbolic feature, namely, what it contributes to a proposition's expression of sense. What it contributes is its occurrence in a proposition (with a sense). The ability to occur in a proposition is the only essential feature of a name; its nature does not matter. So the symbolic feature of a name is contained in the symbol of the proposition as a whole. The symbolic feature of a name is presented by a variable. A variable name is contained in a propositional variable. This dependence can be expressed by construing a variable name as itself a propositional variable, i.e. as a propositional variable with one vacant place.

(iii) Analysis (cf. 3.2's and 4.00's)

It is natural to suppose that thinking is a matter of picturing the world; many philosophers and psychologists have held such an opinion in more or less related forms. But it seems most perverse to claim that sentences of language are pictures. Sentences do not, in the great majority of cases, exhibit the relations they are used to represent. Nevertheless, as we have seen, there are proofs that any signs capable of representing the world truly or falsely *must* be logical pictures, that is, they must be like what they represent. Thus there is a tension between what has been proved *a priori* and what we find in ordinary language. And in the *Tractatus* Wittgenstein used the notion of 'analysis' to resolve this tension.

By the arguments of the two preceding sections, it must be at least possible that there be sentences which are pictures of the situations they are used to represent. Anticipating what has to be said in what follows, let us call such sentences 'fully analysed'. These alone are the sentences which the theory demands: the propositional sign corresponds exactly to the thought expressed, in that it contains one sign for each object in the situation, and these are arranged as the objects are in the postulated state of affairs. If the signs of a fully analysed sentence are correlated with objects, then the sentence is a proposition, and a thought.

But ordinary sentences are not like these fully analysed ones. The words in them do not stand for simple things, but for complex ones, and secondly, the signs in them are not arranged in the variety of relations they may be used to represent, but in uniform, two-dimensional script. Let us consider each of these points in turn.

It seems that ordinary words stand for or name complex objects. But insofar as the sentences in which the words occur are meaningful even if the complex objects represented do not exist, the words cannot be functioning as names, for a name has meaning only in correlation with an existing object. Rather we should say that ordinary words in general *describe* complexes; and, in this case, their function is not incompatible with the theory. We have already seen (2, vi above) how complexes are represented in propositions. A proposition about complexes is equivalent to a number of propositions which describe and assert the existence of those complexes, plus a proposition which gives the alleged relation between them.

For example, the proposition 'The broom is in the corner' is equivalent to the conjunction 'There is a brush. There is a broomstick. The brush is attached to the broomstick, and both are in the corner.' This kind of analysis seems to be justified by the use and meaning of ordinary language, as well as being required by the theory, for it alone explains how the sense of the original proposition can survive the destruction of the complex object, the broom, for example if the handle breaks off. For in this case the first two conjuncts in the analysis are meaningful and true, while the last is meaningful though false, false because one of the relations ascribed to the parts of the complex does not hold.[2]

The analysis would continue until there is no apparent reference to a complex object, but only a description of a complex, i.e. of an arrangement of simple objects. Thus we would eventually reach the general proposition: 'There are objects structured in a broom-like way, and they are in the corner'.

This general proposition contains no names of objects, but signifies a structure and consequently a form. The proposition thus leaves something undetermined, namely, which particular simple objects are in question. So it is that in ordinary language we speak about complex objects without having any idea of what objects we are referring to, and in that sense, with no idea what our words mean. But of course there is the possibility that the blanks in the general proposition can be filled in, thereby making the proposition particular, with determinate sense, i.e. with reference. The requirement that names of simple objects be possible is the requirement that sense be determinate. (There are two equivalent ways of making the general proposition particular: we put in names, or we put in variables, then specifying which value each variable takes.)

There remains the problem, however, how propositions exhibit structure and logical form. The phrase 'broom-like' cannot serve this purpose, nor can any other words for structures and relations from ordinary language. In the complete analysis of a sentence which describes a complex, there must be an actual structure, for this alone can represent a combination of objects. Therefore a single word for a complex must be an abbreviation of the real symbol, which is a picture of the complex. This abbreviation can be expressed in a definition. (We might think, for example, of how we learn the meaning of the word 'broom': we associate with it a particular shape.)

Fully analysed sentences make apparent the sense of ordinary sentences, they correspond to the thought expressed, by actually picturing a state of affairs. Ordinary sentences are abbreviations of fully analysed ones; instead of marking out a structure by names, we write a single word for its general description, and this word usually functions grammatically, and misleadingly, as a name.

But the paradox was: how can what is not a picture represent a state of affairs, if this can be done only by picturing? The answer must be that sentences of ordinary language cannot be *directly* projected onto the world, but only indirectly, via what they abbreviate. It is only what an ordinary sentence is short for which can directly represent a situation, just because it is a picture. Thus we are led to say that in using ordinary sentences we must be employing proper pictures, in accord with the definitions of the words they contain. So it is as was demanded *a priori*; to have a thought *is* to project a picture onto the world. To understand (or mean) an abbreviated sentence we must think its sense, that is, think the situation which it represents, i.e. make a picture of it. The conventions for unwrapping all of the required definitions would be enormously complicated. These conventions disguise thought.

The pictures which are used in thinking the sense of ordinary sentences of language are not found in language itself. There are no fully analysed sentences; Wittgenstein could produce no examples of them. We must infer, then, that the pictorial signs exist in *non-perceptible* thought. Thus all thinking, meaning and understanding takes place in the mind, rather than in speech, or on paper, because language itself does not provide the right materials, namely pictures. But this fact does not belong to logic; in principle thinking could equally well employ perceptible signs arranged into pictures.

5 TRUTH-FUNCTIONS (cf. 4.1–5.1)

A state of affairs can either exist or not exist. A proposition can either assert that a state of affairs exists, or it can assert that it does not exist. That is to say, a picture-proposition can be taken to show how things do *not* stand. In this case, the proposition is called *negative*. A negative proposition is true if the situation represented does not exist, and is false if it does. In specifying the conditions under which a negative proposition is true (and consequently, by exclusion, specifying the conditions under which it is false) we are thereby specifying its *sense*. The sense of a straightforward positive pro-position is given by that condition of reality which, if it existed, would make the proposition true. And now this conception of meaning in terms of truth-conditions carries over and is applied as well to negative propositions.

The focal point of the current section is this: we can express the truth-conditions of a negative proposition not by direct reference to the existence or non-existence of states of affairs, but by indirect reference to them, via the conditions of truth and falsity of the corresponding positive proposition. This latter can be used, as it were, as a base from which to define the negative proposition.

Let us call the simplest kind of proposition, that which asserts the existence of a state of affairs, an 'elementary proposition'. Its sense is given by a possible condition of reality, which is the truth-condition of the proposition. The sense of the negation of an elementary proposition may be defined in terms of (the sense of) the elementary proposition. We do this by giving its truth-conditions in terms of those of the elementary proposition.

In this way, (the sense of) the negative proposition is a function of (the sense of) the corresponding elementary proposition. A *function* takes an object (or set of objects) as *argument* and locates a unique object as the *value* of the function for that argument. (For example, addition is an arithmetical function taking two arguments, it gives 6 as the value for arguments 2 and 4, and so on.) The value of a function for a given argument is said to be a *function of* that argument. (For example, 6 is a function of 2 and 4, since there exists a function which yields 6 as the value for arguments 2 and 4.)

A negative proposition is a function of an elementary proposition, since there exists a function, negation, which yields the negative proposition as value, given the elementary one as argument. Negation is a propositional function, since its arguments and values are propositions. But since the truth-value of the value of the function is always determined solely by the truth-values of the arguments, it is also called a *truth-function*. A negative proposition is a truth-function of the corresponding elementary proposition: it is the proposition which is true when the elementary proposition is false, and which is false when the elementary proposition is true.

There are only two truth-functions of a single elementary proposition, namely itself, yielded by the vacuous function, and its negation. Given two elementary propositions, we can form compounds, such as their conjunction, disjunction, etc. For example, the conjunction of two elementary propositions is the proposition which is true when both of the elementary propositions are true, and which is false otherwise.

For two elementary propositions, there are $2^2 = 4$ different ways in which they can be true or false together; namely, both true, both false, the first true and the second false, and vice versa. Let one of these pairs be argument to a function, then there are two possibilities, true and false, for the value of the function. Thus there is a total of $2^4 = 16$ different sets of four truth-values which may belong to the values of functions of the two elementary propositions. That is to say there are sixteen distinct truth-functions of two elementary propositions.

All sixteen, however, are definable using only negation and conjunction (e.g. 'p or q' = *df* it is not the case that both not-p and not-q). This simple inter-definability is a reminder that all propositions represent the existence and non-existence of states of affairs. This is the essential feature of propositions, and truth-function theory is only a corollary to it. The theory expresses in a clear and advantageous way that elementary propositions may be negated and conjoined.

Truth-function theory allows the sense of compound propositions to be defined in terms of the truth-conditions of elementary propositions, instead of by direct reference to their truth-conditions in reality. But it should be noted that this definition of the sense of compound propositions is philosophically valuable only because it is supported by a precise account of the meaning and truth of elementary propositions, in terms of their relation to reality. The concept of truth-function has a central role in the theory of meaning if meaning is given by conditions of truth. But this conception of meaning requires primarily and essentially an account of *how* an elementary proposition represents the situation in reality which is its truth-condition. And as we have seen, there are convincing proofs that only one such account is possible: the proposition must be a logical picture of a state of affairs.

6 REASON AND NECESSITY

(i) Deductive reasoning (cf. 5.11–5.15)

Our faculty of reason enables us to infer one truth from another, so extending knowledge. If one proposition permits reasonable inference to another, therefore, the truth of the former must in some way guarantee the truth of the latter. Such a guarantee is expected from reason; it belongs to the definition of the concept.

Let us consider, then, how one proposition can guarantee the truth of another. A clear case would be if they are the very same proposition. Suppose the premise of an inference already asserts the conclusion, and perhaps more as well; then it is impossible for the conclusion to be false if the premise is true. Thus the premise guarantees the conclusion, and so is a reason for it. Where such a guarantee exists, resting ultimately on identity, we say that the one proposition can be *deduced* from the other.

This concept of deductive reasoning arises from a particular concept of propositions. We need the idea that propositions (or whatever the smallest units of meaning are) are at first simple and discrete units, which can then be compounded; for then it makes sense to say that one proposition, namely a complex one, *contains* another, namely one more simple. The simplest case would be: 'p' can be deduced from 'p and q'.

But this simple case can be expanded considerably by truth-function theory. Two elementary propositions can not only be conjoined, they can be combined in fifteen other ways to form compound propositions, and various deductive relations hold between these compounds, and between them and the two elementary propositions. The principle is that one proposition can be deduced from another if whatever makes the premise true makes the conclusion true as well. And 'whatever' means here: whatever be the truth-values, true or false, of the two elementary propositions concerned.

Deducibility rests on 'partial identity', on the containment of the conclusion in the premise. But this is not confined to the simple case: 'p' is deducible from 'p and q'. If deducibility is mutual between two propositions, the propositions are identical. No elementary proposition can be deduced from another, for it is essentially the complexity of distinct propositions which is responsible for their logical relations.

(ii) Induction and cause (cf. 5.13's and 6.37's)

Reason must guarantee the truth of propositions, and a clear case of such a guarantee is found in the deductive relation. It can be seen that deductive reasoning does not in fact extend knowledge, for we can only reason to what we knew already, since the conclusion of the inference is already contained in the premise. This is so in a perfectly precise sense: proposition 'q' is deducible from proposition 'p' if the truth-conditions of 'q' are contained in the truth-conditions of 'p' , and this means that 'q' is contained in 'p', since propositions are identified by their truth-conditions.

Reasoning will lead to new knowledge only if we can reason from the truth of one proposition to the truth of another, distinct proposition. In this case, the conclusion asserts more than the premise. But the problem arises whether there can be in this case any guarantee of the truth of the conclusion by the truth of the premise. One thing is clear, that *a priori* consideration of the sense of the propositions reveals no connection between their truth, as it would if a deductive relation held between them. Nevertheless, this does not yet mean that no guarantee is possible, for what has to be ensured is the *truth* of the conclusion by that of the premise, and this might not involve only the meaning of the two propositions.

The truth of a proposition resides in the existence of the state of affairs that it represents. The general problem is therefore: how can the existence of one state of affairs ensure the existence of another? Now if one state of affairs contains another, the guarantee is manifest, and is so simply from the nature of the propositions which represent them. But if the states of affairs are distinct, the guarantee cannot be so simple, but must arise in some way, if it exists at all, from the states of affairs themselves, i.e. from the nature of the world.

The idea would be that the existence of one state of affairs guaranteed the existence of another, distinct state of affairs, so that the truth of the proposition which represented the first state of affairs would, in a corresponding sense, guarantee the truth of the proposition which represented the second. In this case, the ontological necessity is called *causal connection* or *causal necessity*, and the method of inference which it justifies is called *induction*.

Are there, then, any causal connections which justify inductive inferences? So far as logic is concerned, no. For logic investigates the world and propositions *a priori*, and nothing revealed by this investigation suggests that the connection between distinct states of affairs is anything but an accident. Consequently the coincidental truth of any two distinct propositions can only be accidental, and there are no valid inductive inferences, but only guesses, which may turn out right or wrong. A logician will give short shrift to the causal nexus, and to the inferences it is meant to justify. So it is in the *Tractatus*.

But that dismissal might be too fast, even though correct in the end. For it is open to the following legitimate objection: why cannot a causal nexus be discovered, and induction justified, *a posteriori*? When we said that reasons must guarantee truth we did not *mean* 'guarantee *a priori*'. Under this interpretation, deduction surely would be the only valid mode of inference. Rather the nature of the guarantee was left open. Deductive connection is certainly a clear *case* of what we had in mind, but it is not the only one by definition; there remains the possibility of valid inductive inference justified by acquaintance with the facts of the world.

But although induction is not ruled out in one step, it seems to be in a few more. Because a reason must ensure the truth of what is inferred, if what is inferred turns out false, any alleged reason for it cannot in fact have been a reason. Therefore the claim that inductive inferences are reasonable presupposes that their conclusions are true. But what is the basis of this presupposition? If the conclusions are not already known to be true, and if they are there is no need to use induction, then the claim that they are true must rest on inductive procedures. But then induction is being used to establish truths which alone can show that induction is rational. Consequently any attempt to demonstrate the rationality of induction must run in a circle.[3]

(iii) Tautology (cf. 4.46's)

Among the total number of truth-functions of a given class of propositions, there are two extreme cases of propositions which have the same truth-value, true or false, no matter what truth-values be assigned to the constituent propositions. The compound proposition which is always true is called a *tautology*, and the one which is always false is called a *contradiction*. For example, 'either p or not-p' is a tautology; 'p and not-p' is a contradiction.

The tautologies are the logically necessary truths. Their truth is given *a priori*, and hence to logic. The concept of tautology may be seen as making precise sense of two traditional definitions of logical, or more generally, of necessary truth. According to one, a necessary truth is a proposition whose denial is self-contradictory; according to the other, a necessary truth is a proposition true not just in the actual world, but in all possible worlds. For if a tautology is denied, it is necessary to suppose that some one of its constituent propositions is both true and not true. And for the second definition, we may say that a 'possible world' is defined by a possible distribution of truth-values to the constituents in a compound proposition. A tautology, then, is true in *all* possible worlds.

7 THEORY OF KNOWLEDGE

From the assumption that the world is represented by propositions, we have deduced that each proposition pictures a state of affairs, i.e. a combination of objects. A proposition is true if what it represents does exist, and is false if it does not. In order to tell whether a proposition (or a thought) is true or false, we must compare it with reality (see 2.223 and 4.05).

With the expression, 'in order to tell whether a proposition is true or false', we introduce the concept of *knowledge*, knowledge of the way things are in the world, knowledge of the truth or falsity of propositions. It is clear that knowledge is a form of *acquaintance* (German *kennen*, cf. 3.263, 4.021).

The world is known by direct acquaintance. The word 'direct' here is really superfluous; it is sometimes included (for reasons to be discussed in the next chapter) to contrast this knowledge with knowledge which is inferential. According to logic, however, no knowledge is inferential, it all comes by acquaintance. For there are only two kinds of inference, deduction and induction. Deductive inference cannot afford us knowledge which we did not have already, simply because the conclusion of a deductive inference is already contained in the premise (in a precise sense, resting on the criterion of identity of propositions). All other inferences, the inductive kind, would afford us new knowledge were they valid, but it seems they are not. And, even if they were, the ultimate test of knowledge of a proposition could never be simply that it was the conclusion of an inductive inference; since the truth of the proposition would still reside in its correspondence with the facts, and this must be discovered independently and directly, i.e. by acquaintance.

The *Tractatus* contains no detailed discussion of the nature of acquaintance, no discussion, for example, of how much it may be visual. This is because there is no *a priori* information about acquaintance other than the simple fact that it does provide knowledge. Here, as elsewhere, nothing is included in the *Tractatus* as part of the fundamental metaphysics, which does not fall within the province of logic. The position here is analogous with that of objects and their relations in logic space; logic cannot define and investigate them *a posteriori*, this is rather the task of the natural sciences, in particular physics. So it is with 'acquaintance'; further investigation belongs to psychology, not to logic (cf. 4.1121).

But although the *Tractatus* contains no detailed epistemology (and that for legitimate reasons), there still is a theory of knowledge in its metaphysics. What is to be known, the world, is a given status, complete in itself. The act of knowing does not affect what is known; indeed, the word 'act' is inappropriate. Thus knowledge of the world, its objects and relations, must be passive observation or acquaintance.

One explanation, then, of the notable absence of detailed epistemology in the *Tractatus* is the purity of its logical, *a priori* method. Another feature of the book's treatment of knowledge, again a negative one, is the absence of any concern with the great 'problem of knowledge' which has occupied western philosophy since Descartes. This is the problem whether we *can* know whether propositions, particularly those about the external world, are true or false. This problem is not raised in the *Tractatus*; it is simply announced *a priori* that we do have knowledge of the world, by acquaintance. This suggests that either Wittgenstein was not aware of the problem, or that he had an *a priori* solution to it. It is this latter possibility which turns out to be right. But we cannot see what becomes of the problem of knowledge in the *Tractatus* until we examine the way the problem arose in the first place. Such an examination involves detailed study of the origins of modern philosophy, and will be attempted in the next chapter.

8 SUBJECT (cf. mainly the 5.6's)

(i) Mind and body

We have investigated *a priori* the nature of the world, thought, language and knowledge, and we turn now to the nature of the *subject*. The subject whose nature is given *a priori* may be called the 'metaphysical subject' or 'metaphysical self' (usually abbreviated in what follows to simply 'subject' or 'self'). This subject alone is what is given to logic, and is of interest to metaphysics. The concept of subject which belongs to logic must be distinguished from any other notion of subject which may arise, for whatever reason, *a posteriori*.

With that understanding, we can already say what the metaphysical subject is *not*. It is not the human body; for the human body is part of the world, an object among others, which interacts with other objects, and which may be transformed into another complex thing. The human body has no special place in ontology; it no more characterises the metaphysical subject than does any other object in the world. But further, nor can the subject be identified with the human mind, with its psychological processes of feeling, belief, sensation, and so on. For the mind is also more of the world, simply part of what is the case. Certainly the mind is not part of the physical world, its nature is mental and is studied by psychology, not by physics. However, so far as logic is concerned, mental and physical are alike, both being facts in logical space.

Behind this thought that the metaphysical subject is neither the human body nor the human mind is a uniformity in the ontology of the *Tractatus*; there are no divisions in the world, no different categories of being. There is one world, the totality of facts in logical space. Consequently no part of the world, for example mind or body, can be singled out *a priori* as having the special status of belonging to the metaphysical subject. The uniformity established in the first few sentences of the *Tractatus* cannot now be undone. This ontological uniformity is fundamental to logic, re-appearing also as corresponding uniformities in the theories of thought, of language, and of knowledge.

It is a thought familiar from modern science and philosophy that the human body has no special place in nature, and does not belong to the subject (or ego). However, there were originally reasons, to be discussed in the next chapter, for assigning to the mind a special role in relation to the subject, and we are therefore accustomed to thinking of the subject as being at least a mind. But those reasons no longer apply in the *Tractatus* metaphysics, and we are led to the unfamiliar conclusion that the mind too has no special place in the world, and does not characterise the self. Wittgenstein wrote in his *Notebooks*, p. 82:

> The philosophical I is not the human being, not the human body or the human soul with the psychological properties, but the metaphysical subject, the boundary (not a part) of the world. The human body, however, *my* body in particular, is a part of the world among others, among animals, plants, stones etc., etc.
>
> (cf. *Tractatus*, 5.641)

We shall consider later how Wittgenstein is led to say that the subject is the *boundary* of the world (iv below), but first the essential point to note is that the subject does not belong *in* the world: the subject is not related to the world as part to whole. This conclusion is extremely important, and it follows from the foundations of the *Tractatus* metaphysics. The ontology, theory of judgement and epistemology each in turn are flat and uniform, and therefore do not allow for one part of the world to be distinguished from the rest as being or belonging to the self.

So then, what and where is the metaphysical subject? If the subject cannot be defined as part of the world, then it seems that it can only be something *outside*, and related to, the world. Logic seems to suggest that the subject is acquainted with the world, and also represents the world in thought and language. But let us examine exactly what logic has to say about the thinking and knowing subject.

(ii) Thinking (cf. 4.06's, 5.54's, 5.631)

The subject may be identified in metaphysics as that which thinks and knows, and by defining the subject in these ways we draw upon the logic already done. At this stage, however, the *Tractatus* leads to strange conclusions. It does so by default, since, briefly, its account of thinking requires no subject which does the thinking, and its theory of knowledge requires no knowing subject.

Consider first the case of thinking: thought is conceived as the static representation of one complex object by another. Where is there place here for a subject over and above the thoughts and what they represent? A subject is required only if something needs to be done in order for thought to be possible, but in this account of thinking, the only two functions which the subject may appear to have, both turn out to be illusory. The two apparent requirements are that the subject must turn a complex fact into a thought, i.e. into something which represents the world, and that the subject must then turn the thought into a judgement, i.e. into something which is true or false.

The first argument would be that a complex object is a thought only when its elements have been correlated with objects in the world. There is a problem here concerning what an 'act of correlation by the subject' would be like, but the deeper point is that it is not necessary, since an arrangement of a given number of elements is *in itself* a picture, correct or incorrect, of the arrangement of any other set of objects of the same number. When we say that elements of the thought are correlated with objects in the world, this only means that the *thought* is a true or false representation of the arrangement of those objects. (cf. 3.3, 'Only propositions have sense; only in the nexus of a proposition does a name have meaning'.) That a complex object is a thought is independent of anything done by the subject; no 'act of correlation', whatever that might be, is required.

Another way of trying to introduce the thinking subject is to argue that a thought-picture by itself is neither true nor false, but is so only when the subject *affirms that* (judges that) the picture is like, or unlike, reality. But this argument, like the previous one, is mistaken. There is the problem what this 'affirmation by the subject' would be like, but again, the deeper point is that no such act is necessary. For the thought-picture is *by itself* true or false, i.e. already it either agrees or fails to agree with reality (cf. 2.21). Affirmation is at best psychological, and plays no role in the account of thought, meaning and truth (cf. 4.06's).

At 5.541 Wittgenstein considers certain forms of proposition in psychology, such as 'A believes that p' and 'A has the thought p' etc.

He says that if these are considered superficially, it looks as if the proposition 'p' stood in some kind of relation to an object A (which object would be the thinking subject), and continues, 5.542:

> It is clear, however, that 'A believes that p', 'A has the thought p', and 'A says p' are of the form ' "p" says p': and this does not involve a correlation of a fact with an object, but rather the correlation of facts by means of the correlation of their objects.

Since, however, no subject is required to bring about the correlation of facts, the conclusion is that there is no thinking subject. At 5.631 we find: 'There is no such thing as the subject that thinks or entertains ideas'.

We have tried to introduce the metaphysical subject as that which thinks, but there is no need for such a thing. A thought is an object which corresponds or fails to correspond to another object; all is static and self-contained, and there is nothing for a subject to do.

(iii) Knowing (cf. 5.633–5.634)

Knowledge, in the *Tractatus*, is acquaintance with the world. This acquaintance is not necessarily visual, its precise nature cannot be determined *a priori*, nevertheless there is a strong analogy between knowing and seeing: the knowing I is like the seeing eye. Within this theory of knowledge, what can be inferred about the 'knowing I'? Surely nothing, except that it knows, that is to say, that it observes the world. But now the question is this: on what grounds should it be supposed that there are *two* things here, what is known *and* what knows? Wittgenstein writes, 5.633:

> Where *in* the world is a metaphysical subject to be found?
> You will say that this is exactly like the case of the eye and the visual field. But really you do *not* see the eye.
> And nothing *in the visual field* allows you to infer that it is seen by an eye.

The I which is acquainted with the world is not itself part of the world, but then neither can its existence as something outside be inferred.

The underlying problem is again that the subject is required for nothing. The world is already given, and knowledge must be only passive, in no way altering or creating what is known. A passive theory of knowledge, however, requires no subject, neither in nor out of the world. If the knowing subject were active, and in part created what is known, then the existence of the subject could be inferred from those features in the world which derive from the subject and which would therefore be given *a priori*, i.e. prior to acquaintance with the world itself. But this whole possibility is alien to the logic and metaphysics of the *Tractatus*: nothing *in* the world is *a priori*, but only the form of the world (cf. 5.634). In this case, inference to a knowing subject outside the world, is illegitimate.

(iv) Solipsism (cf. 5.6's)

The conclusion so far is that there is no metaphysical subject, since no part of the world, in particular neither the body nor mind, can be identified as the subject, and neither thinking nor knowing requires that there is anything outside the world which thinks or knows. It is an extremely important consequence of the *Tractatus* metaphysics that it apparently fails to include any concept of subject. It is also a consequence hard to accept. At the close of his discussion of the concept in the 5.6's, Wittgenstein writes:

> Thus there really is a sense in which philosophy can talk about the self in a non-psychological way.
> What brings the self into philosophy is the fact that 'the world is my world'.

Such a notion of self belongs with *solipsism*, which may be understood as the view that the self is the only object of knowledge, or the only thing really existent. But we must consider how *any* concept of self can be legitimately brought into philosophy, for as yet we have seen no sign of it. Wittgenstein's explanation appears in these passages:

> 5.6 *The limits of my language* mean the limits of my world.
> 5.62 This remark provides the key to the problem, how much truth there is in solipsism.
> For what the solipsist *means* is quite correct; only it cannot be *said*, but makes itself manifest.
> The world is *my* world: this is manifest in the fact that the limits

of *language* (of that language which alone I understand) mean the limits of *my* world.

5.63 I am my world. (The microcosm.)

This way of introducing the self, however, appears to go directly against the arguments so far discussed. The key question is whether there can be any sense here to the notion of 'my' language. From 5.6 and 5.62 it seems that language is 'my' language because that alone is what I understand; but again, what sense can there be to the notion of 'my' understanding? We have seen that thought requires no thinking subject, and this, so far as I can see, is as much as to say that language requires no understanding subject. Going by this argument, there is no sense in which 'I' understand language, no sense in which language is 'my' language, and hence no sense in which the world which language describes is 'my' world.

Wittgenstein defines the solipsistic self by considering the language which the I understands, concluding that the world which that language describes is 'my world'. A shorter and more familiar route to solipsism, though not the one Wittgenstein takes, is the epistemological one: the world is my world because that alone is what I know; the limits of my knowledge mean the limits of my world. But a similar objection would apply here also; since no knowing subject is required, there is no sense to the notion of what 'I' know, and therefore none either to speaking of 'my world'.

In offering criticisms of the views of the self in the *Tractatus*, my purpose is to establish that *if* those views are indeed problematic and contradictory, this is not because of some error, slip or perversity on the part of their author, but rather because the whole metaphysics of the *Tractatus* is *in fact* deeply antithetical to any coherent and valid concept of self. If this is so, then that it is so, and why it is so, must be clearly grasped. Let us stand back from the arguments, in order to achieve an overall picture of this problem of the self and the world. Let us return to the beginning of the *Tractatus*, its first proposition:

1. The world is all that is the case.

So then, what is the subject? What am *I*?—Supposing, what has been argued in detail, that the uniformity of the world excludes the possibility that the self is related to the world as part to whole, there remain just three possible answers. Firstly, that there is no self, but only the world; secondly, that the self *is* the world; and thirdly, that the self is the *limit* of the world. The line of thought leading to this third possibility is that the subject is not an object in the world, but nor is it another thing outside the world, and what is neither inside nor outside the world is its boundary, or limit.

These three possibilities, that the self is nothing, everything, or the limit of what there is, are each plausible companions to the axiom: the world is all that is the case. And Wittgenstein, in the 5.6's, appears to embrace all of them. But the problem is that they are incompatible with one another. Of the three, the first, that there is no subject, is probably the most consistent with the rest of the *Tractatus* logic, bearing in mind those negative conclusions drawn in the theory of judgement and the theory of knowledge. The basis of the third account, that the self is the limit of the world, is unclear. The limit of the world is significant in the *Tractatus* metaphysics, but it is not clear why this limit should be called 'the self', especially in the light of those arguments which suggest that no self need be postulated. These problems are further complicated by the implication at 5.64, that solipsism is consistent with the view that there is no subject: 'The self of solipsism shrinks to a point without extension, and there remains the reality co-ordinated with it'.

One remark in the 5.6's which might be thought to cast light on these difficulties is the reference to 'the Microcosm' at 5.63 (quoted above). It might be argued that 'the world which is all that is the case', the subject-matter of the *Tractatus* at least until the 5.6's, is *not* what is referred to in the 5.6's; i.e. the world which is all that is the case is not the world that is said to be 'my world'. Perhaps the world which is all that is the case is the Macrocosm, and the world which is my world is the Microcosm. But there are two difficulties in this interpretation. Firstly it is not clear how a concept of self can be joined with any concept of world in the *Tractatus*, whether that world be a macrocosm or a microcosm; and secondly, if the distinction between Macrocosm and Microcosm is grasped as a distinction between two worlds, it becomes mysterious how the self, the Microcosm, can have any idea of the Macrocosm, how the self can represent it in thought, or have knowledge of it (cf. 5.61). No, it is unlikely that anything is to be gained by distinguishing 'the world' from 'my world'; it is more plausible to regard the Microcosm referred to in 5.63 as the 'point without extension' referred to in 5.64, and the Macrocosm would then be the reality co-ordinated with this point.[4]

In conclusion, my argument is that no concept of subject properly belongs with the metaphysics of the *Tractatus*. If, however, the concept is introduced, we are indeed led to the views of the 5.6's: the subject is the whole world, or an extensionless point co-ordinated with the whole, or the limit of the world; views which are incompatible among themselves. If it is true that the *Tractatus* logic does forbid a concept of subject, the question is raised why, on pain of inconsistency, Wittgenstein thought it necessary to have one. The answer to this question is to be found, I suggest, in his discussions of will and value, to which we now turn.

(v) Will and value (cf. 6.37's; 6.4's, parts; and the Notebooks, p. 72–end.)

So far we have seen no sign of activity of the subject, in or upon the world, and this suggests that the concept of 'willing' has no place in the *Tractatus*. Above all, the barrier to introducing the concept of the will is that the subject has no body, and therefore cannot *act*. Because the subject has no body, it cannot act upon the world from within; at best the subject could influence the world from without, but what could the nature of this influence be? There may be an accidental connection between the subject's 'wishing' something to happen and its happening, but this coincidence would be of no interest to logic, and could not characterise the metaphysical subject.

The impotence of the subject also finds expression, as we have seen, in the account of thinking, for the subject contributes nothing to thought. So too the subject has no role in logical necessity, the necessity by which one thought or proposition entails another which it includes; the activity of the subject can be only accidental; no logical necessity exists between acts of will and what happens in the world.

These lines of thought hang together, though it will be clearer why when we contrast the *Tractatus* with another kind of philosophy, in Part II. Judgement must have something in common with the world; now *if* judgement involved the subject, it would follow that the subject has something in common with the world, namely a body, and this would prepare the way for a viable concept of action and therefore of will. And moreover, the concepts of action and will would be linked with the theory of judgement, therefore also with logic, and with 'logical necessity'. But as things are in the *Tractatus*, logic in general precludes activity, and so the concept of will apparently finds no place.

Connected points apply to the *Tractatus* epistemology; knowledge is passive, not an interaction between subject and object. How can a theory of will be made compatible with an epistemology of this kind? Action and will would themselves have to be passive, making no effect on the world. Wittgenstein affirms a theory of this kind. Action is the adoption of an *attitude* to the world; the attitude is 'happy' or 'unhappy'; happiness is being in agreement with the world (see *Notebooks*, pp. 72ff.) He once uses the expression 'looking at the world with a happy eye' (op. cit., p. 86). This brings into focus the harmony between the theory of knowledge and the account of will: to know is to perceive, and to will is to possess a *way* of perceiving, with a happy or unhappy eye.

It is in the quality of the relation between subject and the world, that we find *value*. Wittgenstein writes (*Notebooks*, p. 76):

I will call 'will' first and foremost the bearer of good and evil.

And in the *Tractatus*:

6.423 It is impossible to speak about the will in so far as it is the subject of ethical attributes.

And the will as a phenomenon is of interest only to psychology.
6.43 If the good or bad exercise of the will does alter the world, it can alter only the limits of the world, not the facts—not what can be expressed by means of language.

In short the effect must be that it becomes an altogether different world. It must, so to speak, wax and wane as a whole.

The world of the happy man is a different one from that of the unhappy man.

The will alters the subject itself, that unity of the limits of the world, and the whole world. That the will alters the subject is a deep truth, but since, in the *Tractatus*, the subject does not belong to the world, this truth entails that no part of the world can be influenced by the will.

However, the will can change the self only if there is a self to be changed, and as has been argued, the logic of the *Tractatus* is deeply resistant to the concept of self. At the end of the previous subsection the question was raised why, since logic did not require it, Wittgenstein nevertheless introduced the concept of subject. If this question has a legitimate basis, the answer might be this: unless there is a subject, there is no will, and if there is no will, there is no value, no good or evil, no meaning in the world-picture; but *this* consequence would be untenable. Perhaps it is not that logic provides a place for the subject, rather that the ethics of the *Tractatus* demands one. Wittgenstein wrote in his *Notebooks*, p. 80:

> The thinking subject is surely mere illusion. But the willing subject exists.
> If the will did not exist, neither would there be that centre of the world, which we call the I, and which is the bearer of ethics.
> What is good and evil is essentially the I, not the world.

In this way, there is a tension between logic and ethics: one has no need to postulate a subject, the other must. One aspect of this tension shows in their differing accounts of what the subject is; logic struggles to define a subject which cannot be in the world, but ethics can be concerned with man (see in particular the discussion in the *Notebooks*, pp. 72ff.).

It should be remarked here also that a similar tension exists at the heart of logic itself, in its conception of language. Logic defines language as signs in pictorial combination, and need make no reference to its use by human beings. On the other hand, Wittgenstein believed that his logical results applied to everyday language, which he saw as essentially human, as 'part of the human organism' (4.002). In this chapter I have emphasised the pure logical deduction of the nature of language, and in subsequent chapters I shall continue to point to the non-human character of the *Tractatus* logic. This emphasis is a valid one, particularly in the context of the general aim of this book, which is to relate the *Tractatus* to the modern tradition, and to contrast it with Wittgenstein's later philosophy. Nevertheless, it represents a one-sided view of the *Tractatus*, and of the concerns of its author. It should be balanced by the observation that in his early period Wittgenstein did conceive language as human. This conception did not properly belong with the old logic, however, but rather anticipated the new logic developed later. Wittgenstein wrote the following remark already in 1914, but it could stand alongside his later thoughts:

> When we hear a Chinese, we are inclined to take his speech for an inarticulate gurgle. Someone who understands Chinese will recognise *language* in it. So I often cannot recognise a *human being* in a human being.

(translation of *Vermischte Bemerkungen*, p. 11)

9 THE LIMITS OF LANGUAGE

(i) The general form of proposition (cf. 4.5's; 5.1–6.1)

In his Preface to the *Tractatus* Wittgenstein wrote that the aim of the book is to set a limit to the expression of thought in language; what lies on the other side of this limit will simply be nonsense. The limits of language are determined by the nature of language, by the essence of the proposition. The essence of the proposition is expressed by the general propositional form; every value of this form can express a sense, and every possible sense can be expressed by some value of the form. The general form of proposition may be expressed in words as follows: 'This is how things stand' (4.5). 'This' refers to a picture of a possible state of affairs.

Values of the general propositional form include each and every elementary proposition, and all possible truth-functions of the elementary propositions. Thus:

> 4.51 Suppose that I am given *all* elementary propositions: then I can simply ask what propositions I can construct out of them. And there I have *all* propositions, and *that* fixes their limits.

The apparently larger class of propositions obtained by adding to all elementary propositions all possible truth-functions of them is, however, already implicit in the totality of elementary propositions. Nothing can be said by a truth-function which cannot already be said by listing its elementary constituents and indicating which are true and which are false. Every proposition represents the existence and non-existence of states of affairs; the totality of true-or-false elementary propositions already contains the possibility of expressing every sense.

The superficial paradox that a function, such as negation, does not produce a new object, 'not-p', as value with 'p' as argument, is resolved by distinguishing functions proper from *operations*. So-called 'material functions' (5.44) are completed by an argument to form a new object as value, so that the value contains the argument. Operations, however, only mark differences between forms of propositions already given, one called the base of the operation, the other its result for that base (see 5.2's). The results of all operations with a given proposition as base are already given with that proposition (cf. 5.442 and 3.42). Negation, conjunction, etc. are operations. This is connected with the fact that there are no logical objects (see 5.4, also 4.0312). Wittgenstein uses the concept of operation to define the general form of proposition in symbolic notation, at proposition no. 6.[5]

The general propositional form, which gives the essence of proposition, also expresses the limits of language. Language is limited in two senses. Firstly, in that propositions can only assert or deny the existence of states of affairs. Secondly, the extent of propositions is bounded by the number of elementary propositions that there are.

Both of these limitations of language are imposed by the nature of the world. The world which is all that is the case determines the nature and extent of propositions. Propositions can only truly or falsely represent what is the case. What propositions can express, their sense, are possibilities of states of affairs; all possible states of affairs are given with all objects (2.0124), hence the totality of objects determines the possibility of expression of each and every sense—but this possibility is what is described by the general propositional form.

Further, since the objects in the world are a bounded totality, so too are the elementary propositions which describe their configurations, and so too are the propositions which can be constructed from the elementary propositions (see 5.5561). It is probable that this limitation of the world, and hence of language, does not admit of proof in the *Tractatus*. The idea of totality is already present in the opening sentence of the book: 'The world is all that is the case'. Nevertheless, it is possible to say with what other features of metaphysics it belongs. Firstly, the objects in the world do not change through time (2.027's), and therefore they are not unbounded through time; time neither subtracts nor adds objects. At 4.5 Wittgenstein implies that this fact, or rather what follows from this fact—that the form of reality and hence logical form are given atemporally—is a sufficient condition of the existence of a general propositional form; it is in any case a necessary condition. Secondly, the world is bounded so far as the metaphysical subject is concerned. The subject is not inside logical space, but outside, and it can be outside only what is limited. If the subject is defined as the limit of the world, clearly no inference to the limitation of the world is required. The notion that the world, and hence language, is limited, belongs with the *Tractatus* conceptions of objects in space, time, and subject.

I said above that language is limited in two senses, in its nature, and in its extent. But these two kinds of limitation are distinct only superficially. Both have a common origin, the nature of the world as it is described in the axiomatic first sentence of the *Tractatus*. And we shall see through subsequent chapters that those conceptions of space, time and subject which ensure that language is a bounded totality are the very same as what limits language to pictorial representation of a static world.

(ii) The inexpressible (cf. 4.12's; 6.1–7)

The general form of proposition contains the possibility of expressing every sense, that is, everything that can be expressed by language. There are things, however, which language cannot express. These are of two kinds, one concerning the nature of language, that is, logical form, the other concerning the totality which is the world.

Wittgenstein writes at 4.12:

> Propositions can represent the whole of reality, but they cannot represent what they must have in common with reality in order to be able to represent it—logical form.
>
> In order to be able to represent logical form, we should have to be able to station ourselves with propositions somewhere outside logic, that is to say outside the world.

Propositions cannot represent logical form. Neither can they represent the world *as a whole*. It should be noted that general propositions (using the concept 'all') are not, in the sense here in question, about the totality of the world, and are not excluded from the general propositional form. General propositions may refer to all objects, but they do so, as it were, accidentally; they do not say 'that's *all*', they do not prescribe the limits of reality. The generality-sign is not, however, defined by a truth-functional conjunction, it is rather that a truth-function which has all elementary propositions as arguments is equivalent to a statement of generality, i.e. the generality-sign appears as an argument, not as a function (see 5.52's). All objects can be represented in language, but it cannot be represented that they are all. No representation of the world as a whole can be a value of the general propositional form; propositions are limited to saying that such-and-such is the case in the world, or is not the case, and so on.

Language can express nothing which describes or presupposes

the world as a limited whole. For example: what the solipsist means
cannot be said (5.62); there cannot be propositions of ethics (6.41–
2); it is impossible to speak of the will as the subject of ethical
attributes (6.423–6.43). The subject, value, and the will all are
independent of what is or is not the case; they concern rather what is
outside the world, its limits. Consequently they cannot be represented in language.

It should be seen that the inexpressible is precisely what limits
language. Language is limited by its nature and by its extent; its
limits are given by logical form, and in the sum of all propositions,
which corresponds to the totality of the world. But neither logical
form nor the totality of the world can be represented by language.
In setting the limits to language, therefore, those limits are
transgressed; in the limitation of language, we grasp at the same
time what lies beyond its limits, the inexpressible.

But how should we grasp what is inexpressible? Certainly not by
means of language. Wittgenstein acknowledges this problem in his
Preface to the *Tractatus*, and points to a solution of it: we cannot say
what cannot be said, but we can at least think what cannot be
said. That is to say, what cannot be expressed in language, can
nevertheless be thought. However, this solution is erroneous in
terms of the *Tractatus*, and Wittgenstein does not use it in the text.
According to the logic of the *Tractatus*, thought and language are
not fundamentally different. Propositions of language are thoughts
expressed in a way perceptible to the senses (3.1), and that there are
propositions at all in this sense would seem to be merely *a posteriori*.
Thoughts, like propositions, are logical pictures of facts. Thought is
limited in the same way as language, and for the same reasons. In
the text of the *Tractatus* language and thought are not distinguished
in the fundamental manner of the Preface, and Wittgenstein speaks
indifferently of setting the limits to language or to thought (see
4.114–5, 5.61).

The real answer to the question how we grasp the inexpressible is
not that we think it, for what is inexpressible is also unthinkable, it is
rather that the inexpressible *is shown*, or *shows itself*.

Thus, regarding logical form:

4.121 Propositions cannot represent logical form: it is mirrored
in them.
    What finds its reflection in language, language cannot repre-
sent.

What expresses *itself* in language, *we* cannot express by means of language.

Propositions *show* the logical form of reality.

They display it.

4.1212 What *can* be shown, *cannot* be said.

Logical form is shown in the symbolism which represents reality. A variety of cases is included within this general claim, corresponding to various aspects of logical form, and to its identity with pictorial form and the form of reality. Pictorial form is displayed by a picture (2.172). The rules of logical syntax are shown in the use of signs with a sense (3.33's). Inferential relations between propositions are shown in the structure of the propositions themselves (5.13's). Tautologies show the formal properties of language and the world (6.1's). The propositions of mathematics are equations and therefore pseudo-propositions; but they show the logic of the world (6.2's). Formal concepts, such as 'object' and 'fact', are shown in variables (4.12's). That two signs have the same reference is shown by identity of the signs; there are no propositions of identity (4.24's, 5.53's).

No propositions can represent the logic of language and reality; but meaningful symbolism, of the kinds listed above, shows that logic.[6]

A connected account is given of 'facts' about the whole of reality and its limits. The important concept is that of being *manifest* (*sich zeigen*, literally 'to show itself'). Wittgenstein writes, for example, in 5.62:

What the solipsist *means* is quite correct; only it cannot be *said*, but makes itself manifest.

It is not clear from the text, but it seems likely that something similar would apply in the cases of ethical and aesthetic truths, and truths about the will. All such truths presuppose that the world is a limited whole. This view of the world, Wittgenstein says, is mystical.

6.45 To view the world *sub specie aeterni* is to view it as a whole—a limited whole.

Feeling the world as a limited whole—it is this that is mystical.

And what is mystical is manifest.

6.552 There are, indeed, things that cannot be put into words. They *make themselves manifest*. They are what is mystical.

It would, I think, be incorrect to suppose that the doctrine of showing is merely an *ad hoc* device brought in to resolve the problems inherent in trying to circumscribe language. That language is limited is already implied by the first sentence of the *Tractatus*; but although there are limits to language, language itself cannot draw them, and therefore they must be grasped immediately, not via any representation. It might be said: the subject which understands language must indeed be acquainted with its relation to the world, and this subject which knows reality from the outside does indeed view it as a whole. That the *Tractatus* does not mention the subject in these contexts is connected with its problematic status; no thinking or knowing subject seems to be required. And so, what is understood in language, but by nothing, is shown in language; what is viewed as a limited whole, but by nothing, shows itself. That the inexpressible is shown, hangs together with the rest of the *Tractatus* metaphysics.

Does the doctrine of showing then resolve the tension and apparent paradox which accompany the setting of limits to language, so making the *Tractatus* a coherent whole? Indeed so, were it not for the existence of the book itself; for in the book is written down what cannot be written down.

(iii) Philosophy (cf. 4.11's, 6.53–7)

Philosophy sets limits to what can be said by describing the nature of language, and of the world as a whole. But these things are exactly what is inexpressible. And the paradox of philosophy now becomes clear: in setting the limits to language, philosophy must describe the essence of language—but this description lies outside the limits. The propositions of philosophy must themselves be *nonsense*.

The philosophy of the *Tractatus* consumes its own discourse; the book as a whole is manifestly incoherent. But is it insolubly so? Would it be possible simply to drop the main aim of the book, the setting of limits to language, allowing the logic, the account of language and reality, to remain? It is indeed this aim that causes the trouble, but I do not think that it could just be dropped. As we have seen, the limitation of language *belongs with* the logic of the *Tractatus*, and because language is limited in the way that it is, there can be no philosophical propositions. (No worthwhile piecemeal changes can be made to the *Tractatus*; it correctly and completely fills its own philosophical space.)

Language truly or falsely describes what is the case; this is axiomatic. The form that language must share with reality in order to describe what is the case, and the nature of the world as a whole, which is all that is the case, impose limits on what language can say. Sense is only and all of a certain form. But what defines and circumscribes the sense of language cannot be itself of that form. Language describes the world, but it cannot represent its own means of description, i.e. its relation to the world. This relation is shown *in* language, but cannot be said. Nor can language describe the world as a whole. That the world is a limited whole can be grasped only from outside, not from within; but language describes only what is inside the world, that this is so or that; it cannot describe what is seen from on high—it has a more humble use.

Philosophy has no words to say what it wants to say; so what becomes of it? Wittgenstein has two answers to this question. He writes: 'Philosophy is not a body of doctrine but an activity. Philosophy does not result in "philosophical propositions", but rather in the clarification of propositions' (4.112). As an activity, philosophy points out the nonsense which results when philosophy *tries* to be a body of doctrine, when it misunderstands the logic of language, and fails to perceive its limits. (On this see the 4.00's, 3.32's, and 6.53.)

It should be noted that in this context the account of philosophy as activity is problematic, for the *Tractatus* metaphysics mentions no activity; the world and language are static. Another aspect of the same difficulty arises when we ask what is active. How can it be a human being within the world that grasps the limits of language and acts accordingly? So perhaps it is the metaphysical subject, outside, that does philosophy; but then to whom is it speaking, and with what language? (If philosophy is to be activity, the metaphysics of the *Tractatus* must be changed.)

Philosophy should be a body of doctrines which defines and circumscribes the essence of language and reality; it should be what is written down in the *Tractatus*. But no doctrine of this kind can be written down. This is the paradox, and Wittgenstein accepts it. His own propositions are nonsensical attempts to say what can only be shown, and there remains for philosophy only silence:

6.54 My propositions serve as elucidations in the following way: anyone who understands me eventually recognizes them as nonsensical, when he has used them—as steps—to climb up beyond them. (He must, so to speak, throw away the ladder after he has climbed up it.)

He must transcend these propositions, and then he will see the world aright.

7. What we cannot speak about we must pass over in silence.

2 Tradition and Originality in the *Tractatus*

1 PHILOSOPHY OF NATURE

(i) *Space, time, and causality*

The ontology of the *Tractatus* is spatial. The existence and nature of space are deduced *a priori*, and it is therefore called 'logical space'. The argument that follows is that logical space, in itself and in relation to time and change, shares fundamental features with the space postulated by modern science,[1] and that modern science is a particular form of description of logical space. This connection is the first and the essential indication that the *Tractatus* philosophy belongs squarely within the modern tradition.

The modern philosophy of space, time and change replaced Aristotle's philosophy of nature, central to which was the conception of nature as the Cosmos.[2] In this Cosmos, natural things are ordered in a hierarchy of being, and the place of each thing in the hierarchy is determined by its essential qualities, or essence. Motion is the tendency of an object to reach its natural place in the Cosmos, to realise its inner potential. Motion is 'coming to be'; and time is the dimension of becoming. It was these linked conceptions of change, time and natural things, which were overturned and replaced by modern physics. The concept of the Cosmos gradually subsided: objects were no longer characterised by their place in a meaningfully differentiated chain of being, but rather by their *spatial* properties and relations. One of the forces behind the new emphasis on spatial relations was the insight, achieved particularly in physics by Galileo, that mathematics was applicable to nature. The space of nature was geometrical space, and its lines could be measured by numbers. It was an innovation to regard geometrical properties and relations as the *essential* features of nature and of natural things, in physics, as also in fine art, with the perfection of perspective.

A fundamental feature of the geometrical space postulated by modern physics was that it existed *absolutely*; that is to say, spatial relations were fixed in themselves and were not conditional on any means that we might use to measure them. Similarly, motion and time were taken to be absolute. We shall see that the postulate of an absolute nature had great philosophical implications. These implications are brought out clearly by defining 'absolute' as that which is independent of methods of measurement; an absolute ontology implies, particularly, that judgement should be made by no method, and that knowledge should be achieved by no means, that is, it should be 'immediate'.

This philosophical understanding of absolute is connected with the definitions given in physics. Newton's separation of absolute from relative space, time, and motion, turned on the distinction between what is 'mathematical, in its own nature, without relation to anything external', and what is 'measured by means of the position and motion of sensible objects' (Newton, 1: Scholium to the Definitions, pp. 6f.) Einstein said that by calling space 'absolute' Newton meant that it was 'uninfluenced by the masses and their motion' (Einstein, 3: p. 27). This definition refers to Newton's postulate of rotation in absolute space to explain the results of his famous 'bucket experiment': absolute rotation created forces in addition to those possible in inertial frames of reference, for which Newton's laws of motion were valid. Newton used the concept of absolute space to explain why all geometrical frames of reference were not mechanically equivalent, why those marked by bodies at rest were privileged over those marked by accelerating bodies. Absolute space was the privileged frame of reference, uninfluenced by bodies and their motion; it was pure geometrical space. Absolute space was thus distinguished from any physical frame of reference which we could use to measure it. That is to say, absolute space was independent of our methods of measurement.

Another fundamental feature of natural space, when it came to be identified with geometrical space, was *uniformity*, or homogeneity: each spatial place was qualitatively indistinguishable from any other. This meant that the Aristotelian concept of motion was no longer viable: motion could no longer be conceived as teleological, since there was no reason why an object should be in one part of space (nature) rather than in any other. Motion was thus regarded in the new physics not as a process of becoming, not as the tendency to reach a status, but rather as itself a state, self-contained and self-perpetuating. There was motion, objects could change their position in space, but this change was simply the replacement of one state of affairs by another. And since the time taken for this replacement can be conceived as approaching indefinitely close to no time at all, time is not needed in the description of spatial position. Time ceased to be the dimension of a process and became mere duration, in which one spatial state of affairs may or may not give way to another. In this sense, in modern physics, unlike Aristotle's, the concept of time does not apply essentially to nature.

The concept of change applied within modern physics only to alteration in motion, i.e. to positive or negative acceleration. As can be seen, a radically new kind of explanation of change was needed, and it would not be misleading to say that no such explanation was entirely successful. According to Newton's First Law of Motion, it was the action of *force* on a body which changed its state from rest to motion, motion to rest, or from one state of motion to another. It is intuitively plausible that a body's state of motion or rest should be changed when it comes into contact with a body in a different state. However, there remained the problem of force between distant bodies, apparently unmediated by any mechanical contact; the nature of gravity, particularly, was problematic. The notion of force in Newtonian physics was, and remains, the subject of much debate (see, for example, Koyré, 4; McGuire, 1; and Westfall, 1).

There was an acute underlying dilemma: how could *change* be explained by a philosophy according to which space is uniform, and time mere duration? If, at any time, all things are static, why should they change their state? The principle by which one state of affairs gives way to another can be expected to be obscure. It was called by various names.

Hume wrote 'There are no ideas, which occur in metaphysics, more obscure and uncertain, than those of *power, force, energy* or *necessary connexion.*' (2: VII, pp. 61–2) In the subsequent celebrated passages, Hume subjects these ideas to sustained scrutiny. Power to produce change cannot be observed in bodies, nor is it a real property of matter, nor can it be observed in the operations of our own minds. He concludes:

So that, upon the whole, there appears not, throughout all nature, any one instance of connexion which is conceivable by us. All events seem entirely loose and separate. One event follows another; but we never can observe any tie between them. They seem *conjoined*, but never *connected*. (ibid., p. 74)

Connection can never be observed between 'entirely loose and separate events'; that is, I suggest, between what are *states* of affairs (whether of rest or motion). Hume goes on to argue that the concept of *cause and effect* is derived not from a single instance of conjunction between events, but from regularly repeated conjunctions, experience of which inclines the mind to expect one event, the 'effect', to follow another, the 'cause'. But this concept of causality, and with it those several ideas originally raised for discussion, has only subjective validity and is stripped of all explanatory power. We can say on the basis of experience that certain events regularly follow others, but we have no explanation of this regularity. We can say that things do change and, at least up to now, in a predictable way, but we do not know why. Change, and *a fortiori* orderly change, is not part of the underlying ontology.

It is these linked conceptions of space, time and change which belong to modern philosophy of nature, which characterise also the *Tractatus* philosophy. Firstly, logical space is absolute in the same sense as physical space is absolute, i.e. its relations are given independently of methods of measurement. There is in the *Tractatus*, however, no contrast of absolute space with relative spaces, and this is because logical space is not measured by a *method* at all. In the *Tractatus* theory of judgement, the picture is laid against reality like a measure (2.1512); but this 'laying against' is no method, any suggestion of activity is metaphorical only, the measuring instrument just is or is not the same length as what is measured, they either agree or fail to agree (cf. 2.21). The *Tractatus* thus contains the purest expression of the notion that reality is given absolutely.

Another feature which logical space shares with the space postulated by modern physics is uniformity or homogeneity. All parts of logical space, and all objects in it, are qualitatively indistinguishable, and there is no sense in which one could speak of a reason for objects being arranged in one way rather than in any other. This fact provides one approach among several to the *Tractatus* statements about *value*. The statement that all propositions are of equal value (6.4) might be interpreted as meaning that all possible states of affairs stand at the same qualitative level. Since the world is not hierarchically ordered, no one state of affairs can justify or give sense to any other; and so any concept of value or meaning must apply only to the whole, from the outside, not to one part in terms of another (cf. 6.41).

The *Tractatus* philosophy, like modern physics, makes no essential use of the concept of time in its description of the spatial world. The evidence that this negative doctrine belongs to the *Tractatus* is particularly those passages which refer to what is *already given*, or which in some other way imply that time brings nothing new. Thus: the possibility of occurring in states of affairs is in objects from the beginning, a new possibility cannot be discovered later, etc. (2.01's); the totality of objects itself does not change through time (2.027's). So far as concerns judgement, the proposition is a picture, not a method, and so is not extended through time. Also, compound propositions are already given with the elementary ones (3.42, 4.51, 5.442). The insignificance of time is, in fact, a central doctrine of the *Tractatus*; it justifies the concept of the world as a given, limited whole, and it is presupposed in the definition of the general propositional form.

Finally, change—what happens in the world—is accidental. States of affairs, existing at the same time or at different times, are independent of one another. Wittgenstein wrote:

> There is no possible way of making an inference from the existence of one situation to the existence of another, entirely different situation. There is no causal nexus to justify such an inference . . . *Superstition* is the belief in the causal nexus.[3] (5.135, 5.136–1; see also the 6.37's)

The similarities between the logical space of the *Tractatus* and the geometrical space of modern physics are so deep, that we might suppose they are one and the same; and in a qualified sense this turns out to be so. The qualification necessary concerns the all-embracing nature of logical space. It is introduced *a priori* as that in which relations exist, but although these relations clearly can include geometrical ones, there might be other kinds as well. Wittgenstein seems also to have had in mind, for example, temporal relations and colour relations (see 2.0251).

However, it is unclear whether states of affairs and their pictorial representations could include non-geometrical relations of these kinds. Professor Anscombe has argued (1: p. 27) that no elementary proposition can describe an object's colour, since the predication of two different colours to an object is a contradiction, but according to

6.3751, the conjunction of two elementary propositions cannot be a contradiction. This argument, however, seems too strong, even if it does correctly represent Wittgenstein's intentions in the *Tractatus*. It would also preclude the proposition 'a is left of b' from being elementary, since it contradicts 'a is right of b'. Apparently it must be possible for one elementary proposition to contradict (to be the contrary of) another. In the paper 'Some Remarks on Logical Form' (1929), Wittgenstein acknowledged that spatial relations, and colour properties, exist in scales, and so propositions describing them have contraries. Colour descriptions might be elementary, then, even though they are mutually exclusive. If they cannot count as elementary propositions, this would perhaps be because they have subject-predicate form, while all elementary propositions are said to be relational (see 4.21 and 2.01).

The details of including non-geometrical spaces under the generic concept of logical space would, I think, be problematic. But however this issue be settled, there remains a sense in which logical space *is* the geometrical space of modern physics. For it is not that physics just describes a part of logical space; rather it does describe the whole, but only partly. Logic comprises the possibility of a complete description of reality; it is the great mirror of the world (cf. 5.511). And the status of physics relative to logic is explained in the 6.3's: *physics is a particular form of description of the world*. Wittgenstein writes in 6.341:

> Newtonian mechanics . . imposes a unified form on the description of the world. . . . Mechanics determines one form of description of the world by saying that all propositions used in the description of the world must be obtained in a given way from a given set of propositions—the axioms of mechanics.

For example, physics speaks of colours, roughly, in terms of the motion of particles in space (cf. 6.3751).

There exists a great harmony between the *Tractatus* and seventeenth-century physics; it will appear through this chapter that in an important sense, the *Tractatus* is the true philosophy of that physics.

(ii) Dualism of mind and matter

The modern conception of nature as being essentially mathematical and spatial implied a certain account of the objects in nature. Natural objects came to be regarded as possessing essentially the qualities of extension, shape, position, motion or rest, and number. These were the so-called 'primary qualities' of objects. (Their precise definition and connection was the subject of much debate; e.g. should matter itself be construed as a quality of space?)

Primary qualities of objects were distinguished from qualities such as heat, colour, smell and sound, which were held not to be in objects themselves, but rather in us. The powers that objects have, by virtue of their primary qualities, to produce in us the qualities of heat, colour, etc. were called the 'secondary qualities' of objects. The justification of this innovation in modern natural philosophy, the removal of heat, colour, etc. from natural objects, is to be found partly in the fact that these qualities are not spatial and mathematical. But there is another, connected reason, namely, that they are not *absolute*. For example, the colour of an object varies with the lighting, the heat of an object varies with the relative temperature of the hand; and so on. In general, the point is that qualities of this kind depend in various ways on their mode of perception by a sentient being. They are the product of interaction between the human body, in particular the sense-organs, and other objects. It is this *relativity* of the qualities perceived by the senses, which excluded them from absolute nature.[4]

The qualities of sense-perception were not, however, alone in being excluded from nature; a more drastic separation was inevitable. Modern philosophy of nature made no place for man. In the world of corporeal substance, with its few primary qualities, nowhere were there any characteristics of life; there was no purpose, no intention, no value, so it seemed, no desire, emotion or appetite, no belief, no imagination, no freedom, spontaneity or will, no sensation of pleasure or pain.

The unhappy consequence of the new philosophy was drawn by Descartes: there existed two substances, *res extensa* and *res cogitans*— the first was material substance in space and time, the second was *mind*. And man was split in two, into body and mind. The human body was conceived as mechanical matter like the rest of nature, and then mind comprised everything human which could not be construed as material. Thus, not only was the spiritual soul distinguished from the body and from nature, but so also sensation, perception, desire and will, which would seem so clearly to be bodily qualities and functions, except insofar as the body had been stripped of all sensitivity and life. Cartesian dualism split *natural* man into two; in this respect it was a new conception of man, to be distinguished carefully from the various kinds of dualism found in ancient and scholastic thought.[5]

Cartesian dualism belongs to the foundations of modern philosophy. It reflects the ontological difference between what is spatial and quantifiable and what is non-spatial and unquantifiable, and also the ontological difference between what exists by itself (absolutely) in nature, and what exists only as a result of interaction between nature and man. Also, we shall see, dualism belongs with a theory of knowledge (or better, with a theory of no knowledge), and with the modern distinction between thought and reality, and between appearance and reality.

In the *Tractatus*, however, dualism is conspicuous by its absence. This is a fact crucial for an understanding of the place of the *Tractatus* in the modern tradition. The *Tractatus* does contain allusions to the distinction between mind and matter, for instance in the distinction between thoughts that are, and thoughts that are not, expressed in signs perceptible to the senses (3.1), and there are casual references to body and mind (e.g. in 5.641); but dualism has no central role in the metaphysics, in marked contrast with previous modern philosophy. Already it can be seen that the straightforward ontological aspects of the division between matter and mind have disappeared, since there is in the *Tractatus* no distinction between qualities of objects that exist independently and ones which depend on perception by men, and nor is there distinction between what is spatial and quantifiable, and what is not; the whole world is spatial, and quantifiable, whether it be what we customarily think of as matter, or as mind. We shall see further that the other aspects of the distinction between matter and mind are also made redundant in the *Tractatus*, so that the traditional dualism is no longer to be found there.

2 THOUGHT

(i) Ideas

Our main concern in this section is with the account of thinking which belonged with modern philosophy of nature. By 'thinking' is meant here: the true or false representation of reality. And since, according to the modern view, what is to be represented is corporeal objects in space, the problem is: how are these objects and relations in space to be represented by the subject? The moderns grasped this representation as a *medium* between subject and object, and therefore supposed that thought was to be found in the interaction between man and the world. Modern physiology taught that physical bodies interact, directly or via particles, with the sense-receptors of human bodies, and that the products of this interaction are experienced as *sense-perception*. However, as Descartes emphasised, the concept of sense-perception should not be *defined* as the product of interaction between bodies, since we can experience perceptions when there is no external cause (as in dreams, or delusions) and, we may imagine, could do so even if we had no bodies at all. Descartes wrote:

> I am the same who feels, that is to say, who perceives certain things, as by the organs of sense, since in truth I see light, I hear noise, I feel heat. But it will be said that these phenomena are false and that I am dreaming. Let it be so; still it is at least quite certain that it seems to me that I see light, that I hear noise and that I feel heat. That cannot be false; properly speaking it is what is in me called feeling; and used in this precise sense that is no other thing than thinking. (1: Second Meditation, p. 153)

This account of thinking was taken up and explored by Locke in his *Essay Concerning Human Understanding* (Locke, J., 1). Locke's purpose was primarily epistemological, being 'to enquire into the Original, Certainty, and Extent of humane Knowledge' (I, 1, 2). However, Locke's method involved study of the understanding, the first step being to inquire into the origin of ideas (I, 1, 3). The term *idea*, Locke explains, 'serves best to stand for whatsoever is the *Object* of the Understanding when a Man thinks' (I, 1, 8). The conclusion of the preliminary inquiry into the origin of ideas, Locke expresses as follows:

> Let us then suppose the Mind to be, as we say, white Paper, void of all Characters, without any *Ideas*; How comes it to be furnished? . . . Whence has it all the materials of Reason and Knowledge? To this I answer, in one word, From *Experience*: In that, all our Knowledge is founded; and from that it ultimately derives it self. Our Observation employ'd either about *external*,

sensible Objects; or about the internal Operations of our Minds, perceived and reflected on by our selves, is that, which supplies our Understandings with all the materials of thinking. These two are the Fountains of Knowledge, from whence all the *Ideas* we have, or can naturally have, do spring. (II, 1, 2)

Locke's account of thinking differs from Descartes' primarily in its limitation of the materials of thought to what is given in inner or outer experience. In the Cartesian philosophy, some ideas were given independently of experience, being in this sense innate. These innate ideas were of special relevance to the new conception of nature: ideas of mathematics, the idea of substance, and the idea of God. The problem whether or not there were innate ideas was of enormous importance in the theory of knowledge, which we shall consider in the next section. However, notwithstanding the possibility of innate ideas, it was generally supposed that at least particular material states of affairs were represented, that is to say thought, in perception. The theory of thinking was therefore a theory of perception, one sometimes called the 'representative theory of perception'. The account of thought and perception may be represented as in Figure 1.

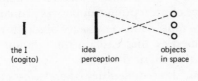

I	idea	objects
the I	perception	in space
(cogito)		

FIGURE 1

(ii) Idealism

Thought was conceived to be the representation of objects in perception. But let us consider what kind of 'representing' this is. How does an idea of perception *represent* a spatial object? The natural answer would be that a perception is *like* the object that gives rise to it, rather as a painting may be like something. And in this case, the veracity or correctness of a perception would be a *matching* between it and a state of affairs in space. However, there is a difficulty in this account, since not all of the qualities given in perception could be taken as resemblances of qualities in corporeal objects. Nothing like the ideas of colour, heat, smell, etc. exist in those objects. Locke wrote:

> The *Ideas of primary Qualities* of Bodies, *are Resemblances* of them, and their Patterns do really exist in the Bodies themselves; but the *Ideas, produced* in us *by* these *Secondary Qualities, have no resemblance* of them at all. There is nothing like our *Ideas*, existing in the Bodies themselves. (1: II, VIII, 15)

There is a difficulty, then, with ideas of secondary qualities, but at least in the case of the primary qualities, we can speak of a resemblance between idea and object. However, this natural move of introducing primary qualities into ideas in fact strikes at the foundations of the whole metaphysics. For ideas should not possess any of the primary qualities, not that of space, and still less that of mass. There are two connected reasons for this. Firstly, ideas are *mental*; they belong to *res cogitans*, not to *res extensa*. If mental entities can be spatial, then the definition of mind as non-spatial is invalid, and the foundations of dualism are threatened. If certain ideas can be spatial, we should have to envisage *two* spaces, one mental (ideal), the other physical. This leads to the second aspect of the difficulty. Perception is understood to be the product of interaction between subject and object, and is therefore essentially observer-dependent. If ideas of perception can possess primary qualities, say spatial ones, we must now envisage observer-relative spatial relations and properties, and explain the relation of these to the absolute space of the physical world.

Notwithstanding these difficulties, there were good reasons for supposing that ideas were, in certain respects, images of material things. For it is only insofar as ideas can resemble material objects, that there is a sense in saying that they are *thoughts* of those objects, i.e. true or false representations of them. In particular, a causal link alone between object and idea would not suffice to make the one a thought of the other. For it is essential to thought that it can be true *or* false, and this distinction cannot be made by the concept of causality alone. Material objects can be part of a causal chain that produces what we call 'false perception', for example illusion, or hallucination, just as much as they can be the partial cause of veridical perception. We need a sense in which a visual illusion *wrongly* represents what is so, even though what is so does partly cause the illusion; hence the need for some notion of resemblance.

There was thus a profound difficulty in the account of thinking which developed with modern philosophy of nature: how can thought, which is mental, non-spatial and relative, represent, be like or unlike reality, which is material, spatial and absolute.

This difficulty, or incoherence, was made much of by Berkeley. Berkeley saw clearly that ideas of perception included the primary qualities, and he stressed that the primary qualities in perception, like colour, heat, etc., were *relative*. He wrote:

> *Great* and *small*, *swift* and *slow*, are allowed to exist no where without the mind, being entirely relative, and changing as the frame or position of the organs of sense varies. (1: I, 11)

Thus Berkeley abolished the distinction between primary qualities and other sensible qualities, insofar as it rested on the absolute nature of the former.

This innovation led Berkeley into direct conflict with the Newtonian philosophy. It involved him in the attempt to show that Newton's postulate of absolute space, time and motion was invalid, and that instead physics could be based adequately on relativity. (See ibid. I, 110–17; and also his (2), which contains a penetrating analysis of Newton's bucket experiment, anticipating arguments used at the end of the nineteenth century.)

In Berkeley's philosophy, the existence of a material substance beyond or beneath ideas in perception was rendered superfluous. Nothing belonging to nature was denied; neither space, time, nor solidity. Berkeley denied only the existence of a material substance in which absolute qualities independent of us were supposed to inhere. Indeed Berkeley held it to be nonsense that such a substance could be thought, since 'an idea can be like nothing but an idea' (1: I, 8). In exploring the modern philosophy of nature and the accompanying account of human understanding, Berkeley concluded that both were, to put it mildly, problematic, and that the postulate of something beyond ideas and those who perceive them is unnecessary and even incoherent—nature became ideal.

(iii) General terms

So far in this section we have discussed the representation of spatial states of affairs in ideas of perception. We turn now to consider theories of a radically different kind of representation, namely, the representation of *classes* of things, in thought, or by general terms of language. Attempts to understand the unity of classes belonged particularly to ancient and scholastic thought, and they were all more or less incompatible with the new modern philosophy. In ancient thought, it was held that natural things were ordered into a particular class by virtue of having something in common, called a 'universal'. Different accounts of universals were given, particularly Plato's theory of *universalia ante rem*, and Aristotle's theory of *universalia in rebus*. For our present purpose, the important point is that *universals were not spatial objects*.

That universals are not spatial is clear in the case of Plato's transcendental forms, but it is true also in the case of universals in nature. It is essential that the universal which is common, say, to all chairs, can exist in many particular chairs at the same time; this is the explanation why those many particulars are the same. But something that can be in many places at once is not a spatial particular. A spatial particular can be broken up and distributed in space, but the universal 'chair' has to be all of it in many places at once. If the universal was spatial, and was broken up and distributed, the original problem of the unity of the class of chairs would reappear in the form: where is the unity in the disparate parts of the universal?

In modern philosophy, however, the ontology became essentially spatial; and so the problem arose what to say of classes, and of the general terms which stood for them. Locke posed the problem, and answered it, as follows:

> Since all things that exist are only particulars, how come we by general Terms, or where find we those general Natures they are supposed to stand for? Words become general, by being made the signs of general *Ideas*: and *Ideas* become general, by separating from them the circumstances of Time, and Place, and any other *Ideas*, that may determine them to this or that particular Existence. By this way of abstraction they are made capable of representing more Individuals than one; each of which, having in it a conformity to that abstract *Idea*, is (as we call it) of that sort. (1: III, iii, 6)

The advantage of this account is that only particular things need be postulated. Locke continues:

It is plain, by what has been said, That *General and Universal*, belong not to the real existence of Things; but *are the Inventions and Creatures of the Understanding*, made by it for its own use, *and concern only Signs*, whether Words, or *Ideas*. (III, III, 11)

Objections to Locke's doctrine of abstract ideas may be made at various levels, but let us for the moment leave aside those which question the whole framework within which Locke was working. Consider rather one of Berkeley's criticisms, which consists mainly of the following quotation from Locke himself:

Does it not require some pains and skill to form the *general Idea* of a *Triangle*, . . . for it must be neither Oblique, nor Rectangle, neither Equilateral, Equicrural, nor Scalenon; but all and none of these at once. In effect, it is something imperfect, that cannot exist; an *Idea* wherein some parts of several different and inconsistent *Ideas* are put together. (1: IV, VII, 9)

To which Berkeley replies simply:

If any man has the faculty of framing in his mind such an idea of a triangle as is here described, it is in vain to pretend to dispute him out of it, nor would I go about it. (1: Introduction, 13)

The particulars to which a general term applies do not, on the whole, share a common feature, indeed their individual features may be incompatible. So the notion that such a feature can be abstracted to form a general idea is problematic, for remember that here 'idea' means a mental image, or picture.[6]

It should be noted that the problem of classes, to which Locke's theory of abstraction was meant to be an answer, has no essential connection with the representative theory of perception or thought described previously. Particularly, it has nothing to do with dualism, for the problem of how things belong to classes is all the same whether those things are mental or physical. Locke's account of the meaning of general terms involves the mind partly because mental ideas are what is immediately given and therefore what need to be classified, and perhaps more importantly, because the strange exemplar of what is common to all triangles, for example, is best thought of as mental rather than ordinary; what we certainly could not make with our hands, the mind, in its mysterious way, can produce.

We have considered, then, two kinds of thought envisaged in the Enlightenment philosophy (particularly Locke's): the first is representation of objects in space, the second is representation of classes of particulars. In the *Tractatus* we find a conception of thought corresponding to the first of these kinds, but there is nothing corresponding to the second. The *Tractatus* ontology is a pure spatial atomism, and there is therefore no place in it for the concept of non-spatial universals.[7] Consequently neither is there a place for general terms in the *Tractatus* theory of the proposition: there are no subject-predicate propositions, all are relational.

(iv) Dualism and language

In the philosophy held in common by Descartes and Locke, material objects in space were represented to the subject as images of perception. It can be seen that language has no fundamental role to play within this theory of representation. As a rule in modern philosophy, words served only to stand for ideas, and it was the ideas, not the words, which directly represented reality. Thus, general terms stood for general ideas, which signified the common elements in classes of particulars. Also, words could be combined to make a proposition, but a verbal proposition only signified a mental one, a combination of ideas, which could truly or falsely represent a combination of things (see Locke, J., 1: IV, v).

It was only towards the end of the last century that language claimed the right to primary consideration. The question gradually crystallised: how does *language itself* truly or falsely represent reality? One approach to this problem was taken by Wittgenstein in the *Tractatus*, but before considering this approach, let us glimpse at the kind of difficulty which arose when the concept of language demanded a place in the modern metaphysics so far described. The point is this: the philosophy of Descartes and Locke already had an account of thought and representation, and so it did not need another one; language interfered with, indeed swamped, the old picture.

Thus, let us grant the three-layered metaphysical picture composed of self, ideas of perception in the mind, and matter in space, and then ask where language can be fitted in as the vehicle of description. Two possibilities are clear: language may describe either the mental realm, or the physical world. Thus we are faced with possibilities which may be represented as in Figure 2.

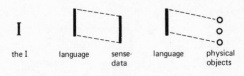

FIGURE 2

The language which describes matter in space (physical objects) may be called the 'physicalist' language, and the language which describes sense-data may be called the 'phenomenalist' language. Notice that what Locke could call 'ideas' are now called 'sense-data', this change in terminology signifying that sense-perceptions in the mind are no longer regarded as *thoughts of* material things. Indeed, as can be seen from Figure 2, there is anyway an uncomfortable surfeit of layers of thought and reality. The consequence was that those philosophers in the early decades of this century who accepted the main assumptions of the Cartesian or empiricist metaphysics, and who then addressed themselves to the contemporary problem of the nature of language, were obliged to simplify the over-burdened and distressing picture with which they were faced; obliged, in particular, to discover the relative status of the two languages now envisaged, and if possible to dispense with one of them. So pressing, indeed, was this problem, that the issue of precisely *how* language did represent whatever it did represent was to a great extent ignored. The main arguments were epistemological, as they always had been in this tradition. We shall discuss them in the next section; the point being made now is that the introduction of language into philosophy struck a great blow at the old assumptions.

(iv) Language in the Tractatus

There is a simpler way of introducing language into the arena of modern philosophy, one which avoids the complications caused by dualism. We consider the use of language for describing physical reality, as in Newtonian physics and the engineering sciences. Language does what it appears to do, namely, gives true or false descriptions of the planets, bridges, watches, and so on. In this case, we have a picture of language in direct relation to the physical world; a picture which may be represented as in Figure 3.

FIGURE 3

The diagram is intended to stress the essential point: that *the medium of representation is now taken to be language itself.* In other words, language has usurped the place of 'ideas' or 'sense-perceptions' as what truly or falsely represents objects in space. Hence there is no longer reason to postulate the mind as a distinct thinking substance; dualism becomes irrelevant to the theory of representation. Further, there is no longer a reason why the vehicle of representation should be regarded as a *medium* between subject and object. Rather the I has equal access to both language and the reality it describes; a fact which could be shown in Figure 3 by moving the 'I' from the far left hand side to a place between language and the objects it represents.

In this way we approach the metaphysics of the *Tractatus*, though there are certain qualifications. Firstly, the status of the subject requires further elucidation (see above, Ch. 1, section 8; and below, Ch. 2, section 4). Secondly, the objects and spatial relations that are represented by language may not include material objects and geometrical relations alone (see above, Ch. 2, 1, i). And thirdly, in the *Tractatus*, the vehicle of representation embraces more than language: only those thoughts which are expressed in signs that are perceptible to the senses, belong to language (see above, Ch. 1, 4, i).

On this last point, however, what matters in the present context is the nature of the true-false sign, not whether such signs are found in language alone. According to the *Tractatus*, the true-false sign, or thought, is in part conventional, i.e. certain objects in the world arbitrarily stand for other objects. The sign cannot be wholly conventional, however; one of its features must non-arbitrarily (i.e. logically, or naturally) represent a feature of the world. This feature is a relation. A thought is thus a combination of signs, and it represents that the objects in the world which are referred to by elements in the thought stand in the relation which is *shown* in the thought. The thought is true if the objects referred to do stand in the relation shown, and is otherwise false. A thought is a spatial picture, in the same space and composed of the same kind of elements as the reality that is pictured.

This account of thought, which uses the notion of conventional representation by signs and, in this sense, of 'language', solves the problems inherent in the earlier accounts given by Descartes and Locke, problems that were emphasised by Berkeley. There is no longer the problem how something without primary qualities can represent matter in spatial relations. Nor is there the alternative problem how spatial relations exhibited (*per impossible*) in mental representations can resemble those in the material world; that is, there is no longer a problem of how what is essentially dependent on human observation (ideas) can represent what is essentially independent (relations in absolute space). In the *Tractatus* account, thought and state of affairs represented both belong in the same, absolute, space.

These considerations suggest the possibility that the *Tractatus* account of thought and representation is the one which *always should have belonged with modern physics*. The whole of absolute space should be represented by a pattern of rigid rods, i.e. something corresponding to the Newtonian absolute frame of reference. And a particular state of affairs is properly represented by a rigid rod, extended in as many dimensions as what is being represented. The importance of isomorphism for Newtonian mechanics was clearly grasped by the great nineteenth-century physicist Heinrich Herz, in his book *The Principles of Mechanics, presented in a new form* (1). This 'new form' was obtained by restricting the axioms of mechanics to concepts which were necessary and sufficient for the explanation of experiment (the concepts of space, time and mass were included, but not that of force), and from these axioms models are made which possess the same logical multiplicity as the phenomena they describe. It is well-known that Wittgenstein was influenced by Herz's work, and he refers directly to Herz on dynamical models when discussing his own picture theory (*Tractatus*, 4.04).[8]

At this stage, some light might be shed on an otherwise puzzling fact about the *Tractatus*, namely, that it seems to prove on purely *logical* grounds that the world consists of simple objects in space, a conclusion that appears to belong to natural science. Perhaps the explanation is this: the logical deduction presupposes that the representation of reality is true-or-false; this presupposition necess-arily leads to an ontology of spatial atomism, but equally, the ontology entails that representation is true-or-false. For the concept of objects in space unlike, in particular, the concept of a universal, already contains the idea of non-being in contrast to being, i.e. a relation between objects can also *fail* to hold. In this sense the ontology of modern science (and of the *Tractatus*) possesses an essential *relativity* which at root is equivalent to the conception of truth-or-falsity as correspondence or failure of correspondence with reality. It is, then, not surprising that in the *Tractatus*, study of this conception should lead back to its origin, modern natural philosophy.

If the account of representation in the *Tractatus* is the only one which properly belongs with modern physics, the whole long and painful story of thinking being mental, observer-relative per-ception, is the story of a deep error. But where does the error lie: in the philosophy of nature, or in the theory of human understanding?

3 EPISTEMOLOGY

(i) Empiricism

The pervasive epistemology in modern times has been that knowledge is gained through the senses: the five outer senses (sight, hearing, touch, smell and taste), and the introspective sense. This theory of knowledge belongs with *empiricism*, and is the defining characteristic of that school of thought. The theory rests upon a very general conception, shared by philosophies which are otherwise radically opposed to empiricism, that knowledge is some form of perception or intuition, a *seeing* in which reality is revealed. Leaving aside this general conception for the time being, let us consider the more specific question: why should intuition be identified with sensible intuition alone?

Arguments for the empiricist epistemology have a dual aspect, according as they focus on the materials of thought, or on knowledge directly. Locke's central argument was of the first kind, and Descartes gave clear expression to the epistemological supports of empiricism.

Having demonstrated that all our ideas originate in experience, Locke was able to proceed with the second stage of his enquiry, 'to shew, what *Knowledge* the Understanding hath by those *Ideas*' (1: I, 1, 3). He wrote:

> Since *the Mind,* in all its Thoughts and Reasonings, hath no other immediate Object but its own *Ideas,* which it alone does or can contemplate, it is evident, that our Knowledge is only conversant about them.
> *Knowledge* then seems to me to be nothing but *the perception of the connexion and agreement, or disagreement and repugnancy of any of our Ideas.* In this alone it consists. (IV, 1, 1–2)

This is Locke's empiricist epistemology, resting clearly on a claim about what there is to be known, a claim which in turn follows from one concerning the materials of thought. As we shall see, Locke's route to empiricism was followed by twentieth-century philosophers, though the argument was expressed by them in terms of language and meaning, not ideas.

In Locke's expression of the empiricist epistemology we can already see the two great and connected difficulties inherent in empiricism, one being the solipsistic predicament, the other being the so-called 'problem of knowledge'. To this problem, and to the epistemological route to empiricism, which makes the problem manifest, we turn next.

(ii) The problem of knowledge

That philosophers should doubt the existence of material bodies in space may be thought by some to be merely amusing or ironical; by others to be great, showing as it does the questioning spirit of philosophy; and by some to be perverse, showing only the inability of philosophers to understand and to accept what is obvious to everybody else and what works; some others may see in the philosophers' problem of knowledge an apparent difficulty or paradox in our metaphysics, but one which is intractable and of no significance outside the confines of the study. No doubt there is something to be said for all of these attitudes; but from our standpoint in the present century, the traditional problem of knowledge can be seen in another light, namely as the focus on a real problem which we have since learnt to solve. The problem of knowledge arose hand in hand with the modern philosophy of nature, that is, hand in hand with a certain conception of what human beings tried to know; and it was indeed a valid problem.

The problem arises, as Descartes explains in his *Meditations*, when we examine the source of our knowledge of natural things, i.e. 'corporeal nature in general, and its extension, the figure of extended things, their quantity or magnitude and number, as also the place in which they are, the time which measures their duration, and so on' (1: First Meditation, p. 146). Such an examination may appear unnecessary now, for it may be obvious that we know of such things. But then, we are used to the concepts involved; rather consider the time when this nature was newly conceived, when the concepts involved were revolutionary, and hazy. On this, Koyré writes:

> We are so well acquainted with, or rather so well accustomed to, the concepts and principles which form the basis of modern science, that it is nearly impossible for us to appreciate rightly either the obstacles that had to be overcome for their establishment, or the difficulties that they imply and encompass. The Galilean concept of motion (as well as that of space) seems to us so 'natural' that we even believe we have derived it from experience and observation (1: p. 3).

Knowledge of natural things seems to be based in the senses, but there are several connected reasons why what is known in this way cannot be the same as what was postulated by the new science. Firstly, our senses often deceive us; an object at a great distance, for example, appears the same size as a closer object that is in fact much smaller. Such cases of deception point to a general and deep paradox for the modern system, namely, that what is given in perception is dependent upon the observer, while what we are supposed to know by perception is independent of us. What is given in perception cannot be the absolute figure and relations of objects in space that are studied in mechanics. Indeed, what is given in perception seems wholly irrelevant to mechanics, so much so that the 'primary qualities' in perception could be ignored altogether, and the mind with its perceptions could be defined as non-spatial and non-quantifiable.

If material things are not given immediately as the objects of perception, the problem begins to bite: how are we sure of their presence? Perceptions can be as they are, and still the question can be raised whether there exists a material reality. Further, the possibility that perceptions need correspond to nothing external is demonstrated in cases of delusion and dreaming. Descartes turns to such cases after considering cases of sense-deception (1: First Meditation). In dreaming we have the same kind of experiences as in waking perception (experiences of colours, shapes, motion, etc.), but they correspond to nothing outside the mind, even if we are convinced of their reality at the time. This shows that the existence of material things which cause perceptions is distinct from the perceptions themselves. But now the problem is this: even in waking perception, how can we know that our perceptions do correspond to material things, how can we know that they are not mere creatures of the imagination?—And that is the problem of knowledge.

One way of stating the problem is this: the empiricist epistemology, which grew to maturity with modern physical science, was not good enough to explain knowledge of the reality postulated by that science. What is given in perception is relative to and dependent on the observer; but nature was conceived absolute and independent. So different are mental perceptions from material reality, that it is conceivable that the perceptions should exist even without a corresponding material world. But according to empiricism, the subject is acquainted only with sense-experience, and consequently the existence of the external world must remain for the subject problematic.

Inadequate though empiricism appeared to be, its supports were firm. One support is Locke's argument, which presupposes that all the materials of thinking are derived from experience. The other is the Cartesian argument, given in the first two Meditations (1), that only what is immediately given in experience is certain, while the existence of bodies in space is open to doubt. These two supports of empiricism are probably in the end the same. For one justification of the claim that experience is the source of ideas is precisely the epistemological conviction that experience is what is immediately knowable; and conversely, what is indubitable according to Descartes is precisely that he *thinks*, for here thinking and perceiving come to the same thing (1: Second Meditation).

(iii) Rationalism

If knowledge of the natural world postulated in modern philosophy could not come from experience, what then was its origin? Part of the answer was already in the new physics: knowledge was fundamentally *mathematical*. Knowledge of the natural world, in practice and in theory, was founded in mathematical intuition and reason. The concepts of mathematics were held not to be derived from the untrustworthy senses, but were rather innate (e.g. Descartes, 1: Fifth Meditation). Hence mathematical truths were *a priori*.

However, mathematical physics was also an experimental science, combining experience with reason. In general it was supposed that mathematical principles must be compared with nature, in order to determine which mathematical laws nature did follow, and which it did not. Notwithstanding the practical success of the experimental method, however, it was epistemologically problematic according to the Cartesian system. Indeed it was problematic how we could tell by experience that there was a natural world at all corresponding to mathematics.

Descartes' solution to the problem was that God's goodness ensured the existence of nature. He wrote:

> For since He has given me . . a very great inclination to believe that they (ideas) are conveyed to me by corporeal objects, I do not see how He could be defended from the accusation of deceit if these ideas were produced by causes other than corporeal objects. Hence we must allow that corporeal things exist. However, they are perhaps not exactly what we perceive by the senses, since this comprehension by the senses is in many instances very obscure and confused; but we must at least admit that all things which I conceive in them clearly and distinctly, that is to say, all things which, speaking generally, are comprehended in the object of pure mathematics, are truly to be recognized as external objects. (1: Sixth Meditation, p. 191)

Descartes' solution to the problem of knowledge is sometimes seen now as rather irrelevant, as though the appeal to God's assurances was an *ad hoc* manoeuvre that swept the real issue aside. However, whatever one might think of the arguments that Descartes employed in reaching his solution, irrelevant it was not. For corporeal matter in absolute mathematical space was truly unknowable by man. Human knowledge is *limited*, in two ways: firstly, in being relative to a particular position inside space; secondly, because it depends on a medium which distorts what is known. Only a being that was limited in neither of these ways could know spatial things as they really are.

Newton wrote:

> Is not the Sensory of Animals that place to which the sensitive
> Substance is present, and into which the sensible Species of
> Things are carried through the Nerves and Brain, that there they
> may be perceived by their immediate presence to that Substance?
> And these things being rightly dispatch'd, does it not appear from
> Phaenomena that there is a Being incorporeal, living, intelligent,
> omnipresent, who in infinite Space, as it were in his Sensory, sees
> the things themselves intimately, and thoroughly perceives them,
> and comprehends them wholly by their immediate presence to
> himself: Of which things the Images only carried through the
> Organs of Sense into our little Sensoriums, are there seen and
> beheld by that which in us perceives and thinks. (2: III, 1, p. 370)

However, God only *as it were* has a sensorium. Newton explains:

> The Organs of Sense are not for enabling the Soul to perceive the
> Species of Things in its Sensorium, but only for conveying them
> thither; and God has no need of such Organs, he being every
> where present to the Things themselves. (ibid. p. 403)

According to the modern view, then, nature was known immediately and wholly by God. And it was by mathematics that men
could share in the divine knowledge. On this, Galileo wrote:

> As concerns the truth, of which mathematical demonstrations
> give us the knowledge, it is that same as that which the Divine
> Wisdom knows. But . . . the manner whereby God knows the
> infinite propositions of which we understand some few is much
> more excellent than ours, which proceeds by ratiocination and
> passes from conclusion to conclusion, whereas His is done at one
> single thought or intuition. (1: p. 115)

Thus an essential feature of the epistemology that accompanied
modern philosophy of nature was *rationalism*: knowledge was
conceived as *a priori* intuition and reason, primarily mathematical,
founded in the divine. (This conception of 'rationalism' is not
intended to be definitive. The customary 'rationalists'—Descartes,
Spinoza and Leibniz—are a heterogeneous group.)

The Cartesian solution to the problem of knowledge was highly pertinent; for the nature described by modern mathematical physics was not accessible to human experience, which was limited by position and distorted by the sense-organs. Knowledge of absolute mathematical nature could not be founded in human experience, but necessarily would derive from God, or from that which in man is god-like. However, this saving theory of knowledge could be believed only as long as conviction in God's existence remained. Descartes' own proofs of the existence of God in his Third and Fifth Meditations (1) belonged to scholastic thought rather than to modern, and subsequently they commanded no general acceptance. And already in Locke's polemical arguments against innate ideas in the First Book of his *Essay* (1), the idea of God, like all others, was held to be discoverable in nature, and consequently the epistemology of revelation became less credible. As Burtt remarks (1: pp. 297–9), the decline of faith in God was the decline of what alone could make sense of the foundations of modern metaphysics, and it was this decline that found expression in the problem of knowledge.

(iv) Phenomenalism

The problem of knowledge can by solved by empiricism only if it can be shown that physical reality is given in sense-experience. Berkeley's spiritual idealism was one attempt to show this. A different kind of attempt was made by the twentieth-century empiricists, particularly the logical positivists of the Vienna Circle. Their arguments were concerned with language and meaning.

We saw above that when language is introduced into the Cartesian metaphysics, it seems necessary to postulate two languages, one describing mental phenomena, the other physical objects. The question arises: what are the relations between these two languages, and which of them is the more fundamental?

The priority of the phenomenalist language is established by the following argument: the signs of language must stand for things that are known to the speaker, but what is known to us is none other than the contents of sense-experience; consequently, the signs of language must signify the contents of sense-experience, and sentences employing those signs must be descriptions of sense-experience. That is, language must be the phenomenalist language.

The first premise expresses the truth that the user of a language must know what it means, otherwise it will not be a language for him, but mere marks or noises with no meaning. And if it be assumed, as it was throughout the tradition described in this chapter, that a meaningful sign is distinguished from a mere mark or noise because it is correlated with some thing, then that general truth assumes the particular form: the user of language must be acquainted with the objects for which its signs stand.[9] Add to this the empiricist premise that we are acquainted with sense-experience, but apparently not with physical objects, and the priority of the phenomenalist language over the physicalist language is proven.

Language must describe sense-experience. What, then, is the status of the physicalist language? According to the above argument, any language that appears to describe something beyond what is immediately given is either deceptive in this appearance, or is no language at all. In the case of ordinary language that describes physical objects, the choice between these two alternatives is clear: the language must, in the end, describe what is given in experience. So it was proposed that each proposition about physical objects could be analysed into propositions about sense-experience, propositions that specify what experiences would be had by an observer in such-and-such a position and in such-and-such circumstances. *Phenomenalism* was the claim that this analysis would be possible.[10]

Physical reality is not, however, the only category that apparently lies beyond immediate experience. There are also the inner experiences of other people, past events, the entities postulated by theoretical science; and so on. In short, very little is immediately given, only the present, inner experience of the subject. But, there is a proof that *all* language must be restricted to the description of the immediately given. Consequently, phenomenalism must be just the final stage in a larger programme of analysing one form of discourse into another. This larger programme included 'philosophical behaviourism', the view that statements about other minds are reducible to statements about behaviour. It included also reductionism in science, the proposed analysis of statements referring to 'unobservables' into descriptions of experiments. Also, statements about the past were held to be translatable into statements about the present. When all discourse was explicitly in physicalist form, the whole would then be translated into the phenomenalist language.[11]

The force behind this whole programme was summed up in the so-called Verification Principle of Meaning. According to this, the cognitive (or descriptive) meaning of a statement is given by the method of its verification in sense-experience. Thus, unless a particular kind of statement could be shown in the final analysis to be verifiable by sense-experience, it would follow that such statements had no meaning. This is the verificationist criterion of meaning: unverifiable statements are cognitively meaningless, i.e. they describe nothing, and are incapable of truth or falsity. So the stakes of the reductionist programme were high, being no less than the meaning of the major part of everyday discourse, and the whole of science. Hence the effort to provide analyses of these forms of language. However, such a protective attitude was not extended towards metaphysics, theology and ethics, which were abandoned as indeed meaningless in the above sense.[12]

The combination of the verification principle and the companion criterion of meaning entails that all and only meaningful statements are verifiable (at least in principle). Thus there can be no meaningful statements that describe a reality beyond the reach of our knowledge. So the problem of knowledge is solved, solved by limiting meaning (or understanding) to the narrow bounds of immediately given sense-experience.

The major problem then was: is language in fact limited in that way? Are descriptions of other minds no more than abbreviated descriptions of behaviour? Also, are scientific theories no more than descriptions of observations and experiments? Examples of these kinds of analysis were, to put it mildly, thin on the ground. And the final phenomenalist stage was certainly no less problematic. It could be put in this way: the problem of knowledge was solved at the expense of creating a new *problem of meaning*. How can we give sentences meaning that is prohibited by the empiricist criterion? And this is analogous to the old problem of knowledge: how do we know what empiricism dictates we cannot know? Both meaning and knowledge seem to reach beyond the narrow limits of sense-experience. And now the culprit responsible for both problems seems likely to be what is common in them: empiricism. Or better, the culprit was the whole metaphysics of which empiricism was just a part.

The principle of verification had a relatively short life. The programme it demanded *a priori* appeared to be largely fantasy— and the only reward at the end was solipsism. Nevertheless, the principle was a very *clear* expression of a theory of understanding and knowledge which had been current for centuries; and this clarity performed the service of showing that the theory was no longer credible. Moreover, in the new empiricism there was an indication of a radically new conception, namely, the explanation of meaning in terms of *methods of verification*.

The verification principle can be derived in two ways, and comparison of the two is instructive. The first way we have already considered; the argument is that sense-experience is what we are acquainted with, so that is what language must describe. Propositions truly or falsely represent sense-experience; either they are 'elementary', i.e. descriptions of a simple condition of experience, or they are truth-functions of such elementary propositions.

Regarded in this way, logical positivism stands at its closest to the *Tractatus* metaphysics. Both prove *a priori* that language must consist of elementary propositions together with all their possible truth-functions. But the nature of the elementary propositions were radically different in the two cases: the positivists made only empiricist demands on them, so that elementary propositions had only to be (never mind exactly how) descriptions of sense-experience; Wittgenstein, on the other hand, tackled the problem of how the proposition truly or falsely describes the world, and concluded that elementary propositions were pictures of particles in space. Roughly speaking, the positivists made language describe the Cartesian mental realm, while in the *Tractatus* language describes objects in absolute space , the world of modern physics. But this difference between the *Tractatus* metaphysics and logical positivism itself presupposes common acceptance of much in the modern philosophical tradition.

But there is another aspect to logical positivism, which distinguishes it from previous expressions of empiricism, and also from the *Tractatus* metaphysics. This is the emphasis on evidence or verification. The positivists saw that evidence played a crucial role in knowledge. But they saw also, and this was the great and perhaps most original insight, that the concept of verification was central to the *meaning* of a proposition; that asking how a proposition is to be verified is one way of asking what the proposition means. This insight, however, was completely stripped of its true significance by the old framework within which the positivists were thinking; or, better, the old framework prevented its true significance from emerging. For there is no room in empiricism for the concept of evidence or verification, no room in the theory of knowledge, and still less in the theory of judgement.

It was supposed that judgement, the proposition, represented a possible state of empirical reality, i.e. its truth-conditions. Consequently if evidence plays any role in determining the sense of a proposition, it must do so by determining its truth-conditions. Hence a proposition must state and be equivalent to its evidence. In other words, a proposition is a truth-function of whatever evidential propositions determine its meaning. These evidential propositions must in turn be truth-functions of whatever propositions determine their meaning, until in the end all propositions are shown to be truth-functions of propositions which are *not*, in their turn, based on any evidence, i.e. propositions that describe immediate sense-experience. Thus in the final analysis the concept of evidence, as opposed to the concept of representing a state of reality, has no place in the theory of meaning.

An analogous result follows in the theory of knowledge, if the insight that evidence enables inference from one kind of proposition to another (e.g. from another person's behaviour to his inner experience), is combined with the dogma that inference is valid only if it is inductive or deductive. For this conception of valid inference implies that evidence cannot take knowledge beyond what is immediately given, and therefore has no fundamental place in epistemology. Deductive evidence already asserts the conclusion (that is why it is a self-contradiction to affirm the premise and deny the conclusion). Inductive evidence, on the other hand, cannot be known to be valid unless an independent check is made on the truth of the conclusion; for the truth of the conclusion cannot be guaranteed by the truth of the premise alone, which is distinct from it. And so knowledge can never be based on evidence; it must always be, in the end, non-inferential, direct or immediate.

These linked definitions of inference and knowledge belong with certain preconceptions in ontology, and also in the theory of judgement. It is presupposed that reality is already given (as objects of some kind). Then judgement is essentially the representation of this reality. Hence also, the only kind of knowledge that can be envisaged is acquaintance with reality, or with the coincidence of judgement and reality. And the concept of inferential knowledge can make sense only if nothing can be known by inference which is not or could not be known directly, without inference. And this is what the definition of inference as either deductive or inductive ensures: knowledge is immediate. And according to empiricism, this means that knowledge is sensible intuition; and neither inductive nor deductive reasoning can go beyond its limits.

The definition of reason as deduction or induction characterises empiricism. Perhaps its earliest clear formulation was Hume's distinction between demonstrative and moral reasoning (2: IV, II, 30); and it was further clarified by the positivists in the twentieth-century using the new truth-functional logic. But this conception of reason, in the sense of inference, also characterises philosophical systems other than empiricism, for example, the *Tractatus*. Indeed, it is perhaps not incompatible even with rationalism. For what is essential to rationalism is the postulate of *a priori* intuition, called 'reason', into a non-empirical reality, and it does not follow from this postulate that the concept of inference from one proposition to another, for example in mathematical proof, has any fundamental epistemological role. It is probable that none of the philosophical theories described in this chapter have any use for the concept of reason, in the sense of inference. The essential point, I think, is that the concept of *method*, in judgement or in knowledge, is wholly alien to modern metaphysics. But we shall return to the concept in Part II.

(v) The Tractatus solution

The introduction of language into modern metaphysics solves the problem of knowledge. The main reason is that linguistic signs must be conventionally correlated with objects in the world. Applying this argument to the *Tractatus* metaphysics, we find an argument that runs as follows:

To understand the meaning of a proposition is to know what state of affairs it represents. This knowledge does not imply acquaintance with the state of affairs (which, in case the proposition is false, does not exist), but it does imply acquaintance with the objects in the state of affairs, which are named by the signs in the proposition. So to understand the meaning of a proposition requires at least *that* much acquaintance with the reality it represents. But then, it seems, there is no sense in which it would be 'impossible' to tell whether what a proposition asserts about objects of acquaintance is true or not, i.e. whether the objects do or do not stand in the relation shown in the proposition. The suggestion that the reality with which a proposition deals might be in some radical way beyond reach of knowledge, appears to be nonsense. In particular, since physical things in space are represented by language, it follows that they are objects of acquaintance.

Although an argument of this kind probably could be expressed by the *Tractatus* logic, there is little or no evidence in the text that Wittgenstein subscribed to it, and there is some evidence that he would not have done. Consider, for example, in 4.002:

> Man possesses the ability to construct languages capable of expressing every sense, without having any idea how each word has meaning or what its meaning is.

Behind this remark is the claim that words in ordinary language are general descriptions of complexes, which do not name particular (simple) objects. In this case, men do not know the meaning, i.e. the reference, of their words. Nevertheless, the argument against scepticism is still valid in the sense that what our propositions assert is knowable . If they assert only that a collection of simple objects has some gross structure, then we can indeed know whether or not they do have that structure, even though we have not named, and are not acquainted with, the particular objects in question. The conclusion still holds, then, that insofar as language describes physical objects, we are acquainted with them, at least as complexes. On this, Wittgenstein wrote in the *Notebooks*:

> Even though we have no acquaintance with simple objects we *do* know complex objects by acquaintance, we know by acquaintance that they are complex. (p. 50)

It should be noted, however, that consideration of what may or may not be possible for the human eye, or other means of perception, is hardly relevant to the *a priori* logic of the *Tractatus*. At one place (3.263), Wittgenstein does speak of knowing the meaning of a primitive sign, by which he presumably means being acquainted with the object for which it stands.

The status of scepticism in the *Tractatus* is further complicated by the fact that, according to the conception of language and its limits in the book, the sceptical doubt is literally nonsense (see 6.51). Language can express nothing about the world as a whole, or about the logic of language. Scepticism about the existence of the world, or about the relation between language and the world, is therefore meaningless. It would seem, however, that the sceptic is *shown* to be wrong. In the sense of the *Tractatus*, the world is *manifest*. Its existence is shown also in meaningful propositions, in language itself. Further, by the argument already considered, if the sense of propositions is understood, it is possible to tell whether they are true or false. Consequently scepticism about knowledge of truth or falsity implies scepticism about meaning, and also about thinking. But doubt whether thought and language are meaningful is absurd. (Compare Descartes: I can doubt everything, but not that *I think*.)

The conclusion is that we are directly acquainted with physical reality. But then what has become of the traditional arguments that such acquaintance is impossible? Two sets of powerful arguments now confront one another: if, as it seems, our language describes physical reality, then we must have acquaintance with it; on the other hand, there are the old arguments that physical things are beyond our acquaintance. But what are those arguments?— Consider those of the form: judgement about experience cannot be mistaken, but judgement about physical objects can be mistaken, and this shows that only experience is immediately given, not physical things. But what is a 'judgement about experience'? This notion in modern metaphysics is, in one respect, a gross error, since there is no coherent account of what such a judgement would be. For experience *is* judgement; it is a thought about physical reality, it is not itself the subject-matter of judgement. Or, it may be that a judgement about experience is some faded image of a perception, which agrees or fails to agree with a present experience. But that is the point: any judgement about anything can indeed be right or wrong. Sense-experience only appears to be incorrigible because we have not thought through what it would mean to make a judgement about it. It is true that when *I say* 'I have such-and-such an experience', then I cannot be in error. But to understand why this is so, we need a radically different account of judgement from that which characterises modern metaphysics. Descartes was right in not doubting the *I think*, but why? Is this judgement a special picture, or a picture of something special, or rather a different kind of thing altogether?

'Judgements about physical objects can be mistaken' just means that judgements are made about physical objects. It is because we make judgements about physical objects, but not about experience, that we can be wrong about physical objects and not about experience. The requirement that judgement about physical objects in space can be right or wrong is, of course, met by the *Tractatus* metaphysics. But this does not exclude acquaintance with them.

Why did corrigibility ever seem to exclude acquaintance? It was only because the conditions that determined the truth or falsity of judgements about physical reality were held to exist beyond reach of knowledge, quite distinct from the judgements, i.e. ideas of perception, themselves. But this separation of thought and reality was problematic. As Berkeley saw, and as Wittgenstein later proved, thought and reality must be of the *same kind*. According to the *Tractatus*, thought and reality have the same form, they exist in the same space. In the *Tractatus* all judgements are corrigible just because they are judgements; but judgement and reality exist together, and we are equally acquainted with both.

Corrigibility of judgements about physical objects was not, then, the reason why acquaintance with physical reality was held to be impossible. Corrigibility only seems to have this consequence if it is already assumed that physical objects lie beyond what we are acquainted with. The fundamental problem was, I think, rather this: human beings only experience the results of interaction between themselves and nature, but nature itself, according to modern philosophy, exists independently of us. Thus, what a man is acquainted with is relative to his means of perception, and cannot be identified with the absolute physical world.

The fate of *this* argument in *Tractatus* metaphysics is of great importance, though also rather obscure. Insofar as language is used and understood by men, they must have acquaintance with what it describes, including physical reality. So far, then, the *Tractatus* points to a solution of the problem of knowledge. However, it seems also that man as thinking and knowing subject is of no concern to logic. The subject defined by logic is stripped of all human qualities: it has no body, no organs of sense, no point of view in the world. Rather the subject is transcendental; it knows an absolute world, not by any kind of interaction. Regarded in this light, the *Tractatus* pays a high price for solving the problem of knowledge; indeed, in an important sense the problem is not solved, insofar as it was a problem for human beings, not for a transcendental subject. The question how human beings could know the absolute world postulated in the *Tractatus* is not raised. The conflict between the relativity of human experience and the absoluteness of the world is therefore left unresolved. The issue here is at root the same as the problem whether the absolute system of measures which represents the world of the *Tractatus* is really *human* language at all, a problem which has been noted in the first chapter (section 8, end of v).

The logic of the *Tractatus* excludes the problem of knowledge.

Thought and reality must have the same form, and therefore knowledge of reality is no more problematic than knowledge of thought. But it can be seen that this same logic makes thought, in a profound sense, unnecessary. In order to compare thought with reality, I must be acquainted with reality; but if I am acquainted with reality, what is the purpose of thinking about it? Is this a pastime? No; the concept of thought or judgement (hence also the concept of language) has a proper role in metaphysics only if judgement constitutes the *medium* by which reality is grasped and known. So in this respect, the account of judgement given by Descartes and Locke was a good one, for sense-experience constituted both the medium of thought and a means of knowing, and was distinguishable from reality itself. The problem was that it was too distinguishable; experience and reality belonged to completely different categories of being. Consequently neither the account of thought, nor the account of knowing, was satisfactory. Judgement must be a true medium. Therefore it must be distinguishable from reality, but not a separate form of being. These requirements cannot be met, however, if judgement is regarded as a static form, for this form will inevitably be either the same as or different from the form of reality. Rather, judgement must be conceived as an interaction between subject and object, that is to say, as a method.

Any reality described by language must be known. The twentieth-century empiricists inferred from this that language must describe sense-experience. The alternative inference, more akin to what we find in the *Tractatus*, is that we must have knowledge of objects in absolute space. Whichever way the argument turns, the problem of knowledge is solved by placing great demands *a priori* on the nature of language. Its nature and limits are rigidly defined. The new problem arises: is language of the kind which is demanded? And if the answer to this question is 'No', then *all* the fundamental assumptions of modern philosophy are called into question.

4 SUBJECT

(i) The cogito

Descartes wrote in his Second Meditation:

But what then am I? A thing which thinks. What is a thing which thinks? It is a thing which doubts, understands, affirms, denies, wills, refuses, which also imagines and feels. (1: p. 153)

The subject performs the function of thinking, or it is a substance in which thoughts occur. This definition of the subject was severely shaken by Hume in his *Treatise of Human Nature* (1). Hume argued that if 'substance' be defined as 'something which may exist by itself', then perceptions in the mind are themselves substances, and no 'thinking substance' need be postulated (I, IV, v, p. 233). A perception can exist by itself, and the scholastic notion of a substance needed to support them is unnecessary. (It might be noted that this rejection of the scholastic notion of substance from the theory of the mind corresponded to the gradual decline of the notion in physics, and its replacement there by the concept of spatial, massy atoms.) Hume then turned to the view proposed by Locke (1: II, xxvii, 9), that the self is something we are always aware of as a perception. There is, Hume says, no constant or invariable impression which could give rise to such an idea of self; and further, all that we can find on introspection is always some particular perception. He writes:

> For my part, when I enter most intimately into what I call *myself*, I always stumble on some particular perception or other, of heat or cold, light or shade, love or hatred, pain or pleasure. I never can catch *myself* at any time without a perception, and never can observe anything but the perception. (op. cit., I, IV, vi, p. 252)

The *Tractatus* account of the self is similar to Hume's, in that there appears to be no need for a thinking subject. Hume's argument that perceptions are complete in themselves is related to the argument which the *Tractatus* logic seems to imply, that thoughts or propositions are self-sufficient entities which require for their existence no contribution from the subject (see above, Ch.1, 8, ii). Hume's second argument, that the subject is not an object of perception, recurs in the *Tractatus* in the following form:

> 5.631 There is no such thing as the subject that thinks or entertains ideas.
> If I wrote a book called *The World as I found it*, I should have to include a report on my body, and should have to say which parts were subordinate to my will, and which were not, etc., this being

a method of isolating the subject, or rather of showing that in an important sense there is no subject; for it alone could *not* be mentioned in that book.—

In modern metaphysics, the subject became that which thinks. But there is no need for such a thing; thoughts are complete in themselves. Nor is the thinking subject to be found, as it were, among thoughts, among perceptions, or in the world. The only role the subject was given, was superfluous.

(ii) Solipsism

The Cartesian *cogito* defines the subject; it defines also what belongs to the subject, as opposed to what does not, that is to say, mind as opposed to matter. It is because the mind is the medium of thought that it characterises the subject. Further, the existence of material things may be doubted insofar as it is not given immediately in thought, i.e. in sense-representation. And it is because the mind is indubitably known, while corporeal nature, including the human body, is subject to doubt and may not exist, even though the I and its thoughts do exist, that Descartes concludes that he is essentially mind and not essentially body, nor any other corporeal thing (1: Second Meditation). In this way, the subject ceased to be the whole human being, but was mind alone.

The Cartesian distinction between the I and the not-I presupposes that corporeal nature is distinguishable from mind, and that corporeal nature can be known to exist. That is to say, the distinction presupposes dualism and a solution to the problem of knowledge. However, these two requirements became increasingly difficult to reconcile with one another, and consequently the division between subject and object became problematic. In the *Tractatus*, as previously in the modern tradition, the distinction collapses more or less completely.

In the seventeenth century it was supposed that each man was limited to his own experience, mind; but each man was also assured that there was an independent world conforming to his experience, and common to all men. This knowledge could not come from experience itself, but was rather in some way given by God. The absolute world inaccessible to the senses was God's world; He created it, and it was known immediately and wholly by Him. The divine assurance had several forms: God is no deceiver; out of His goodness, God would create the right correspondence between human experience and nature; in mathematics, men possess something of the divine knowledge, absolute and *a priori*; and also, the Creation is revealed in Scripture. There was no *problem* here. The problem arose, rather, with the subsequent decline of faith; for then the whole edifice became uncertain. And there were two solutions to the uncertainty: either nature must be reduced to what is given in (my) experience, or, the subject must be elevated above the empirical, so that nature itself is its dominion. Either way the effect is the same: the I assumes a god-like position, it surveys everything, neither from a particular point of view, nor by organs of sense. With the decline of belief, the I ceases to be human, or finite mind, and becomes transcendental.

The first great philosopher to embrace atheism seriously was Hume; and Hume also demonstrated the inadequacy of human experience and reason. As is well-known, it was Kant who picked up the pieces and welded them back into a coherent metaphysics. But in order to do this, Kant postulated the transcendental subject as the source of *a priori* cognition; the human being was not enough.[13]

The concept of transcendental subject appeared in various forms throughout subsequent nineteenth-century German idealism. It appears also, though in a less spectacular guise, in the early twentieth-century philosophy we have so far discussed, logical empiricism and the *Tractatus* metaphysics.

These twentieth-century philosophies solved the problem of knowledge in distinct but analogous ways: language is made the means of representation, and everything that is described by language is immediately known. Dualism therefore collapses, since there is no longer a difference of category between thought and reality, and there is no longer a distinction between what is immediately known and what is mediately known. Thus the twentieth-century empiricists no longer called sense-experience 'mental', rather it was 'neutral', and what we know as mind and matter is (logically) constructed out of it.[14] Similarly, there is no fundamental dualism in the *Tractatus*; any distinction between mind and matter would be made *a posteriori*, for nothing in logic requires it. The solution of the problem of knowledge and the subsequent collapse of dualism makes the limits of the self problematic. Applying the Cartesian criterion that the subject is defined by thought, it seems that now the subject should be defined by language; but language is commensurate with the whole of reality. Or again, applying the Cartesian criterion that the subject is defined by what is immediately given, it follows that everything now belongs to the subject, that everything is the subject's own states. These lines of thought appear to be close to the solipsism in the *Tractatus*: language is *my* language, the limits of my language mean the limits of *my* world; the world is my world, I am my world (5.6's). Similar kinds of conclusion pressed on the logical positivists, though their resistance to them was greater.[15]

Although the transcendental subject of the *Tractatus* (as also that implied by logical empiricism), is in certain respects the descendant of the subject postulated in the Kantian and neo-Kantian systems, one fundamental difference should be noted. Kant saw that the thinking subject is *active*, and at least in part creates the objects of its knowledge. This insight was fundamentally opposed to the previous assumptions of the modern tradition, which we have discussed, and which are found still intact in the *Tractatus*. In the *Tractatus*, so far as I can see, there is no sign of Kant's 'Copernican revolution'. The subject in the *Tractatus* has no means of thought or knowledge, and in no way produces the world. All possibilities in the world, all that can be known, all that can be meaningfully said or thought, is already given in the form of objects; the world is absolute, independent of the subject.[16]

The *Tractatus* gives one expression to what was inevitable in modern thought, the elevation of the subject to a god-like position. Man made the modern world-picture with God in mind. Nature was conceived from the divine point of view; it was grasped as an absolute whole, with its essential laws and limits defined. There was a fundamental ambiguity in the status of the subject from the beginning.

Wittgenstein knew the direction in which his logic was leading. He wrote in the *Notebooks* 'There are two godheads: the world and my independent I' (p. 74). But let us ask, finally, why two godheads are required? What is the purpose of this 'I', when the world is complete in itself, when even the representation of the world requires no subject? As we have seen (Ch. 1, 8), Wittgenstein seems to waver in the *Tractatus* between retaining the I (though, indeed, as the world itself), and dismissing it altogether. The issue was a great one, for without the I there is no meaning of value in the world. Perhaps the distant ancestor of this problem in the *Tractatus* metaphysics was the seventeenth-century debate whether the absolute nature postulated by philosophy required the existence of God.

5 SURVEY AND CONCLUSIONS

So far we have considered various philosophical theories, most of which belong to modern thought, and have seen how they are connected more or less directly with the *Tractatus*. This final section has two connected aims; one is to bring together the themes discussed so far, making explicit the logical connections between them, and the other is to suggest an historical perspective for Wittgenstein's early philosophy, and by implication, one for his later philosophy. With these aims in mind, the section falls into two parts: the first concerns modern metaphysics, in which, until this century, language played a comparatively minor role, and the second focuses on language, bringing together various conceptions which are either in the *Tractatus*, or which share certain key assumptions with what is in the *Tractatus*.

Firstly, then, let us consider modern metaphysics. According to the philosophy that has been dominant, in varying forms, in Europe for the past four centuries or so, man is essentially a thinking substance or subject, that is, he is presented with perceptions, images, ideas, etc.; some of these perceptions are caused by the interaction of material bodies in space with the sense-organs of the human body. An important feature of this picture is the dualism between two categories of being, mind and matter. Dualism has many and various aspects; they are intimately connected, but may be distinguished in the following ways.

Firstly, dualism is a distinction between what is spatial (matter), and what is non-spatial (mind). Objects in space possess the primary qualities of extension, mass and inertia, which can be described by mathematics. Secondly, dualism distinguishes what exists absolutely (matter) from what is relative to man (mind). Thirdly, dualism reflects the distinction between thought and reality. The mind contains perceptions of the external world, which are veridical if they show the world to be as it in fact is, and which are otherwise illusory. In this representative theory of perception there is, therefore, a theory of truth as being correspondence between thought and reality, and a theory of judgement, which has no name, but which is the ancestor of the recent conception that the meaning of a sentence is given by its truth-conditions, and particularly, which is the ancestor of the *Tractatus* theory of the proposition. Fourthly, dualism contains a theory of knowledge, for the subject knows material things in space via his perceptions of them. And finally, dualism distinguishes between subject and object: the mind essentially belongs to the 'I', but material things, including the human body, do not.

All of these aspects of dualism in modern philosophy were problematic, perhaps insolubly so. What forced the adoption of dualism in the beginning appears to have been the modern understanding of nature, expressed in physics and mechanics. Nature was conceived to be essentially spatial and material, absolute, independent of human activity, the domain of mathematics. This conception of nature made no place for the whole man; only the human body was part of nature, a mechanical thing like other bodies, while what we have learnt to think of as 'mental processes', the emotions, belief, perception, feeling, will—which make our life—had to belong to another realm of being, the mind. But it was exactly because the mind was defined in opposition to an independent reality, exactly because the mind became the receptacle for whatever did not fit into the new mechanical nature, that there never would be a coherent answer to the question how human beings, or mind, related to the world; that is, there was no coherent account of understanding or thought, nor of knowledge, nor of human action, will and value.

Thus, what is non-spatial cannot be a true or false representation of what is spatial. Consequently either dualism is retained and the account of understanding left obscure, or spatial qualities are allowed into mind, so that dualism is retained in a radically weaker, though still problematic form, being between relative mental spaces and absolute physical space. Secondly, what account could there be of human knowledge of material reality? Material things are not given immediately in sense-perception, which is relative to position in space and to the particular human sense-organs. Nature was defined as being independent of human beings and their perception; therefore their knowledge of it was ruled out. Knowledge comes from *interaction with the world*. The moderns saw this; that is why knowledge was supposed to derive from interaction between the human body (the sense-organs) and the rest of nature. But the knowing subject was *not* the human body, it had no interaction at all with anything, but simply 'observed' the products of the material interaction. And the problem was then whether the subject could know that what it passively observed was indeed the product of a material interaction, or rather just states of its own imagination.

The insight that human knowledge is interaction was buried in the assumptions of modern thought, neglected because it was incompatible with an absolute ontology. An absolute world cannot, by definition, be known by interaction, but must be known by direct and passive observation. So the 'I' was not identified with what acts, but with what passively observes. But all that the subject could know in this way was its own mental states, not nature itself.

Difficulties lay upon difficulties. The distinction between subject and object was also threatened. The distinction between mental states which belong to the subject, and material states which do not, presupposes that mental states are truly the medium by which material reality is represented. But the subject can never know that this presupposition is a valid one. The distinction between inner and outer cannot be made by the subject, and it threatens to dissolve altogether. Subject and object, appearance and reality, coincide. In this and related ways, the tradition tended towards solipsism, and towards realism, the doctrine that the subject directly observes reality as it is, without any medium, or other method.

The problems of thought, of knowledge, and of the distinction between subject and object, all spring from the dualism of mind and matter. There were other problems, not concerning the relations between mind and matter, but the two categories themselves. For example, the question arose whether there was need to postulate a thinking subject apart from perception or thought itself. Also, there was a profound problem in physics, namely, the principle of change in a nature containing *states* of affairs. Things changed their states under the action of 'force'; but is this to say any more than that things do change, and perhaps also, that we expect them to? If the concept of change is not grounded in nature, it must belong to us alone, for no concept can be grounded in our relations with nature.

Those difficulties in modern philosophy that arose specifically from the dualism between mind and matter were solved by the *Tractatus* metaphysics, and the key to this revolution was the introduction of language as the vehicle or medium of representation. In the *Tractatus* the division between thought and reality is no longer the problematic one of category, but is only the conventional difference between objects which are names and objects which are named. Most importantly, thought and what is represented in thought are in the same space, this being the condition under which representation is possible. It follows that everything which is represented in thought, and thought itself, is spatial, and consequently the traditional distinction between spatial matter and non-spatial mind is no longer valid. Whatever dualism is hinted at in the *Tractatus* for example, by the separation of psychology from physics, would need a new explanation, perhaps in terms of an *a posteriori* distinction among forms of description or forms of space. The epistemological aspect of dualism also collapses, and with it the problem of knowledge. There is in the *Tractatus* no distinction between immediate and mediate knowledge; all knowledge is immediate, there is no medium between subject and object. That the subject is acquainted with the world follows from the existence of thought or language, firstly because thought or language belong to the same category as reality itself, and secondly because insofar as thought or language is understood the subject must know the conventional relation between their signs and objects in the world.

The price paid for a solution to these difficulties is, however, high. Implications which were concealed in the belief that dualism was coherent, are now laid bare. Thus, all that happens in the world is wholly accidental and contingent; or, what comes in the end to the same, there is no possible interaction between the subject and the world. The subject does not belong to the world, it is neither body nor mind. The subject is super-human; it observes the whole world, being limited neither by means of perception, nor by a particular point of view within the world. It has been argued that transcendental epistemology belonged with modern philosophy from its conception. Knowledge of absolute nature independent of man was derived from innate ideas, given by God and verified by divine assurance. Subsequently, the source of *a priori* cognition was identified as the subject itself, elevated to a transcendental status. Following the tradition of post-Kantian philosophy, the subject in the *Tractatus* is transcendental, but more in conformity with the original presuppositions of modern thought than with the Kantian philosophy, this subject is not active; the world is already given as absolute, and is simply observed. Insofar as the world is absolute, however, the question arises whether the subject is indeed necessary at all. Wittgenstein wavers between having no subject, postulating that the subject is the limit of the world, neither inside nor outside, and identifying the subject with the whole world. Or better, for there is no *wavering* in the *Tractatus*, the subject is postulated in all these three ways.

And so, what began as a complete metaphysics, a conception of man, of nature, and of man's place in nature, became transformed eventually into a philosophy in which there is no man, no human understanding or knowledge, but only an absolute world, indistinguishable from subject, or without subject at all. If we were to draw a picture of the *Tractatus* metaphysics, to be compared with the picture of the Cartesian (see above Figure I, section 2, i), it would consist only of spatial objects, with no thinking subject, and with no medium of representation and knowledge separable from the world. It would be only this:

objects in space

FIGURE 4

But this metaphysics, if the reader will bear with me, is no philosophy we can use at all; it does not make the necessary discriminations. The *Tractatus* marks the *end* of a tradition. This tradition has its origin in modern philosophy of nature, a philosophy which could prepare no proper place for human experience, because it aspired to, and supposed it had been granted, and eventually usurped, a higher view. The immediate influences on Wittgenstein's thought reflect the roots of his philosophy. It was the last of the Newtonian physicists, particularly Herz, who guided Wittgenstein to his account of representation, the one best suited to modern natural philosophy; and it was a philosopher in the Kantian tradition, Schopenhauer, who showed Wittgenstein that the subject must be transcendental.

Let us turn now to the concept of language in relation to the *Tractatus*. As we have seen, the main differences between the *Tractatus* and previous modern philosophy resulted from the introduction of language into metaphysics. It was the contemporary preoccupation with logic and language that Wittgenstein shared with Frege and Russell, who were perhaps the greatest conscious influences on Wittgenstein's thinking. The conception of language in the *Tractatus* was dictated by the axioms of modern philosophy: the proposition was proved to be a static, spatial measuring rod, a true-or-false representation of a spatial state of affairs.

This theory of language is not, however, the only one which belongs with the modern tradition. Another is Locke's view that the meaning of a general term is an idea in the mind, one produced by abstracting from the particulars to which the term applies, the feature which they have in common. This modern account of general terms shares certain assumptions with those accounts belonging to ancient and scholastic thought, even though it grew in opposition to them. The older views explained the meaning of general terms by saying that the terms referred to something found in, or instantiated by, many particulars, this something being called a universal. What ties together the ancient and more modern views is that both conceive description of things as involving perception of natural classes, and both conceive the meaning of a general term to be what holds such a class together as a unity. Thus, according to these views, description is, at bottom, passive. For our use of words only reflects what is already in the nature of things (even if we chose what it is, in the nature of things, that we wish to describe). In brief, both ancient and modern views of general terms express the conviction that the meaning of a word is an (already given) object.

This same conviction reappears in the *Tractatus* account of language, though applied to a different kind of description, a kind which perhaps emerged clearly for the first time in modern philosophy, namely, description of spatial arrangements of objects. The two kinds of description have, in their traditional forms, little in common: general terms indicate how things fall into classes, propositions represent how things are spatially related. But the *Tractatus* theory of the proposition shared with the traditional theories of general terms the conviction that language simply reflects and is wholly conditioned by what already exists in the nature of things. In this respect, the view that the meaning of a general term is an object associated with a class is of a piece with the view that the meaning of a proposition is a spatially complex object.

The general conviction that language describes what is already given, and is to be understood by acquaintance with the objects it stands for, gives rise to more piecemeal philosophy than the great theories so far considered. We might ask naïvely what objects words refer to, being particularly inclined to do so when those objects cannot be seen, heard or touched. Some order is introduced by grouping together words with similar meanings, such as colour words, numerals, words referring to mental processes, and so on. Between such groups we find no logical, deductive connections, and so it seems that the reality described by language divides into categories, each independent of the others. In this way, kinds of object come to be described by their negative characteristics: the mind is not spatial, not mechanical, not public; numbers are not physical, not mental, neither spatial nor temporal; value cannot be identified with natural qualities, nor with affections of our minds, nor of God's, it is neither physical, nor mental, nor spiritual.[17] There are also other ways of conceiving what reality language describes. We seem to know very well what we mean by saying, for instance, that the Earth is a ball floating freely in space, so we may repeat the sentence to ourselves, observing what we mean by it; we shall come across pictures in the mind's eye, which show what we are talking about and what we mean. And very often the use of a word suggests a picture of its meaning: for example, it is as if an intention were something *inside* a person; we cannot observe it, but he tells us it is there. There are various ways in which we can make or imagine pictures which seem to show what language means. Ontology done in these piecemeal ways draws on intuition and imagination; at times it is banal, otherwise it lapses into metaphor.

The burden of such a free approach to ontology and meaning falls heavily on the shoulders of the theory of knowledge, for account must be given of how the various realms of being postulated to explain the meaning of language are known. The accounts varied, but they could only be variations on the theme of *intuition*; for what existed was the state of some reality, and no matter what manner of being it had, it must be known by direct acquaintance of some kind. All such epistemological theories of direct access modelled their terminology on that used for ordinary perception of day-to-day things; memory is to be conceived as the direct seeing into the past, value is apprehended by a special 'moral sense', the mind by the 'inner eye', and the truths of mathematics by some intuition appropriate to them. All such accounts disregarded the role of evidence or proof, and generally of method, in knowledge—but we are familiar with this tendency from what has gone before. (I should say that these epistemologies are criticised here only because they express this tendency; each no doubt contains a truth. Some of them, particularly, served as necessary correctives to the dogmatic and at times tyrannical claim of empiricism and positivism that human knowledge is limited to perception by the five senses.)

The *Tractatus*, therefore, shares fundamental assumptions about language with a wide variety of other philosophies, ancient and modern, general and particular. What ties together the various and sometimes incompatible conceptions of language and meaning may be summed up as follows: words have meaning because they are correlated with objects of some kind, objects already existing in reality.

The theory of language given by the twentieth-century empiricists also shared this assumption, the objects described by language being in this case the contents of sense-experience. That propositions must describe what is immediately given in experience follows from modern empiricist epistemology. It can be seen that both major theories of language produced in the early decades of this century were dictated by the axioms of modern philosophy: empiricism demanded that language describe sense-experience, physics demanded that language describe arrangements of objects in space. However, neither of these demands were satisfied by language; at least, not apparently. Therefore both the empiricist verification principle and the *Tractatus* theory were obliged to incorporate the notion of analysis; analysis would reveal that ordinary language was, despite appearances, of the kind demanded and proved *a priori*. The empiricist analysis was epistemological, going from (what appears to be) the mediately given to the immediately given; analysis in the *Tractatus* was spatial, leading from complex to simple. Both kinds of analysis were truth-functional, reflecting shared acceptance of the conviction that meaning was given by truth-conditions.

These early twentieth-century concerns with language, however, marked the end of the modern tradition which dogmatically steered them, for the introduction of language destroyed the dualism on which that tradition was founded. The world was unified under language, and we were brought next to it. And from these considerations there emerged, as might be hoped, glimpses of a new philosophy. The *Tractatus* made clear some profound truths about language and its relation to reality: the proposition contains arbitrary elements, signs, but also has an essential feature, something spatial, in common with what is represented; this common feature is both natural, in the nature of reality, and *a priori*, in the nature of judgement itself. And in the empiricist verification principle too there are glimmers in the dark, for it expresses the new idea that meaning is determined by a *method*, an idea which implies, though this could not be seen at the time, that judgement is active and extended through time, and is no longer the static representation of what is already given. If these insights into language in the *Tractatus* and the new empiricism are combined with rejection of the concept of a transcendental, isolated and passive subject, a concept which emerged so clearly in these philosophies, then we already have much that will aid understanding of Wittgenstein's later philosophy.

It is to this philosophy that we now turn. We shall find that the *Tractatus* metaphysics is overturned, not piecemeal, but in one movement of thought. The purpose of this chapter has been to show that if the *Tractatus* falls, much falls with it. If the *Tractatus* metaphysics collapses, so do the axioms of modern philosophy to which it gave expression, and along with those axioms go their various implications, including those which are not found in the *Tractatus* itself. These implications include dualism of mind and body, empiricism, the problem of knowledge, and solipsism. The axioms of modern philosophy were crystallised in the *Tractatus* theory of language, intended to be a theory of human language, but prevented from being so by its origin. It is the rejection of this theory of language which leads into Wittgenstein's later philosophy. It is not this theory alone, however, that will be replaced, but also various accounts of language, ancient and modern, which share deep assumptions with what is in the *Tractatus*. Thus the *Tractatus* prepares the way for a turning-point in Western thought, away from assumptions at least as old as the modern age, towards a new mode of philosophy. The young Wittgenstein's work was able to perform this service, because of its purity and integrity.

Part II
The Later Philosophy

Part II

The Later Philosophy

3 Turning Our Whole Examination Round

I THE CONCEPT OF 'METHOD' IN MEASUREMENT

(i) Ways of measuring

A group of men want to measure the objects around them. They use similar measuring rods, and try to find out which objects are the same length as them. This is what happens: one man places his rod against the object to be measured; another does the same, but also sets up a microscope with which to view the ends of rod and object; a third man glances at his rod in his hands, and then at the object some distance from him; a fourth puts down his rod after looking at it carefully, and then goes to look at each object in turn; and lastly, one man takes his rod and bends it to fit whatever he is measuring. When the men report their findings, there is disagreement among them. Some say of a particular object that it is the same length as their rods, others that it is not. And we may suppose as well that no two of the men agree on the results for all the objects measured.

So which of this assortment of results is right? Well, the men were trying to determine which objects were the same length as their rods, so we can say: 'a man's result is right if he says that rod and object are the same length when in fact they are'. But now consider the question which, if any, of the men went about finding his results in the right way. What is the *right method* for measuring an object with a ruler? One answer which might be given is the following: 'It does not matter which method of measurement is used, all that matters is that one finds the right result, and that has just been defined'.

But then let us look closer at this definition of 'the right result', which is being made to carry all the weight. What does it mean to say: 'rod and object are the same length'? Of course it seems obvious what this means; we are to imagine the rod laid flat against the object, so that their ends coincide. However, this understanding of equality of length seems to presuppose a *particular method* of measurement. And if this is indeed the case, there is something radically wrong with the suggestion that it does not matter which method of measurement is used, as long as it leads to the right result. For we can understand what a right result is only if we are given a method of measurement. If, when we enquire after this, we are referred back to the concept of obtaining the right result—if, to put it briefly, the right method is defined as the one which produces the right result—we shall end up understanding nothing, neither what the right result is, nor how to obtain it.

The moral of this tale is of great importance in metaphysics. At the heart of metaphysics there are concepts which in certain respects are analogous to those involved in measuring. I mean the concepts of judgement, truth, reality; and others intimately connected. We find in metaphysics propositions of this kind: 'the world is represented by judgement; a judgement is true if it describes the world to be as in fact it is; if it agrees or corresponds with the world'. Such definitions or postulates say as yet very little; they express in general terms, for example, what the purpose of judgement is conceived to be. But they contain already the seed of false metaphysics, for they speak of the right result of judgement, that is to say, of truth, without mentioning the concept of a *method* for obtaining this result, that is, without mentioning the concept of method of judgement.

The connection between measurement and judgement is affirmed in both periods of Wittgenstein's philosophy. In the early period, the concept of method was assumed to be irrelevant; judgement is a rigid measure which in itself is a true or false representation of reality. Wittgenstein wrote in the *Tractatus*:

2.1512 It (the picture) is laid against reality like a measure.

2.21 A picture agrees with reality or fails to agree; it is correct or incorrect, true or false.

But this conception of judgement, also of thought, and of meaning, is questioned in the later work. Attention is directed to the concept of method. The *Blue Book* begins as follows:

What is the meaning of a word?
Let us attack this question by asking, first, what is an

explanation of the meaning of a word; what does the explanation of a word look like?

The way this question helps us is analogous to the way the question 'how do we measure a length?' helps us to understand the problem 'what is length?'

And the *Investigations* contains clear statements that our understanding of *what* is being measured presupposes *how* it is measured. For example:

One judges the length of a rod and can look for and find some method of judging it more exactly or more reliably. So—you say—*what* is judged here is independent of the method of judging it. What length *is* cannot be defined by the method of determining length.—To think like this is to make a mistake. What mistake?—To say "The height of Mont Blanc depends on how one climbs it" would be queer. And one wants to compare 'ever more accurate measurement of length' with the nearer and nearer approach to an object. But in certain cases it is, and in certain cases it is *not*, clear what "approaching nearer to the length of an object" means. What "determining the length" means is not learned by learning what *length* and *determining* are; the meaning of the word "length" is learnt by learning, among other things, what it is to determine length. (II, xi, p. 225e)

Let us consider the implications of defining judgement without reference to method. We shall see that these implications are characteristic of the philosophies already described in Part I.

A method of judgement is a practice which involves signs, for example, words and sentences of language. We refer to the method by which a sentence, say, is used, when we speak of its *meaning*. The meaning of a sentence is what is essential to its use in making judgements, and the method of its employment is precisely what is essential. Such a method can be explained to someone; we instruct a child, 'Say this here (in such-and-such situation), but not here', and so on. And sometimes we can explain when a particular sentence should be used by referring to what we call 'evidence', or 'reasons'. Evidence gives us the right to make a judgement; it signifies the method for estimating truth.

To obtain false metaphysics from the otherwise correct and harmless conception that truth is agreement with reality, we define any concept which pertains to method of judgement in terms of truth, i.e. in terms of 'the right result'. In particular, then, *meaning* and *evidence* must both be defined in terms of truth. Such a definition of meaning is peculiarly complex, since method itself is defined as an object. The definition of evidence in terms of truth is, however, relatively straightforward. Since method must lead to or guarantee truth, evidence must signify the method of making a judgement by guaranteeing the truth of that judgement. How can the truth of a judgement be guaranteed? To ask an analogous question: how can the result of measuring an object with a ruler be guaranteed? If someone said: 'We could measure the object first, find out the result, and then we would know what the result would be if we measured again', we should be amazed at the triviality of the reply. And this triviality would become a mistake if the person thought he was telling us *how* to determine a result. However, the reply is analogous to and no worse than the widely-held view that the best evidence is deductive. For this is to say, the best evidence already contains the inferred proposition. Indeed, perhaps deduction is the only valid kind of inference. For how could one proposition guarantee the truth of another, quite distinct proposition? Perhaps there is valid inductive inference, but its nature is obscure, unless it can be construed as a concealed deduction. For what is fundamentally obscure in this account of reasoning is the *method* by which we discover that a proposition is true; the only permitted 'method' is already to know that the proposition is true.

If truth is determined by no method, it must be a *state* of correspondence between proposition and reality. This state is absolute and self-contained, and therefore is not conceived as the result of applying a method, or indeed, as a 'result' at all. And so there is no use here for the notion of method, save perhaps to define it trivially as what brings about the state of correspondence.

It can be seen how meaning must be defined in accordance with this static conception of truth. A judgement must be an object like the fact it represents, so that it either coincides with the fact or fails to coincide. In a similar way, a ruler must be like what it measures, it must have *length*; this length is conceived as an object like the ruler itself, but more pure, stripped of all accidents of composition—'Look at the ruler, there you see its length'. Any sign that can be used in making judgements about the world must have something in common with the world. This common element is what is essential to the sign; it is the *meaning* of the sign. Meaning is an object, like the judgement-sign itself, but purer. And which object it is can be simply defined: the meaning of a judgement is given by the fact which would make it true (with which it would correspond) and may therefore be defined as the representation of the conditions of truth of the judgement.

Evidence is defined as what guarantees truth, and must therefore be deductive, or possibly inductive. Meaning is defined as a kind of object, the representation of truth-conditions. These theories of evidence and meaning combine together as expressions of the assumption that the concept of truth is fundamental. They affirm that truth is not grasped by any method, but is rather an absolute state of correspondence between judgement and reality. Without this conception of truth, definitions of evidence and meaning in terms of truth, since they are definitions of method in terms of result, are useless because circular.

It is plausible to conceive equality of length as an absolute state of correspondence in the above sense; one has only to look at a ruler laid alongside an object to see why. But now think instead of measuring length, not with a ruler, but by means of a theodolite, or think of telling the time by a clock, or of measuring electric current with an ammeter. In these cases we appear not to have a grasp of when a measurement is right or wrong, independently of the methods of measuring we employ. Particularly, it would not be plausible to suppose that a correct measurement is some state of correspondence between the measuring instrument and what is being measured. Rather this supposition is most natural in the particular case of measuring short lengths with a ruler. But it may also seem that this case makes manifest what is essential to measuring; so that other kinds of measuring are made to approximate to this case, or they are ignored, or they are made into philosophical problems and paradoxes.

The theory of judgement which excludes method has little to say about human beings. At best we passively observe, or passively receive impressions of what is already given. Although even this 'we' is out of place, for there is apparently no reason for the single 'I' to suppose that anything it observes is a subject of the same kind as itself. The implication is that the subject is passive and isolated. The nature of being human is inevitably obscure in this static philosophy, still more so the nature of human community, for men do act, and they rely on common methods in their judging and knowing.

The *Tractatus* gives a clear expression to the idea that judgement is a static measure, and its logical consequences are drawn out.

However, as we have seen in the second chapter, the same idea, and many and various of its consequences are to be found also in other major systems in the history of philosophy. Wittgenstein's later philosophy stands opposed to the *Tractatus* and to these other systems. The interpretation of judgement is changed into the dynamic alternative, according to which judgement is essentially a method. As we shall see, this fundamental change brings in its wake radical re-thinking of other philosophical concepts. The central concerns of philosophy—meaning, understanding, truth, 'subject', knowledge, and so on—are to be grasped by means of the concepts of method, activity, and practice.

The difference between the old and the new philosophies has been represented as primarily concerned with the concept of judgement. This accords with Wittgenstein's method, in both periods, of using the theory of language to enter the larger sphere of philosophy. However, it is clear that change in the concept of judgement is just part of a change which is broader and more general. So far as I understand, the general difference in conception may be described in the following way: the old metaphysics is *timeless*, it permits only states, objects, and 'instantaneous acts'; certainly states and objects may exist in time, and may perhaps pass in and out of existence, but this is wholly incidental to their nature, and to the understanding of their nature. By contrast, *time* and *change* are essential to the new philosophy; time, or what happens though time, is essential to what there is, and to our understanding. This general difference assumes more particular forms within each traditional concern of philosophy. And these can be brought out in the following series of questions:

Is existence being or becoming?
Is truth absolute, or relative to men and time?
Is knowledge a passive awareness, or is it rather a way of acting?
Is the understanding passive or active? Does it only observe what is already given, or is it creative?
Is the self inactive, separate from reality, or does it rather engage with reality in action?
And lastly: is the meaning of a sign an object? Or is it method (use)?

All of these metaphysical concepts stand in line, each equivalent to each; woe or paradox or both betide the philosopher who gives incompatible interpretations of them. If reality is a process of

change, but knowledge is static, then we shall have no knowledge—
for we cannot keep pace with what is to be known. If the subject,
particularly man, is active in reality, then that reality cannot,
without creating problems, be construed as absolute being. And so
on.

(ii) Relativity physics

In this subsection, comparison will be made between Wittgenstein's
later philosophy and the relativity physics of Albert Einstein. This
comparison may aid understanding of some general principles in
Wittgenstein's later philosophy, by relating them to an idea which is
already seventy years old and to which we are becoming accustomed. And further, Einstein's departure from seventeenth-century
or Newtonian physics is of particular relevance to the theme of this
book, for we have seen that there are strong connections between
that physics and various metaphysical theories which belong to the
modern tradition, empiricism, 'rationalism', and the *Tractatus* logic.
What we find is that Einstein's revolution in physics, like the
revolution in Wittgenstein's later philosophy, turns on the concept
of method in measurement.

Near the beginning of his celebrated 1905 paper,[1] Einstein gives an
analysis of the concept *time*, noting first that every judgement about
the time of an event refers to the simultaneous occurrence of two
events, for example the arrival of a train at a platform, and the
coincidence of the hour-hand of a watch with the number '7' on its
dial. Einstein then focuses on the as yet undefined notion of
simultaneity. We might suppose that simultaneity of events can
simply be observed, so that there would be no need for definitions.
However, when we consider more closely what is involved in the
observation of simultaneity, we find that certain assumptions are
being made. We say that two events occur simultaneously when,
situated equidistant from each, we see both occur together. But this
criterion presupposes that light travels to us from each event at the
same speed. And further, if the criterion is to be used as a basis for
judging simultaneity and hence time, the constancy of the speed of
light between any two places (relatively at rest) is not so much an
assumption, but rather needs to be *stipulated*, for otherwise we should
need an independent measure of velocity, and hence of time. Using
the above definition of simultaneity, we may define the 'time of an
event' as follows: set clocks of identical construction so that the
positions of their hands simultaneously coincide, then the time of an

event anywhere in space is the reading of the hands of one of these clocks taken and placed in the immediate vicinity of the event. Here it may be supposed that identical clocks, once synchronised, will remain synchronised.

There is nothing yet in this analysis to disturb Newtonian ideas of space and time. Einstein remarks only that our concept of simultaneity, and hence of time, turns on a certain method of determination, which involves certain assumptions or stipulations. In brief, the concept turns on a method, and the method involves a theory.

Thus, in both Einstein's critique and Wittgenstein's it is proposed that the nature of measurement and judgement is not to be explained on the basis of an undefined notion of identity or correspondence. Rather, judgements of dimension and equality in dimension presuppose methods, which must be clarified. The question is brought into focus: *how do we measure?*

This emphasis on methods of measurement is found already in the writings of the physicist Ernst Mach towards the end of the nineteenth century, especially in his rejection of the Newtonian concepts of absolute space, time, and motion (Mach, 1: II; VI and VII). Einstein wrote on the concept of space:

Why is it necessary to drag down from the Olympian fields of Plato the fundamental ideas of thought in natural science, and to attempt to reveal their earthly lineage? Answer: In order to free these ideas from the taboo attached to them, and thus to achieve greater freedom in the formation of ideas or concepts. It is to the immortal credit of D. Hume and E. Mach that they, above all others, introduced this critical conception. (2: p. 142)

There is, however, an important difference between Mach's thinking and Einstein's. Mach was a positivist, and limited the concept of what is measurable to what is observable by the senses; in this respect he followed Hume's empiricism. But Einstein came to reject (if, indeed, he had ever accepted) this empiricist or positivist feature of Mach's emphasis on measurement. Einstein's view comes out well in a conversation with Werner Heisenberg in 1926; Heisenberg was explaining the philosophical background of his recent work in the new quantum mechanics, when Einstein protested: 'But you don't seriously believe that none but observable magnitudes must go into a physical theory?' Heisenberg was surprised, and asked Einstein whether this wasn't precisely what he had done with relativity. Einstein replied:

> Possibly I did use this kind of reasoning, but it is nonsense all the same. Perhaps I could put it more diplomatically by saying that it may be heuristically useful to keep in mind what one has actually observed. But on principle, it is quite wrong to try founding a theory on observable magnitudes alone. In reality the very opposite happens. *It is the theory which decides what we can observe.* (Heisenberg, 1: p. 63; italics added)

This last proposition is the real insight to be gained from the focus on measurement and on the methods and theories which it presupposes.[2]

Both Einstein and Wittgenstein were led to the problem of method in measurement partly by positivist writings. Einstein was directly influenced by Mach, and Wittgenstein indirectly influenced by him, via the members of the Vienna Circle, on whose philosophy Mach had been a formative influence. But both men went on to free the new insight from its empiricist source, with which it is, indeed, deeply incompatible. If measurement or judgement is a method, then knowledge is an activity, not passive observation, and the nature of the reality known will depend on what methods are employed. So there is, in particular, no pre-given reality called 'sense-experience' which all judgement must in some way reflect; rather the concept of sense-experience arises through a particular method by which we judge.

Einstein's analysis of time employs a new philosophical method. Its implications in physics are broad, and intimately linked. Similar implications will be found, in various forms, in Wittgenstein's later philosophy which, as we have seen, draws on the same new method.

In pursuing the consequences of his analysis of time, Einstein inferred that measurements of both temporal and spatial dimensions were relative to the system of spatio-temporal coordinates used for measurement, or, that they were relative to the spatio-temporal position of the observer. This relativity arises particularly under the assumption that no matter what (non-rotating) frame of reference is used, *the speed of light is constant.* This assumption is one aspect of the fundamental difference between Einstein's mechanics and Newton's. It is a matter of what is held constant, and what is allowed to vary. Newton said that the spatial measuring rod is constant (i.e. 'rigid'), and allowed the speed of light to vary between reference frames. As a consequence, the absolute distance between any two points is the same regardless of frame of reference, and so is the time of an event. But Einstein holds the speed of light constant, and as a consequence, space- and time-intervals are both relative to frames of reference; rods and clocks themselves are no longer rigid. The point may be put instructively in this way: the measuring instrument must be rigid; for Newton it was an atemporal spatial rod, for Einstein it is the speed of light, something spatio-temporal. The measure is now a movement, not an object.

The relativity of measurement in Special Theory is demonstrated simply in the following thought-experiment. Suppose that an observer A is situated at rest relative to two places X and Y midway on the line between them, and judges, according to Einstein's definition of simultaneity, that lightning strikes X and Y at the same time. Suppose further that at the time the lightning strikes X and Y, as judged by A, another observer, B, passes A with some velocity towards Y along the line XAY. As light travels from X and from Y to A, B travels away from X and towards Y. Light from Y will therefore reach B before light from X reaches B, and therefore he will judge that the lightning strikes Y earlier than it strikes X; unlike A, who judges the two events to be simultaneous. Thus each observer has his own time measure. And further, B will differ from A in his measures of distance. We have supposed that according to A, he is situated midway between X and Y. But according to B, A is not situated midway between those two points; light travelling from X takes longer to reach B than light travelling from Y, and so he judges that the distance AY is less than the distance AX. In brief, as B moves with uniform velocity relative to A, A judges that the measuring rod B uses contracts, and his clock slows down.

It is clear that the inference of relativity here depends on the constancy of the speed of light. Particularly, B is to judge that light from X and from Y has the same speed, notwithstanding his motion relative to X and Y. In Newtonian mechanics, this supposition is not made. In Newtonian mechanics, B agrees with A that the distances AX and AY are the same, and he also agrees with A that lightning strikes X and Y simultaneously, not because he sees the events occurring simultaneously, but because he adds and subtracts his own velocity along the line XAY with the velocity of light coming from X and from Y respectively.

The difference between Newtonian mechanics and relativity

theory can be brought out by comparing the so-called 'principles of relativity' that apply in each case. These principles, strange as it may seem from their titles, affirm constancies. They state that the same laws of nature apply in all Galilean coordinate systems (i.e. systems in which the law of inertia is valid) which are relatively at rest or in uniform motion. In Newtonian mechanics, the principle of relativity is restricted, in that it does not include the invariance of the speed of light, which adds or subtracts like any velocity with that of the coordinate system. The simple Newtonian theorem of additive velocities underlies the Galilean transformations, rules which relate positions in space and time in different coordinate systems. According to the Galilean transformations, both time and the separation between two points in space are identical in all frames of reference. Einstein, however, broadened the restricted principle of relativity so as to include the invariance of the speed of light.[3] In consequence the Newtonian theorem of additive velocities was abandoned, and the Galilean transformations were replaced by more complex ones, the Lorentz transformations. Thus we have a new principle of relativity, the Special Theory: general laws of nature are covariant with respect to the Lorentz transformations. According to these transformations, time measures vary between reference frames as a function of position and velocity, and distance measures vary as a function of time and velocity. The Lorentz transformations have the effect that one velocity is invariant between all frames of reference, namely, the velocity of light.

For our present purpose, there are two instructive ways of regarding what the Special Theory of Relativity affirms and implies. It implies that there is an overall constancy in the results of measurement taken by different observers; that is to say, different observers agree on the laws of nature, even though the particular measures of spatio-temporal relations they obtain are relative to their position. But there is, I think, a deeper interpretation which underlies this first one. Namely, the principle affirms that the *methods* of measurement used by different observers are *the same*, while the *results* of measurement made by those observers are *relative* to their position. To say that the methods of measurement are shared between different observers means a variety of connected things: they use rods and clocks of the same construction, they use the same physical theory, the same assumptions and stipulations, in order to construct and interpret their measurements. A special case of sharing the method of measurement is that all observers receive *light* at the same speed. This is a special case because light is the *medium* between observer and object, it is the means by which observation is made. Thus, holding the methods of measurement constant, the results of measuring depend on the relative spatio-temporal positions of observer and what is observed; that is, in this sense, the results represent an *interaction* between observer and observed. By contrast, in classical mechanics, results of measurements made in different reference frames are indistinguishable, and in this sense there is but one *absolute* frame of reference. Space- and time-intervals are absolute values, not dependent on any method by which they are measured. Another aspect of this same point is that the Lorentz transformations become the Galilean transformations as the speed of light approaches infinite value, that is, when there is no medium between observer and observed, but direct, immediate acquaintance.

In the new mechanics, there is no longer the idea that measures are correct insofar as they coincide with an absolute quantity being measured. Rather, results obtained by one observer may be verified by results obtained by another. However, the comparison involved in such verification is not straightforward. Nothing yet can be inferred from apparent conflict, or from apparent record. For comparison to be possible at all, it must be assumed or established that different observers use the same method to obtain their results. And comparison of results obtained by the same method by different observers must take into account the differences between the observers, i.e. their relative positions in space and time.

A general feature of the ontology of Special Theory is, as we have seen, that what is measured depends on the methods of measurement employed. But one particular feature of the ontology is also of special relevance to the theme of this book, namely, that space and time now form a unified continuum.[4] This conception is opposed to Newtonian mechanics, in which the four-dimensional continuum divided naturally into two independent ones, three-dimensional space, and one-dimensional time. The fusing of the concept of time into that of space may be partly grasped in the following way: measurement of space involves methods, which take time, and consequently measurement itself and what is measured are inseparable from time. Space is separable from time only if its measurement is explained in terms of static correspondences.

Let us now consider the implications of relativity physics for the concept of 'the observer'. The fundamental implications, indeed, appear so trivial that they hardly bear stating—unless, that is, we remember the history of our subject. The observer has a place *in* space and time; he has a particular *point of view* inside what he observes. Secondly, Einstein speaks naturally from the start of a *plurality* of observers, one at rest, others in different relative motions, etc. It is because the observer is now in some part of space and time, that other observers can be in other parts. Thirdly, the observer is no longer passive. He does not simply observe how things are independently of himself, but takes up rods and clocks and other measuring instruments and uses them in certain ways. What he observes then partly depends on the instruments he uses, how he uses them, and how he stands relative to what he is observing. The observer is now active, an agent. The possibility is raised that the observer may be defined by his position in space-time, and further, that this position may in turn be defined by the measurements which are taken from it. These measurements define a point of view in space-time, and this point of view is the observer.

The above points belong to the philosophical foundation of Relativity Theory, and it can be seen that they contradict the philosophy, or rather the various incompatible philosophies, which surrounded seventeenth-century physics. Seventeenth-century physics contained deep tensions which inevitably gave rise to incompatible epistemologies. The postulate of absolute space and time already implied a rationalist transcendental epistemology, while the experimental method required an account also of empirical knowledge. Empiricism struggled to show how human beings could have ideas of, and know, the absolute nature postulated by physics. Human perceptions were meant to be measures of spatial relations, but they were not rigid, and because the mind was non-spatial, they were not even rods. Again, human perceptions were relative to men, and could afford no knowledge of anything absolute. In the *Tractatus*, Wittgenstein made a philosophy consistent with the modern view of nature, but in so doing what was incompatible with that view was ignored, namely, human experience. The measure was an absolute one, and the subject itself was transcendental.—In relativity physics, however, there is no being postulated *a priori*. What is given is the activity of measuring agents inside space and time. The resulting relativity in the results of measurement is accepted; what stays constant is the method.

Relativity physics corrects a conspicuous imbalance and dichotomy that has existed in modern thought between natural philosophy and moral philosophy, the philosophy of man. Modern physics presented the philosophy of man with the enormous and indeed impossible task of explaining the relation between the nature it had postulated and what was left of man, mind. Philosophy, particularly in the empiricist tradition, devoted itself to the study of human understanding and knowledge; it became the under-labourer to physics. And despite all the problems, the physics itself was hardly questioned; it was 'absolute' in more than one sense of the word. But such a relation between physics and philosophy no longer exists, because contemporary physics has *its own account* of how human beings represent and know its domain. Men act in certain ways, using certain instruments and theories. Man's place is already prepared in the foundations, it does not need to be added as an after-thought, which indeed never would be possible.

And the same movement of thought which liberates philosophy from the old problem of knowledge at the same time frees the concept of understanding from the tight grip of positivism, that blend of physics and empiricism. While it was supposed that nature was wholly described by physics, the understanding could do no more than represent those few qualities postulated by physics. Even the content of sense-experience was of interest only insofar as it conveyed the position and movement of matter. But if understanding is our activity, then it does not follow at all that understanding is limited to what is found in physics. The activities of concern to physics by no means exhaust all human activity. And the implication is that as men act in other ways, they discover different aspects of the world, and of their place within it. The same point is that the measuring instruments employed by physics are by no means all that is available to us. The human being himself, particularly, is a greater measure, is sensitive to more, than a rod or a clock alone.

The philosophical principles of Einstein's physics which have been described are found also in Wittgenstein's later philosophy, though in a more general form. Wittgenstein was concerned with the concept of judgement as a whole, and therefore with what lies at its foundations, activity and communication between people in language. Einstein, on the other hand, was concerned with measurement only of space and time, and that by means of the instruments of physics. The connection between contemporary physics and contemporary philosophy, as it is expressed by Wittgenstein, corresponds to the connections between Newtonian physics and the various modern philosophical traditions. The unity between physics and philosophy in modern times, however, was made by fixing together more or less compatible parts; the new unity is a truer one, more akin to the relation between the particular and the general case.

2 A NEW CONCEPTION OF LANGUAGE (cf. §§1–80)[5]

(i) *Meaning and activity (cf. §§1–37)*

Wittgenstein begins his *Philosophical Investigations* with a passage in which St Augustine describes his learning of language. The words give us, Wittgenstein suggests, a particular picture of the essence of human language, namely this: the individual words in language name objects—sentences are combinations of such names. Wittgenstein continues that in this picture of language we find the roots of the following idea: Every word has a meaning. This meaning is correlated with the word. It is the object for which the word stands.

The conception of meaning which Wittgenstein describes here belongs with the philosophy described above in Part I. The general conception that language serves to name and describe objects has been given various, often opposed, expressions. For example, in the *Tractatus*, names stand for spatially simple objects, and other signs, including most belonging to ordinary languages, are disguised descriptions of complexes. In the empiricism of the Enlightenment, general terms stand for abstract ideas in the mind. In one ancient version of the theory of universals, the object named by a word such as 'circle', perhaps also those named by words like 'table', is a supernatural form. This is to say, philosophers have given various accounts of the signs of language and of the reality they represent, guided by reflection on the use of those signs, by ontological convictions, by epistemological arguments, and so forth. Indeed such considerations sometimes required certain qualifications to be made to the general and underlying thesis, as in the *Tractatus* for example, where the logical connectives are said *not* to stand for objects. But what matters for the moment is not the differences between these and related theories, nor the qualifications that they may contain; what matters here is rather what they have in common. What they all have in common is what Wittgenstein calls 'a particular picture of the essence of human language': that the signs in language represent objects. This picture of language is, as it were, pre-philosophical; it underlies subsequent detail and argument.

Wittgenstein immediately confronts the conception of meaning he has described with the facts of the matter. He asks us to think of the following use of language: someone goes shopping with a slip marked 'five red apples', and the shopkeeper counts out five apples, comparing them with a colour chart on which the word 'red' is written. He continues:

> It is in this and similar ways that one operates with words.—'But how does he know where and how he is to look up the word "red" and what he is to do with the word "five"?'—Well, I assume that he *acts* as I have described. Explanations come to an end somewhere.—But what is the meaning of the word "five"?—No such thing was in question here, only how the word "five" is used. (I, 1)

'Well, I assume that he *acts* as I have described.' This assumption marks the beginning of Wittgenstein's investigations. Philosophy now begins with what men do, and rests its explanations there. So there is to be no explanation of human activity and use of language in terms of something prior, in terms of objects which are grasped by the understanding and named in language.—The question arises why explanations should come to an end in human action. The answer is partly that any philosophical explanation must come to an end *somewhere*. But why in action and language? Perhaps because this is now where our greatest certainty lies.

In §2, Wittgenstein summarises how the conception of meaning he has described manages with the facts of our use of language. He writes:

> That philosophical concept of meaning has its place in a primitive idea of the way language functions. But one can also say that it is the idea of a language more primitive than ours.

The concept that meaning is correlation between word and object is part of a 'primitive idea' of language. This primitive idea is, I think, the one which misinterprets notions such as *name, description, object* and *fact*, so that the use of language in human activity is not fundamental, or is, indeed, denied altogether. This idea includes not only a certain conception of meaning, but also equally primitive conceptions of understanding, of learning language, of the purpose of language, of truth; and so on. The second kind of mistake referred to in §2 would be this: properly understood, language has a variety of functions, of which naming objects and stating facts are but two; and so the concept of meaning suggested is appropriate only to a language more primitive than ours, one in which these two are the only purposes to which words and combinations of words are put.

Analogous criticisms apply to the conception that measuring consists in offering up an object to the quantity being measured. This conception is too narrow, for it acknowledges only certain cases, such as measuring short lengths with a ruler, and ignores or makes problematic other measuring activities. But this too narrow view of meaning encourages and is encouraged by a more radical misconception, according to which measurement is essentially a state of correspondence between objects, so that there is no method in measurement. And this is the misconception which spreads, so that measuring is not seen as a human activity, for all the measuring agent need do is passively observe, and *a fortiori* measuring is not seen as a human activity among others, such as building a shelter, the giving of orders, and so on.

Wittgenstein explores the various errors implicit in the idea that words stand for objects by comparing it with a series of simple systems of communication. They are between a builder and his assistant. The builder uses building-stones: there are blocks, pillars, slabs and beams. The assistant has to pass the stones, in the order the builder needs them. For this purpose, they use a language consisting of four words, 'block', 'pillar', 'slab' and 'beam'. The builder calls them out, and his assistant brings the stone which he has learnt to bring at such-and-such a call. Just this is the first system of communication, described in §2. An extension is imagined in §8: there is a series of words, say the letters of the alphabet, which are used as the shopkeeper used the numerals in §1, and there are two words, 'this' and 'there', used roughly as we use those words, and finally, there are a number of colour-samples. The builder gives an order like: 'd—slab—there', at the same time he shows his assistant a colour-sample, and when he says 'there' he points to a place on the building site. From the stock of slabs the assistant takes one for each letter of the alphabet up to 'd', of the same colour as the sample, and brings them to the place indicated. On other occasions, the builder gives the order 'this—there'; at 'this' he points to a building-stone; and so on.

Wittgenstein's descriptions of men acting and speaking on a building site must count among the simplest of propositions to be found in a philosophical work. They direct our attention to the origin of meaning. We may suppose that the essential function of words is to stand for things. But what do the words used by the builder and his assistant stand for? Well, the claim is that *meaningful signs* stand for things; that is why they are not mere noises. But it is presumably because the sounds 'block' etc. are used in certain activities that we want to say in the first place that they do have meaning. And therefore the claim that meaningful words stand for objects, if it is to be correct, must be compatible with, indeed it must *rest on* the fact that words have meaning because men use them in their activities. And therefore it is wrong to say that what is *essential* to language is that its signs stand for objects; if we are to speak of what is essential here, it would rather be the *use* of signs.

We may indeed say that words stand for things; that such-and-such a word signifies a kind of building-stone, another a number; and so on. On this Wittgenstein writes at §10: 'But assimilating the descriptions of the uses of words in this way cannot make the uses themselves any more like one another. For, as we see, they are absolutely unlike'. This assimilation reaches its peak in the dictum: all words stand for things. As though all words had meaning in the same way, by correlation with some object, and only the objects were different. And with this thought we are on the way to misconceiving the nature of the correlation, as though it were a state of affairs.

It may also be said that signs are names insofar as they may be attached to objects, like labels. But even if a sign can be used as a label, this does not mean that its meaning is just a matter of being attached (by hand, or by some act of the understanding) to an object. It is rather that the activities into which the use of a word weaves, which give the word meaning, may involve collecting, fetching and carrying things, and men may find it useful to fix the written word onto these things, perhaps to help them remember, for example, how to carry out a particular order. Whether it is useful depends partly on men, partly on their interests, and partly on the use of the word in question. And it can be seen that the use of some words, such as the demonstratives 'this' and 'there', precludes their being attached to any one thing or any one place. This means that under one legitimate interpretation of the claim that words stand for things, according to which words can be attached to things like labels, the claim is too narrow; it is appropriate only to a language more primitive than our own, indeed more primitive than the simple language of the builders.

The conception that meaning is the representation of objects finds expression in the claim: all sentences are descriptions or statements of fact. This claim fares badly when compared with the language of the builders, for it contains only commands, and no statements at all. Or is it that commands are essentially (insofar as they mean anything) descriptions? It might be said: 'what is essential to the meaning of the sign "slab" is that it describes a kind of building-stone, and it is only because of this that it may be used to give orders'. But why say this? It is certainly true that *if* meaning is the representation of objects in reality, then any sentence must do at least that before it can do anything else. The bare minimum, the description of reality, might be called the proposition-radical; and this can be made into a statement, command, question, etc. But this reasoning is now baseless. Sentences have meaning because they are used in human activities; depending on the kind of use they have, we may classify them as statements, commands, greetings, confessions, and so on. There is a variety of kinds of sentence, and diversity also within kinds; no essential form, called description, underlies this variety and diversity.

Kenny suggests that the picture theory of the *Tractatus*, although presented there as a theory of the indicative proposition, is really a theory of the proposition-radical, and he argues that the shift to Wittgenstein's later period could be described as the taking of interest in moods other than the indicative (1: p. 122). But Wittgenstein had already written in 1913: 'Assertion is merely psychological. There are only unasserted propositions. Judgement, command and question all stand on the same level; but all have in common the propositional form, and that alone interests us' (*Notes on Logic*, p. 96). The change from the early to the later period would, I think, be better described as the rejection of this idea of the common propositional form. For what gives sentences meaning is not their representation of how states of affairs are, should be, or might be, but is rather their use in our activities. And this change, which brings uses of language other than description out of the shadow cast by the old logic and into the light, is not an amendment or addition to the *Tractatus* theory of meaning, but is rather the complete overthrowing of it.

If words have meaning because they stand for objects, then to teach someone the meaning of a word is to show him the object that it stands for. This teaching could be called 'ostensive definition', for it defines the meaning of a word by pointing. And it is true that in teaching the meanings of words such as 'chair' and 'two', we do use gestures to direct a child's attention to things. But if we teach a child the meaning of the word 'two' by pointing at two chairs and saying the word, how is the child to know that it is the number of things that we are calling 'two', rather than the chairs, or the material from which they are made? So perhaps a single ostensive definition will not do; we should show the child also two cups, two apples, and so on, so that he can abstract the common element in all these cases and discard their differences. In this way the understanding can pinpoint the object or property called 'two', even though our hands are unable to.

But there is another way of conceiving what happens when the meaning of words is taught by means of gestures and examples. When we show a child two chairs, two cups, two apples, applying the word 'two' in each case, we are initiating the child into a *practice*; we are encouraging him to *do* something, to apply the word 'two' in some situations and not in others, to classify these sets of objects together, but not those, and so on. The use of gesture and example is certainly a way of showing the meaning of a word; but what is being shown is not an object, not even an abstract object—it is a way of acting and speaking. That is why if a child carries on by himself, using the word 'two' correctly as we have shown him, then we say that he has understood what we were teaching him.

Our question may be expressed in this way: what is the connection between language and reality? Answers to this perplexing question have been mysterious, obscure, or inexpressible. But what Wittgenstein now proposes is this: the connection is made by us, and not by means of queer and instantaneous mental acts, but in our activity. Our activity is itself the connection. And those features in the use of language which encouraged and were emphasised by the conception that meaning is essentially a correlation between word and object, do not constitute the essence of language, though they may sometimes accompany our practice and use of words. Thus:

37. What is the relation between name and thing named?—

Well, what *is* it? Look at language-game (2) or at another one: there you can see the sort of thing this relation consists in. This relation may also consist, among many other things, in the fact that hearing the name calls before our mind the picture of what is named; and it also consists, among other things, in the name's being written on the thing named or being pronounced when that thing is pointed at.

Wittgenstein's reply to the philosophical question, 'what is the relation between words and things?', is to tell us to look. The relation is before our eyes, in what we do every day.

What appears in the first paragraphs of the *Investigations*, up to §37, is so simple that it might be thought obvious. Certainly Wittgenstein does not *argue* that words are used by people in such-and-such ways, but he assumes it, and apparently assumes it will be obvious to his readers too. But although this starting-point may seem natural for philosophy now, some of its implications are more controversial, for they strain, stretch, and break conceptions to which we are accustomed. If the concept of meaning has its origin in human practice, then so too does the concept *truth*, and the concept *object*, and also the concept *understanding*, and *certainty*. Activity must be fundamental in these cases, if it is fundamental to meaning; for the major concepts of philosophy all stand in line. One of the major obstacles to following Wittgenstein's later philosophy is, I think, to suppose that his beginning is more simple than in fact it is. A misunderstanding of particular relevance is the belief that emphasis on the use of language in human activity is a prelude to, or perhaps an amendment to, a philosophy of language of the old kind, which does not mention human activity at all. As though the use of language were important only insofar as it brings about correlation between words and objects, and enables, for instance, correspondence between proposition and fact; as though the process mattered only because it leads to a certain status. But the significance of the beginning of the *Investigations* is, I think, precisely that the concept of use of language in human activity cannot be discarded in favour of something more fundamental. This view of what is fundamental is the new conception of language.

(ii) Critique of the traditional conception (cf. §§38–80)

The conception that words have meaning because they represent objects is misleading, for it directs attention away from the use of words in human activity. But the same conception fosters a more radical error, namely, the denial that words are used at all, except in the trivial sense that they are used to stand for objects. This denial appears fully-fledged in those various philosophies which try to explain how language is in a state of correspondence with reality.

These philosophies have been considered in some detail in Part I; we saw that they divide into those concerning general terms, and those concerning propositions. Various explanations of general terms all presupposed that the particulars to which such a term applies have something in common. In ancient and scholastic thought, this presupposition led to various ontologies of universals; in modern thought, it supported the doctrine of abstract ideas. Systematic study of the true-false proposition, particularly in the *Tractatus*, led to the conclusion that propositions are combinations of names which stand for simple objects. The ontology belonging with this conclusion was spatial atomism. The theory of universals (in its various forms) and the theory of the proposition as picture both belong with the philosophical conception that words have meaning in their static representation of reality. And in certain of these doctrines, the reality which words stand for is itself essentially static and unchanging; for example, in the doctrine of *universalia ante rem*, and in the ontology of the *Tractatus*, in which only the configurations of objects are created or destroyed, while the objects themselves persist.

These philosophies are the systematic expressions of the pre-philosophical idea that words name and describe things. And it is remarkable that although the pre-philosophical idea is suggested by observation of the use of certain ordinary words, like 'table', 'chair', and people's names, the philosophical interpretations of the idea leave ordinary language or daily experience, or both, far behind. Instead the arguments lead to signs that no-one has ever seen or heard, to 'simple' objects, or to ideas in the mind, or to transcendental forms, and so forth. These philosophical arguments are themselves convincing demonstration that the notion that signs stand for objects does not fit well with the language and reality of daily life.

Wittgenstein's critique of these philosophical theories of language begins at §38, and continues until about §80. The deductions that have led to familiar theories of meaning and being are undermined, always by standing on the ground laid down in the first pages of the *Investigations*: language has meaning because men use it in their activities, therefore not because it reflects objects or states of affairs which are given independently (absolutely, unconditionally). No ontology explains the use men make of language, for what we describe in language is to be grasped via the means of description. So, for example, whether an object is 'simple' or 'complex' depends upon which of various methods of decomposition we have in mind, methods that are revealed in our descriptions of the object, and in the practices or experience which underlie those descriptions. Thus, a physical object may be complex because we can break it apart with our hands, or by other mechanical means, or by chemical methods, or by using the apparatus of contemporary particle physics, and so on. Conversely, an object may be called 'simple' in that it cannot be broken apart by such-and-such a method; but there is no sense in the notion of an 'absolute simple'.

Of Wittgenstein's arguments against the traditional theories of meaning, I shall discuss in detail only one, selected because it undermines several of those theories at once, and because the idea against which it is directed is seductive, and pervasive among philosophers and non-philosophers alike, and because it is particularly relevant to other themes in Wittgenstein's philosophy. The argument is directed against the idea that the instances to which a general term applies must have some feature in common, in virtue of which the term applies.

'The meaning of a word is an object; it is the object for which the word stands; the word is correlated with the object.' So then, the correlation required to make a general term must be a series of separate correlations, for in this way the term would apply to many things. But this suggestion (which belongs to the doctrine called 'nominalism') cannot be right, for a series of separate correlations would simply produce a proper name which happened to apply to many things; just as many men are called 'John' because they have each been separately so christened. We have here no account of why, given that a general term applies to certain things, it then applies or fails to apply to others.

'The meaning of a word is an object.' So then, if a word *seems* to apply to many things in virtue of its meaning, this can only be because the object which is its meaning is found in many things. Thus, the many particulars to which a general term applies each have *something in common*; this common thing is the meaning of the term.

The problem is to know what this conclusion means. Does it

mean, for example, that all chairs *look alike*? For what *does* it mean if it does not mean that?—But all chairs just do *not* look alike, not in shape, colour, etc. In this plain sense in which all items collected by a general term might have 'something in common', they do not. As §66, Wittgenstein considers the proceedings we call 'games', and invites us to *look and see* whether there is anything common to all. And there is nothing: what we find instead is a 'complicated network of similarities overlapping and criss-crossing: sometimes overall similarities, sometimes similarities of detail'. Wittgenstein goes on to characterise these similarities as 'family resemblances'.

The issue whether there is something in common to all games is not settled by finding that there is, or that there is not, a satisfactory definition of the word 'game'. For the issue is all the same whether we consider the word 'game' or any other form of words with the same meaning, namely, do they signify a common element which holds the class of games together? The demand for a common element underlies the demand for definition, rather than the other way round. And the source of the demand for a common element includes, among other things, the idea that the meaning of a word is an object.

For how can this conception of meaning cope with the use of general terms? A general term is used for describing many particular things, and these descriptions are each right or wrong. Or, we can say, the repeated use of a general term is subject to a *rule*, or *method*. But the *method* in description is precisely what the theory of meaning under consideration denies; that is what it means to say: the meaning of a word is an *object*. Faced with the method in judgement that the use of general terms implies, the theory has two ways of escape: either it holds that the many applications of a general term are wholly separable from one another—but this leads to an untenable nominalism—or it says something equally wrong but more obscure and therefore more tenable, namely, that although it seems that a general term applies to many things, in fact it applies to only *one* thing. The conclusion is a strange one, for we began with many things, and with many uses of a word, and now we have only one thing, and one correlation of a word with it. Many particulars turn into one universal, and our method for using a word becomes an object. If there is bewilderment with the conclusion, it can be weakened. It may be said that there really are many particulars, but they are still, in some sense, one, for they are all exactly alike in some respect. And then it will also be said that to follow a rule in using a word is to use it always in the same way, so that in a sense we use the word only once after all. But this idea, freed from the strict denial of method and use, is simply wrong, for the things to which a general term applies are not all alike, and in this sense our use of a general term is not always the same.

The traditional explanations of the meaning of descriptive terms—the various theories of universals, nominalism, the doctrine of abstract ideas—all express the idea that the meaning of such a term is an object. They try to explain away our methods, and substitute objects. The mistake here shows in the paradoxes to which the theories have given rise.

Once we see that description belongs with human activity in the world, we should not be surprised that general terms brings together things that are more or less alike for our purposes, not things that 'exactly resemble one another' (whatever that means). But we are not accustomed to seeing the collecting done by a word as of the same kind as collecting done by men. For the idea that a general term means one thing is as much as to say that there is no collection at all; and the weaker idea, that the things to which a general term applies are all alike, means that things are by their own nature in classes that are perfectly defined, so that men have nothing to do but perceive and name those that interest them. However, the answer to the philosophical question, 'how do many things come to be in one class?', is simply this: men put them there. Plato was right when he said that a third element, something universal, not particular, is required to unite two things—but this third element is our practice.

As we saw in Part I, incompatible ontologies were necessary to explain the meaning of general terms on the one hand, and true-or-false combinations of words on the other. The ontology in the latter case had to be spatial; in the former case it could not be. It is possible now, however, to bring both kinds of description together: the collecting of things into classes is part of our activity, and so is the measurement of spatial (and other) relations. Therefore logic no longer has use for the radical distinction between subject-predicate and relational propositions. Both kinds of proposition are unified under the concept of method (which is spatio-temporal). Wittgenstein turns to the general concept of judgement as method, or rule, from §134 onwards; but first he re-interprets the nature of the logician's task, and it is to this discussion that we turn next.

3 LOGIC AND PHILOSOPHY (cf. §§81–133)

(i) Philosophy as logic

The great revolution in European thought that occurred within and around the seventeenth century was the gradual separation of philosophy from theology, and the rise of modern philosophy of nature and of man. Modern philosophy tended to fall into two parts, reflecting the separation of man, or mind, from nature. Increasingly natural philosophy came to be regarded as an independent science, and philosophy was confined more to the study of human nature, knowledge and understanding. Among the major changes during the late nineteenth century was a move away from the study of man and his psychological processes, towards the study of signs and their use in judgement, i.e. towards *logic*.

Logic in this broad sense coincides with what is now often called the 'philosophy of language'. In another sense, logic is particularly the study of *reasoning*. These two aspects of logic were united, however, in Frege's work. For it was in his search for satisfactory definitions of mathematical proof and certainty that Frege was led to the study of signs. Frege saw (after Leibniz) that a rigorous definition of proof required a well-defined calculus, such as the *Begriffsschrift* (see Frege, e.g. 1: §§90 and 91). In this way logic became narrowly defined, as being the truth-functional and predicate calculi. These logical calculi were used also in the more general study of language, for example in explicating the notion that meaning is given by truth-conditions, and in defining the 'logical form' of general propositions, or of propositions containing so-called 'definite descriptions'. Frege's interests remained for the most part with logic in the restricted sense and its relation to mathematics, though he did develop a philosophy of language expressed in concepts drawn largely from his logico-mathematical enquiries. The task of approaching the concepts and problems of modern philosophy via the study of signs and language, with the aid of the new logical calculi, was left to those who followed Frege, particularly Russell and the young Wittgenstein. The impact of logic on modern philosophy has already been considered in Part I, with particular reference to the *Tractatus*.

The logical philosophies of Frege, Russell and Wittgenstein contained several doctrines concerning the nature of signs used in judgement and the meaning of those signs. Perhaps the most general assumption, one which underlies several suppositions to be mentioned below, may be expressed in this way: the meaning of a sentence is its representation of a possible state of reality (physical, mental, mathematical); and therefore at least some words in a sentence name or in some other way signify objects in that reality.

Concerning this general assumption, Frege saw clearly that the meaning of a sentence, the thought it expressed, was *neither physical nor mental*. The thought expressed by a sentence is not an idea in the mind, for ideas are transient, dependent on and private to the thinker; but thoughts (or meanings) are permanent, not dependent upon apprehension by a subject, and they may be shared. By such arguments, Frege freed the theory of meaning from psychology, and brought it closer to logic. However, neither is the thought expressed by a sentence a perceptible, material thing. Particularly, it is not the sentence itself, since, for example, the same sentence may express different thoughts depending on the context of its use. A sentence may express a thought, but it is not the thought itself. Frege concluded: 'So the result seems to be: thoughts are neither things of the outer world nor ideas. A third realm must be recognized' (3: p. 302). Thought or meaning is an entity (some kind of object)—but it is neither physical nor mental.

Frege's deduction of the 'third realm' accepts uncritically the dualism of mind and matter, and is for this reason (among others) not found in Russell's logical empiricism, nor in the *Tractatus*. However, other of Frege's insights were taken over by Russell and Wittgenstein, directly or in related forms. For example, Frege supposed that meaning must be *precisely defined*. One support of this demand can be expressed in this way: signs represent a condition of reality which must itself be precise, consequently signs better represent reality the more their meaning is precisely defined. In short, if meaning is an object of some kind, it must be well-defined. Frege compared classes with areas of a plane, saying that a concept without a sharp boundary would correspond to an area that in places shaded vaguely into the background; but this, he says, would not really be an area at all, and similarly a concept that is not sharply defined is wrongly called a concept (2: vol. ii, §56).

Another doctrine characteristic of the early logical philosophy is that a proposition must have certain features in common with the reality it represents. The meaning of a sentence has a certain logical form which mirrors the state of affairs represented, for example, both contain the same number of elements. In the *Tractatus*, logical form is pictorial, and is identical with the form of reality. Similar, though perhaps less systematic, concepts of logical form were employed particularly by Russell.

Logic rested on the assumption that language signifies a reality already given in the form of objects. But this is precisely the assumption which, as we have seen, is rejected in the *Investigations*. The old logic must therefore be dismantled, and this task begins at §81. Criticism is aimed particularly, though not exclusively, at the *Tractatus* logic. Criticism is made first of the 'normative' aspect of logic, its tendency to compare the use of words with games and calculi which have strict rules. This tendency, we have seen, springs directly from the idea that words are used to describe a reality which is already given, and therefore itself precisely defined. But now that this idea fundamental to the old logic has been abandoned, there is no longer need to require that words should be used according to 'exact' rules, nor that rules should be definable in advance. The flexibility of various kinds which characterises our use of language is no more answerable to logic.

However, although the old logic demanded that signs be used according to fixed rules, the deeper claim was that signs are not used at all, save in the trivial sense that they stand for things (or classes, or relations). The denial of use found expression in the various postulates of meanings-as-objects; particularly Frege's thought in the 'third realm', and Wittgenstein's logical picture of facts. These are the underlying dogmas criticised next:

> 94. 'A proposition is a queer thing!' Here we have in germ the subliming of our whole account of logic. The tendency to assume a pure intermediary between the propositional *signs* and the facts. Or even to try to purify, to sublime, the signs themselves. . . .

Logic defines what is essential to representation. But when we consider ordinary language, we find that it falls short of what logic demands. The signs that alone can represent reality: *where are they?*

> 105. When we believe that we must find that order, must find the ideal, in our actual language, we become dissatisfied with what are ordinarily called 'propositions', 'words', 'signs'.
> The proposition and the word that logic deals with are supposed to be something pure and clear-cut. And we rack our

brains over the nature of the *real* sign.—It is perhaps the *idea* of the sign? or the idea at the present moment?

The 'real sign' would be, for example, the picture-proposition postulated in the *Tractatus*. But there are apparently no such signs.

'To measure is to lay an instrument alongside what is measured. The measure must have well-defined boundaries, like a ruler. Indeed the idea of a ruler whose end-points faded away indeterminately is clearly absurd; such a thing could not be used to measure anything.' But suppose a man wants to compare the length of a field with its width, so he paces one way, counting the paces, and then the other, and makes his comparison. This is a case of measuring. Is it accurate? Well, we know of more accurate ways, and also of less accurate ones. Or is there an ideal in mind, the measure made by an absolutely rigid rod, laid alongside what is measured? But then consider this case: we judge the height of a tree very accurately by triangulation, using a theodolite. Where is the measuring rod now? Someone convinced that there must be one might say that it is in his head. And perhaps even as he makes measurements, he imagines himself struggling to erect an enormous ruler alongside the tree, convinced that this act of the imagination is the real measuring, while the business with the theodolite and the trigonometric tables is in some queer way quite incidental. Even so there will be problems, for what instruments is the man to imagine when he is measuring astronomical distances, or time, or electric current?

How could we argue with the demand that judgement must involve special objects: precisely defined, perhaps neither physical nor mental, perhaps exact copies of whatever is represented. Certainly no such objects are to be found in ordinary language. But this will likely be admitted, or even insisted on. The perfect objects essential to judgement belong elsewhere, perhaps in the mind, or outside space and time altogether. To argue against these postulates is less important now than to realise another way of conceiving the whole problem.

(ii) Logic as grammar

Wittgenstein writes at §107 that the more narrowly we examine actual language, the sharper becomes the conflict between it and our requirement; the conflict becomes intolerable, the requirement is in danger of becoming empty.

Logic conflicts with the facts of language. Logic must be rejected, but it cannot be amended piecemeal. No negotiation with the facts is possible, because logic purports to deduce *a priori* what the facts *must be*. If we take a stand and say that language in fact is not as logic demands, we thereby reject logic altogether, and begin instead with language as we find it. Wittgenstein writes:

> 108. We see that what we call 'sentence' and 'language' has not the formal unity that I imagined, but is the family of structures more or less related to one another.—But what becomes of logic now? Its rigour seems to be giving way here.—But in that case doesn't logic altogether disappear?—For how can it lose its rigour? Of course not by our bargaining any of its rigour out of it.—The *preconceived idea* of crystalline purity can only be removed by turning our whole examination round. (One might say: the axis of reference of our examination must be rotated, but about the fixed point of our real need.)
>
> The philosophy of logic speaks of sentences and words in exactly the sense in which we speak of them in ordinary life when we say e.g. 'Here is a Chinese sentence', or 'No, that only looks like writing; it is actually just an ornament' and so on.
>
> We are talking about the spatial and temporal phenomenon of language, not about some non-spatial, non-temporal phantasm. But we talk about it as we do about the pieces in chess when we are stating the rules of the game, not describing their physical properties.
>
> The question 'What is a word really?' is analogous to 'What is a piece in chess?'

The old logic is rejected because its account of language and its use is wrong. This account was guided by the conception that signs must represent a given status in reality, a conception which is just part of a still more general philosophical picture, according to which time, change and activity are irrelevant to order and being. So general is this picture that in a certain sense it cannot be refuted by argument, for it would simply deny the premises of any attempted refutation, substituting its own. The picture can be denied only by saying: *the facts* are not of the kind demanded. In principle this stand could be taken in connection with any major issue in philosophy, but in accord with his dominant concern in both periods, Wittgenstein makes his stand in connection with the nature of language. Insofar as language is not in fact a static, fixed representation, the general picture that order and being is a status stands refuted, and arguments may proceed against its other various implications.

The old logic is replaced by a different study, which Wittgenstein sometimes calls 'grammar', and sometimes 'logic'. Grammar begins with the use of language in human activities. Grammar studies the meaning of signs, as did the old logic; but the nature of meaning is differently conceived. Logic as grammar does not place demands on language and its use. For example, our methods of judgement may be more or less precise, but there is no question of an ideal precision which is unconditional on men's purposes. Still less does grammar demand that signs in language be of a certain kind, nor does it postulate intermediaries between language and the world. Or rather, there is such an intermediary, but it is not an object hidden in the mind, or elsewhere; it is our acting. The order of action lies at the basis of logic as grammar; in this way grammar makes a new interpretation of the original word, 'logos'.

Grammar, like the old logic, is a way into the traditional concerns of philosophy. For example:

371. *Essence* is expressed by grammar.
373. Grammar tells what kind of object anything is. (Theology as grammar.)

By studying methods of description, we learn what it is that is described. In this sense, ontology is grammar. Grammar is also an epistemological study, for the conditions under which judgement should be made with assurance are exactly what is specified in a method of judgement. These conditions may be, for example, that certain evidence is at hand. Thus:

353. Asking whether and how a proposition can be verified is only a particular way of asking 'How d'you mean?' The answer is a contribution to the grammar of the proposition.

Let us now consider how philosophy as grammar differs from philosophy as logic. Grammar and logic rest on different conceptions of meaning, and consequently they lead to opposed interpretations of major concepts in philosophy. But how far do they imply differing views of philosophy itself?

(iii) The rejection of philosophical system

The old logic was what Wittgenstein later called 'sublime'—but grammar is not. It is here, I think, that we find the fundamental difference between Wittgenstein's views of philosophy in his two periods. He writes:

> 89. These considerations bring us up to the problem: In what sense is logic something sublime?
>
> For there seemed to pertain to logic a peculiar depth—a universal significance. Logic lay, it seemed, at the bottom of all the sciences.— For logical investigation explores the nature of all things. It seeks to see to the bottom of things and is not meant to concern itself whether what actually happens is this or that.—It takes its rise, not from an interest in the facts of nature, nor from a need to grasp causal connexions: but from an urge to understand the basis, or essence, of everything empirical. . . .

Logic was an *a priori* science; it was knowledge prior to acquaintance with the facts of the world. Logic showed the relation which must hold between signs and the world, if judgement is to be possible at all. Logic at the same time deduced the nature of the world itself, and of the metaphysical subject, and so forth; it comprised a whole philosophy. However, philosophy as logic was not *a priori* in the original sense of the term which belonged, particularly, with the Platonic philosophy, and later with the rationalist tradition in modern thought. That is to say, logic did not postulate a super-empirical reality, knowledge of which is already present at natural birth (that is, innate). There is no reality outside the world of the *Tractatus*. Rather, logic dealt with the *possibilities* of the world, by prescribing the limits of the meaningful (cf. §90).

The limits of the meaningful are given in the essence of thought and of language, expressed in the general propositional form: 'This is how things stand'. And at the bottom of the deduction of the essence of thought and language, there lay the simple assumption: thought truly or falsely represents the facts in the world.

> 95. 'Thought must be something unique.' When we say, and *mean*, that such-and-such is the case, we—and our meaning—do not stop anywhere short of the fact; but we mean: *this—is—so*. But

this paradox (which has the form of a truism) can also be expressed in this way: *Thought* can be of what is *not* the case.

It is a truism that thought represents the facts. However, the significant preconception of the old logic was that 'the facts' are already given, i.e. as existing *states* of affairs. And in this case, thought, and the expression of thought in language, must lay across the world as a picture of it. The requirement that representation be pictorial is particularly clear in the case of false propositions, but is no less strong in the case of true propositions. The preconception that truth and falsity are relations between thought and a world given as status leads inevitably to the heart of the *Tractatus* logic. Wittgenstein continues:

> 96. Other illusions come from various quarters to attach themselves to the special one spoken of here. Thought, language, now appear to us as the unique correlate, picture, of the world. . . .

And so logic found the *a priori* order common between thought and the world. It gave the essence of the world—the arrangement of simple objects in space—and the essence of thought—the pictorial combination of signs.

It can be seen that what underlies the normative tendency of logic is the same as what underlies its being sublime. The fundamental assumption is that signs have meaning because they represent a reality that is already given. For then it follows that there is a well-defined ideal, the *perfect* reflection of reality, to which our use of language approximates. But this ideal is none other than what is defined and demanded by sublime logic, which knows in advance what language *must be*.

But how does a theory of meaning turn into a sublime philosophy? Let us try to answer that question along with another: why is grammar, embodying as it does what can be called a theory of meaning, *not* sublime?

Wittgenstein's explicit indication why philosophy can no longer be sublime is that it does not now have the right *language*. Consider this passage from §97:

> We are under the illusion that what is peculiar, profound, essential, in our investigation, resides in its trying to grasp the

incomparable essence of language. That is, the order existing between the concepts of proposition, word, proof, truth, experience, and so on. This order is a *super*-order between—so to speak—*super*-concepts. Whereas, of course, if the words 'language', 'experience', 'world', have a use, it must be as humble a one as that of the words 'table', 'lamp', 'door'.

This is surely hard for philosophers to accept, that their words should be reduced to the level of 'table', 'lamp' and 'door'. And how can it be so? The philosopher is not concerned with a particular table, nor indeed with all tables, but with all things. (Aristotle: metaphysics is the science of being *qua* being.) And the same goes for experience, truth, and the rest.—But Wittgenstein is saying something about the *origin* of these philosophical words. Their origin is earthly. A word has meaning in human life.

There are several ways of expressing why philosophy no longer has a super-language. The old logic belonged with certain conceptions of being and of intelligence (deity, subject), which characterised the modern philosophical tradition. This we have considered in Part I. Being, matter in space, was absolute and essentially unchanging. Therefore it was known by transcendental intelligence, not by men. Thought must be conceived as a static form, a rigid measure, which reflects the state of being. And this is the assumption, expressed as a doctrine concerning language and meaning, that was taken up by the old logic. The assumptions of the modern tradition carry with them a conception of philosophy. As ontology, philosophy reveals the essence of being; natural philosophy gives a complete and final account of the essence of natural phenomena. Philosophy wants to describe the world as a whole, as it appears from the outside. Therefore *a priori* psychology is transcendental; as science of the understanding, philosophy draws limits around thought, by defining what is essential to thought. These pretensions of philosophy appear more or less explicitly in, for example, Newtonian physics and cosmology, in Locke's empiricism, and also in the Kantian system.

Just as the logic of the *Tractatus* gave clear expression to the assumptions of modern philosophy, so also it clearly expressed the aspirations which were part of that philosophy. Logic was 'sublime'. This clarity of expression would be one reason why the more detailed the discussion of sublime logic becomes, between §89 and §133, the more it is addressed specifically to the logic of the *Tractatus*.

And further, there is reason to say that the *Tractatus* logic meant the end of the modern conception of philosophy, as it did the end of particular assumptions in the tradition.

In the *Tractatus*, language displaced sense-experience as the medium of thought. Language was now a truly rigid measure. But at the same time, language had also to be the vehicle of *philosophical* thought; and here, the *Tractatus* logic came headlong into conflict with the modern conception of philosophy. For philosophy required a super-language, but logic said: there is no such language. Wittgenstein wrote at the end of the *Tractatus*:

> 6.54 My propositions serve as elucidations in the following way: anyone who understands me eventually recognizes them as nonsensical, when he has used them—as steps—to climb up beyond them. (He must, so to speak, throw away the ladder after he has climbed up it.)
>
> He must transcend these propositions, and then he will see the world aright.

There is no transcendental language for philosophy to use. The ending of the tradition in the *Tractatus* was profound in many ways. Language is essentially and only a measure of states of affairs; it can say that this is so in the world, or that. But language can say nothing about the world as a whole, nor about the essence of the world, nor about the relation between itself and the world. And so language cannot circumscribe its own limits. Language has, one can say, a humble use.

But why can there be no super-language now? After all, the reasoning in the *Tractatus* hardly applies any longer. Certainly, grammar does not pretend to give the essence of language, from which it might follow that language can do nothing but 'state the facts' (whatever that now means). It is by all means true that language is not a rigid measure, so one might ask, what should it not be used for? At least *not* for circumscribing its own measure! But if grammar does not pretend to give the essence of language, or of anything else, what should it want with a high language?

Grammar is a view of the origin of meaning. Words have meaning in human life. And how should we, in our life time, propose to describe the whole of reality and its essence? We see too little of it; and we have evidence that what is given to human beings changes, so that what we do see is not necessarily the rule for the whole. How should a man suppose that he is entitled to know everything? Wittgenstein writes of the urge behind the old logic, at §92:

> '*The essence is hidden from us*': this is the form our problem now assumes. We ask: "*What is* language?", "*What is* a proposition?" And the answer to these questions is to be given once for all; and independently of any future experience.

These same questions, nevertheless, and others related to them, are the concern of philosophy as grammar; as Wittgenstein indicated at the beginning of his Preface to the *Investigations*. But the difference is: there is now no answer to be given 'once for all'. However, what language is now to be used for philosophical investigation? As we have seen, Wittgenstein denied philosophy its traditional superior language. One possibility seems to be that the traditional language be retained, but used with qualification. In this way it might be proposed, for example, that 'language is related to the world in such-and-such way', but it is added that no final or complete or unique account is intended. The propositions of philosophy would then not pretend to be pronouncements from above, but discourse from within. But there is clearly a tension here between theory and method, and no such tension is found in Wittgenstein's own work. What we find in the *Investigations* is not a philosophical language, but a *philosophical style of writing*. This style is what Wittgenstein offered in place of what had to be taken away from philosophy. Wittgenstein's language is drawn in general from daily life. The language is not used to state results, for the aim is not to bring static truth into focus. What truth there is is found in the quality of movement itself; the writing moves always, round, sometimes back on itself, showing things from several points of view. The writing is a dialogue; the reader is not told what is the case, he is taught rather by being drawn into the investigation. The reader must make his own contribution, which is guided, but not determined; the reader finds himself with a freedom of thought not usually granted by writers of philosophy. Wittgenstein describes and explains his style in the Preface to the *Investigations*. The style and the philosophy expressed make a unity. Indeed, the style of the *Tractatus* was also in harmony with its philosophy. It may also be said: the new philosophy studies our ways of using language, not by saying what they are, but by *showing* what they are. And in the

Tractatus too Wittgenstein had said that philosophy could not be put into words—despite his having done so—but could only be shown. But now *showing* is *doing*, and there is in the *Investigations* no longer a contradiction between what is written and what the philosophy says can be written. Philosophy studies our uses of words; it has no special words for this purpose, for all words may come under its scrutiny (cf. §121). Philosophy as grammar is a vagabond; neither its tools nor what it can do with them are fixed.

But does this mean that philosophy makes no substantial claims at all? In one sense, it seems to me, it must do. Even critical philosophy, including that in the *Investigations*, cannot proceed from a vacuum. Philosophy has to begin with an assumption. Consider, for example, what Locke wrote at the beginning of his *Essay*:

> I presume it will be easily granted me, that there are such *Ideas* in Men's Minds; every one is conscious of them in himself, and Men's Words and Actions will satisfy him, that they are in others. (I: I, 1, 8)

And Locke presumed right; no-one quarrelled with this assumption until much later. As another example, the *Tractatus* begins with the postulate: 'The world is all that is the case'. And in the first section of the *Investigations*: 'Well, I assume that he *acts* as I have described. Explanations come to an end somewhere.' Propositions of this kind stake a claim to what is fundamental; they exclude other propositions from the basis of philosophical enquiry and explanation. Thus philosophy begins with an assumption, around which grows a system of thinking; to understand a philosophy, its assumption is what one has to grasp. Wittgenstein begins his later philosophy with human activity, and on this basis he develops an account of language and meaning, and subsequently also accounts of other concepts central to philosophy. For example, at §241:

> It is what human beings *say* that is true and false; . . .

And at §281:

> Only of a living human being and what resembles (behaves like) a living human being can one say: it has sensations; it sees; is blind; hears; is deaf; is conscious or unconscious.

These are examples of the philosophical theses which are, and which I think must be, found in the *Investigations*. They develop around the theory that words have meaning in human activity, the same theory which provides the basis for critical philosophy.

But still it may be thought that what we have here is not really a *theory* about meaning. And it certainly is strange to say that we *assume* that men act. Perhaps there is no assumption, and no theory, but simply a description of what obviously are the facts. Even so, is it also simply a 'fact' that philosophy should now begin with activity, rather than with, say, ideas in the mind, whose existence, after all, no-one would want to deny? It is perhaps plausible to say that the philosophy we are now inclined to believe simply states the facts of the matter. One consequence of this view is that we set the history of philosophy in a queer, though not unfamiliar, light. It appears as the history of one error following another, with perhaps occasional insights showing through, which has at last found its way to the truth. At least, this is what follows if we assume that 'the facts' do not change. We can say: the facts are obvious to any man with healthy senses and sound mind; they are accepted without further ado. But how constant are these facts, through time, and between men at any one time? Men's way of life changes; they discover more, do new things, cease doing others; along with these changes come changes in concepts and belief. The facts change. Philosophy as grammar does not propose a system of doctrines, in that there is no absolute and final truth to which it aspires. What is systematic is the method, which makes use of certain insights. Philosophy tries to show what is now before our eyes; it offers a point of view.

Wittgenstein writes:

> 126. Philosophy simply puts everything before us, and neither explains nor deduces anything.—Since everything lies open to view there is nothing to explain. For what is hidden, for example, is of no interest to us.

What is open to view is what we do, and what we say; this is where Wittgenstein proposes that explanations come to an end.

This may seem to imply that philosophy cannot go beyond what is natural and human, in other words, that transcendental philosophy is banished. If so, Wittgenstein's later philosophy would belong to the long tradition which includes, for example, Hume's work, and Kant's. There is something to be said for this assimilation, but more, I think, which counts against it.

It is a matter of where we are to put our feet. Wittgenstein says, it seems to me, that we start with what men do. What is denied is the possibility of *beginning* elsewhere; as though we had a stand-point outside from which to grasp daily life. This position contrasts with that of Hume, and again with that of Kant. Hume sought to base his philosophy in human nature, but at the same time he wanted to measure man against an independent standard. This can be seen clearly, for example, in his discussion of human reasoning. Early in the *Enquiry* (2), Hume lists the principles of association of ideas, which appear to have 'an equal influence on all mankind'; they are resemblance, contiguity in time or place, and cause or effect (op. cit., III). These are the principles by which men infer and reason. Now what Hume *might* have gone on to say is this: 'These are the ways in which men reason, *therefore* they are the principles of reason'. But Hume did not say that; instead he went on to show, in the following section, that our reasoning in terms of cause and effect, which rests on experience of contiguities, is after all *not* reasoning, because it fails to meet a certain standard; in brief, the premise fails to guarantee the conclusion. Compare what Wittgenstein writes on the same subject (*On Certainty*, §196):

> Sure evidence is what we *accept* as sure, it is evidence that we go by in *acting* surely, acting without any doubt.

What underlies this change in conception of reason is a fundamental change in the conception of thought. Hume's analysis of reason follows directly his definition of thought as a collection of discrete entities, namely ideas; Wittgenstein's concept of reason follows from the postulate that thought, or meaning, is to be found in ways of acting. And this same fundamental change in the concept of thinking reappears in a new conception of philosophy and its ground.

Consider also the Kantian philosophy on this subject of human reason. Kant succeeded where Hume had failed, in proving that reasoning about experience in terms of cause and effect is valid; but he was able to reach this conclusion only by explaining (justifying, deducing) the legitimacy of our reason in terms of something not human, nor natural at all, namely the activity of the transcendental intelligence. Hume's philosophy and Kant's both belong to the tradition which Wittgenstein rejects; the former because it measures human activity against an *a priori* standard, an independently defined essence of thought and reason, the latter because it explains or justifies what men do from the outside.

It can be seen now that what at last bases philosophy truly in man, or rather, in men, at the same time throws out all attempts to draw *limits* around human understanding and reason. The drawing of such limits requires what men do not possess. In the famous passage at the end of his *Enquiry* (2), Hume says that any book which contains neither abstract reasoning concerning quantity or number, nor experimental reasoning concerning matter of fact and existence, should be committed to the flames; 'for it can contain nothing but sophistry and illusion'. But how does Hume know that without reading them? Because he has a preconceived idea of the essence of thought and reason, independent of what men do in fact think, and how they do in fact reason. And what was the justification of this idea? Or to ask the question now more pressing: how might *we* try to justify such an idea? 'So is it that we can, after all, speak and know of things beyond experience, even beyond the possibilities of experience?' But what is *experience* now? We find out what men experience by seeing what they do and what they say. We do not know the possibilities of experience from the start.

Hume's philosophy and Kant's shared a certain assumption with the speculative metaphysical systems they were each concerned to reject, and in this respect all belong to the same tradition as the sublime logic of the *Tractatus*. Those who say: 'Philosophy must strive to go beyond experience, for that is where the important questions lead', and those who reply: 'Philosophy cannot exceed the limits of experience', together accept the premise that experience is a given and limited whole. Metaphysics and the rejection of metaphysics as nonsense are but two poles of the same movement of thought.

So are there then no limits? Words have meaning in human activity. So how should the limits of language be drawn? If we knew the general form of proposition . . . ; but what is the general form of what men do? Or again, how should we stand outside life, not indeed just outside our own life, but outside all life, so as to grasp its entirety? We are indeed limited. What a man does and what he says are limited; the limits of knowledge are the limits of action. Some of these boundaries we can define, concerning for example, place, time, the nature of our bodies, but we do not know them all in advance, and our idea of them is constantly, and with good reason, changing. And the limits to what we know (or do, or say) are not the limits of what can be known; on the contrary, the finiteness of human beings is just that they are not everything, and do not know everything. Our experience is limited in that it is, so we believe we know, only part of a greater whole.

In his later work, Wittgenstein rejects the attempt to build philosophical systems of thought which grasp and fix reality from a transcendental viewpoint. These great systems are seen now as an illusion, and our attention is directed back to earth. He writes:

118. Where does our investigation get its importance from, since it seems only to destroy everything interesting, that is, all that is great and important? (As it were all the buildings, leaving behind only bits of stone and rubble.) What we are destroying is nothing but houses of cards [*Luftgebäude*] and we are clearing up the ground of language on which they stand.

Already Wittgenstein anticipated this idea in his *Tractatus*; for it was perhaps the last great philosophical system of this kind, but it proved its own impossibility, the meaninglessness of its own language. Insofar as Wittgenstein's later view of philosophy is correct, if there are to be philosophical systems now, they can be only provisional and experimental, without dogmatic assertion and demands for belief.

131. For we can avoid ineptness or emptiness in our assertions only by presenting the model as what it is, as an object of comparison—as, so to speak, a measuring-rod; not as a preconceived idea to which reality *must* correspond. (The dogmatism into which we fall so easily in doing philosophy.)

4 Judgement

1 MEANING AND UNDERSTANDING (cf.§§134–242)

(i) Following a rule

Wittgenstein begins the *Investigations* by criticising one conception of language and offering another in its place: the signs of language have meaning not because they are correlated with objects, but because men employ them in their activities. Our task is to pursue the consequences of this change in the conception of language, and in this chapter we turn to the theory of judgement.

The connection between the old conception of meaning and the theory of judgement can be brought out immediately by asking what kind of object was supposed to be the meaning of a sign. As we have seen, the meaning of a general term, that is, a universal, or an abstract idea, marked off a class of particulars from other particulars; not any class, not just a 'random' group, but one already in the nature of things. Also, the complex object supposed to be the meaning of a sentence was able to represent truly or falsely the relation of things in space. That is to say, *objects constituted meaning insofar as they reflected the order of reality*; this order was non-temporal, and already given, which is why it could be grasped in an object.

The theory of judgement explains how meaningful signs mark the order in reality. In abandoning the idea that signs are meaningful because they stand for objects, we abandon at the same time the idea that judgement simply reflects an already given order. Our task now is to make a new conception of judgement. The meaning of a sign is its use, but not any usage can make a sign meaningful: the use of a sign through time must be ordered, not random. If the use of a sign is to constitute judgement, there must be 'correct' applications of the sign, contrasted with 'incorrect'. Or to put the requirement another way: *the sign must be used according to a rule (or method)*. The concept 'rule' in Wittgenstein's later philosophy replaces the various old concepts of static ordering, such as 'universal', 'idea' and 'picture'. To understand this fundamental change, we must examine what is meant by the term 'rule'.

Wittgenstein's discussion of rules begins at §134, with reference to the *Tractatus* notion of general propositional form, and lasts until §242. The aim of this discussion is partly negative and partly positive. Criticism is directed against the old view, that signs signify a pre-given reality, that truth is correspondence with that reality, that the understanding is passive. But what matters now is not so much the old view at its most rigorous or pure, for that has been already rejected earlier in the *Investigations*. At its purest, the old view demanded that language be a picture of reality, or that it should signify a common element in all members of a class. These demands have been rejected. What must be laid aside now are various watered down versions of the old theory. They make their appearance as misconceptions of what it means to follow a rule. For although the essential feature of the old theory is its denial of method in judgement, it implies at the same time certain misinterpretations of what it is denying. These misinterpretations try to grasp method solely in terms of objects and 'instantaneous acts', that is, solely in terms of what is permitted in the old theory. They must be cleared away so that we can see properly what is involved in the ordering of reality through time, according to a rule. As would be expected, the main point to be made is in principle simple: *the rule is not given in advance*.

The simplest account of the rule for using a sign would be that the sign itself determines its application. This account does not, of course, have in mind the ordinary signs of language, so let us suppose for the moment that when we use those ordinary signs, what is essential is that in some way we are employing samples or pictures of things. Even so, the attempt to explain meaning in terms of the intrinsic nature of a sign only works if it is supposed that the sign is not *used* at all. For the idea was that we hold up the picture and say: 'This is how things stand'. And if the question is pressed *how* things are meant to stand, the reply is only that we should look at the picture. Nothing is *done* with the picture, so there is no question of doing different things with it. But once we grant that signs are employed, for example in our activities of collecting things together, we see that the signs themselves can dictate no method of application, and therefore no meaning. Any object, picture or sample, can be used in a variety of ways. It is this use which is the source of meaning, not the object itself. And it follows then that an account can be given directly of the meaning of ordinary words and sentences of language, not merely a secondary account, deriving from some theory of images and pictures in our heads. These images and pictures are the 'real signs' belonging to the old theory of meaning; they are the elusive phantasms we abandoned earlier.

It is also no explanation of the rule for using a sign that it is used 'in the same way every time'. For this is either false, in that, for example, the things to which the word 'chair' is applied are not all alike, or it is vacuous, in that we simply substitute for the expression 'used according to a rule', the expression 'used always in the same way (or with the same meaning)'.

Another possibility is that the rule for the use of a sign is simply what we intend its use to be. According to this view, a child who is learning the use of the word 'chair' by being shown examples, must try to see what meaning his teacher has in mind. Let us suppose that the child goes on to make a mistake, applying the word 'chair' to a sofa, say. The suggestion is that this is a mistake because it conflicts with the meaning that was intended, and which has already been given to the word.

Wittgenstein considers this suggestion using an analogy with continuing an arithmetical series (see §§185ff.; also §§143ff.) Suppose we teach a child to expand the series ' + 2', by showing him the beginning of the series, and encouraging him to carry on by himself, giving perhaps guidance to his first attempts. He then proceeds correctly up to 1000, but continues: 1004, 1008, 1012. We should point out his mistake, and the pupil may correct what he has done. What must be defined, however, is the sense in which a 'mistake' has been made. Or alternatively, we can ask: why is 1002 the *right* number to write after 1000? According to the possibility we are considering, the answer would be that this is what we meant him to do when we told him to continue the series ' + 2' from the examples given. Here meaning is conceived as some manner of intention which singles out in advance the expansion of an arithmetical formula, or, in general, the correct use of a sign.

The reply here is that we cannot lay down all the steps in advance because there are infinitely many of them. It may be true that when I gave the instruction to expand the series ' + 2', I *meant at the time* that he should write 1002 after 1000. But even though I meant the step then, still I did not take it then; and if I did, there are countless others that I did not. I meant the step at the time insofar as, if someone had asked at the time what was to be written after 1000, I would have replied '1002'. And we can affirm this hypothetical proposition because as soon as the issue is in fact raised, I say without hesitation: 'Of course, write 1002 after 1000'. But there is no need to say that an issue which can be settled at any time without further ado must have been settled already.

On the whole, once we learn to use a sign in a particular way, we proceed as a matter of course. We have no choice, but not because we have already travelled that way before, rather because no other way occurs to us.

The temptation was to say: the correct use of a sign is determined by the meaning which we gave the sign. But the opposite is so: it is the correct use of a sign which determines its meaning. And what we wanted to call an *act*, is rather a *process*. Signs have meaning because we use them, not the other way round.

The method by which a word is used is not laid down in advance; neither in an object (picture or sample), nor in that the word is simply used always the same way as before, nor in that we stamp the word with a particular meaning which then dictates its use. The rule is made through time, in practice. Meaning is not an object, nor anything else that is already given.

The practice from which words derive their meaning is our understanding ('understanding the medium of ideas'). But it might be objected: 'while what shows that a man understands something, say a word, or an arithmetical formula, is his correct practice, his understanding is not the practice itself, but is rather something that lies behind, and indeed explains, what he does or says'. Understanding is in this way taken to be a mental state, acquaintance with some kind of idea or other object, which underlies practice; or which, indeed, may not ensue in practice at all. But the so-called 'objects' of the understanding are properly described as rules, principles, processes, all essentially extended through time. We speak of understanding an object only insofar as it participates in some movement; it is a bad joke to say that one understands something commonly regarded as inert, like a walnut, or a corpse. It may be inferred, then, that understanding is an activity, not a state.

When we say truly of someone that he understands, for instance, the rule for expanding an arithmetical series, what we say is true at the time, regardless whether or not he happens to be then writing out the series correctly. But it does not follow that what we say is true because the person is in some state, namely, that of understanding. This is only to represent a whole pattern of activity as a state of mind which exists whenever we have occasion to remark on it.

'The essential thing about coming to understand is that we grasp (abstract) the rule.' Of course; but what does that mean? It does not mean to find an expression of the rule, for example an arithmetical formula, for the possession of such a formula is neither a necessary nor a sufficient condition of being able to continue the series. Otherwise we should not need to teach children as we do; we could, for example, just give them formulae for the multiplication tables from the start. What is being taught is not the expression of a rule; it is not an object at all, not even an abstracted one. It is rather a practice. In teaching a child we show him the practice, we do it ourselves, and then leave him to try on his own, offering guidance when necessary. The child is learning to *do* something, and there are no ready-made objects of the understanding which we can give to him.

It may be felt, however, that Wittgenstein's analogy between understanding a word and being able to continue an arithmetical series is misleading in an important respect. The series of numerals associated with the expression '+2' is a conventional one, and therefore knowing the formula alone is no help in knowing the series. But in contrast, a series of judgements *made about the world* is certainly not just conventional; it is rather held together by an independent regularity. For example, repeated uses of the sentence 'This is red' mark a regularity in the world, and understanding how to use the sentence is a matter of perceiving this regularity. It would follow then that there is a truly informative expression of the rule for using the word 'red', namely, a table with the word written opposite a sample of red. And understanding the word is acquaintance with such a table in the imagination, a mental state which underlies and explains the practice of making judgements.

The possibility is, then, that to follow a rule in using a word is to read off its use from some expression of the rule, perhaps in the form of a table relating word to sample. Wittgenstein's discussion between §156 and *c.* §171 concerns just this possibility. At §162, he considers the following definition: reading is *deriving* the reproduction from the original. He describes a case in which a man derives a handwritten text from a printed one, consulting a table with printed letters in one column and cursive letters in the other. At §163, it is imagined that the man follows a more complicated rule than reading off simply from left to right; instead the derivation follows a criss-cross pattern. But now suppose further that the man does not keep to a single method of transcription, but alters his method as he goes along. The problem is: how is the line to be drawn between this kind of procedure and a purely random one? And the problem in insoluble while we try to describe the process of derivation independently of the results of the derivation. For in this way we fail to capture the distinction made *in practice* between what counts as deriving and what is only random.

An expression of a rule, say a table, cannot be the rule itself. The rule is made in practice. And an interpretation of such a table, say a system of arrows linking the items in it, cannot determine the rule either. An 'interpretation' of this kind, like anything else, will be given sense by its use. Whether and how a man is deriving something from a table is shown by what he does; his practice *is* the derivation. Rules are made in practice; but not *any* practice counts as forming a rule, only the right ones, for example doing *this* (and we do it). At §201, Wittgenstein speaks of the difficulty which arises when we try to define the rule by tables and always need more tables to interpret previous ones. He continues:

> What this shews is that there is a way of grasping a rule which is *not* an *interpretation*, but which is exhibited in what we call "obeying the rule" and "going against it" in actual cases. . . .
> 202. And hence also 'obeying a rule' is a practice. . . .

Any mental process which may be involved in understanding the meaning of a word, whether it be a feeling of recognition, or a feeling of being guided by what is seen, or the inspecting of some sample in the imagination (or in the hands), can belong also with a wholly random use of a word, practised without reason or intelligence. Whether someone *in fact* recognises what is around him depends upon what he *does*, for example upon what things he collects together, with his words or with his hands. Only if a man's judgements and actions are of a certain kind do we say that he is 'going by regularities in the world'. Our concept of regularities in the world is of a piece with our concept of regularities in human action. This is an aspect of the harmony between reality and thought.

The rule is not laid down in advance; it is made by following the rule, and that is a creative practice. When teaching the meaning of a word, we give a limited number of examples of the word's use. What must be taken away by the pupil, however, is the ability to make a potentially unlimited number of judgements. So there will be, as it were, something left unsaid, the path that is to be, that *will be* followed. But this cannot be said. The path cannot be grasped, because it has no limits, and is not present; knowledge of the path is not an act, but an activity, marked by sound judgement. There is an inclination to say, however, that in some sense the path already does exist. Confusion arises when we try to imagine the use of a word as extended through time, and so into the future, and yet also as something which can be grasped *now*. The solution here is that we do now grasp the use of a word, in that we have used it and can use it; but this does not mean that nothing remains to be done in the future (as though now we could rest on our laurels). In teaching we allude to *what is to be done* with a word. But the nature of this 'allusion' must be clarified. In teaching, we give examples, perhaps definitions, samples, pictures. But does this show the pupil *every* application of the word? Maybe so, but this only means that he will later carry on correctly by himself. And if he does not, we give more examples, more definitions and pictures to explain the earlier ones. The purpose of all this is to help the person *do* something. The allusion to the future is encouragement, and persuasion.

It has been argued that the concept of following a rule cannot be explained in terms of perception of regularities in the world, since following a rule and perceiving regularities come to the same thing. In a similar way, the practice of following a rule is not supported by *reasons*. Reference to teaching and instruction, to one's own or to others' past practice, can provide a reason for continuing the rule in such-and-such way, but only on condition that this way is indeed following the rule, and whether it is or not is judged from the practice itself. The concepts of understanding and of acting with reason are applied on the same grounds. Wittgenstein writes:

> 211. How can he *know* how he is to continue a pattern by himself—whatever instruction you give him?—Well, how do *I* know?—If that means 'Have I reasons?' the answer is: my reasons will soon give out. And then I shall act, without reasons.

We have exhausted the reasons for our practice of, for example, using a word, once we have described, in the various ways in which it is possible to describe, the fact that we are following the rule for its use. We can for instance, point to our training and say, 'I am just carrying on as I was taught', or 'Look, I am guided by comparing things with this sample', etc. But if someone then asks: 'But why call *this* "the same way as before"?', or 'Why do you think *this* is near enough to the sample?', and so on, then sooner or later we should have to pass by these questions, and act regardless.

Reason is not a 'super-cause' responsible for our continuing the rule. Indeed there is no word in the traditional philosophy for what enables us to carry on as we do. For the concept of creative ordering by practice is a new one, and one which underlies new interpretations of the traditional intellectual or cognitive faculties.

Saying that understanding is practice seems to conflict with the fact that understanding is a conscious or mental process. But let us consider more closely the nature of this fact. We do not ascribe consciousness to machines, not even to very complicated machines, but to animals, and particularly to men. What we know is that the behaviour of animals, unlike the operation of machines, is varied and flexible, marked by whole bodily expressions of purpose, hesitation, doubt, surprise, confidence, and so on. And human beings can give account of themselves; they, uniquely, can say what they are doing, and why. If we now feel that facts of this kind have nothing essentially to do with being conscious, we are perhaps thinking that mental processes, including understanding, lie behind action rather as steam lies behind the movement of a locomotive. But no such process can be what we in fact call 'understanding'.

We could also express the objection in this way: 'understanding is something *more than* the mere ability to use words'. And certainly it is, for understanding involves the activity in which words are used. But the word 'mere' in this objection indicates that the use of language is being wrongly regarded as just a sign of what is really important, the inner processes of understanding and meaning. If we do say that understanding is something 'more than' activity and speech, and more than any other grounds we might use in ascriptions of understanding (writing, calculating, etc.), we should remember that this does not mean that understanding is some inner process independent of these grounds, which enters into explanation of them.

When we say that someone understands something, we are not describing his behaviour and speech. Even so, the statement what is so, and the description how we discover what is so, are not independent. According to the new theory of meaning, a synonymy or analysis is not what we are seeking; indeed they are to be avoided. A concept is clarified not by giving definitions, not by purporting to say what object, process or state of affairs the concept signifies, but rather by describing the conditions under which the concept applies or fails to apply. The description of these conditions will not be synonymous with the word whose meaning is thereby explained; this is to be expected. Understanding is not the same as speaking and acting, but it cannot be separated from them. It is not as though in describing the use of the word 'understanding', or rather, in giving vague and general indications of its use, by pointing to the importance of speech and action as grounds of ascriptions of understanding, we had quite neglected the essential thing, some inner state of process which is the understanding. Behaviourism was right in drawing attention to the central importance of bodily movement within our concept of mental life, but was wrong in trying to analyse descriptions of mental life into descriptions of behaviour. This error was not, however, a small one. It grew out of a whole mistaken metaphysics, apparent in the theory of meaning as the necessity to find states of affairs for descriptions to represent: 'if psychological propositions do not describe something behind behaviour, then they must describe the behaviour itself'. In the sense of 'description' at work in this dogma, however, psychological propositions describe nothing (and neither do physical object propositions).

'But still something is lost from understanding, if it is reduced in some sense to behaviour'. It would be better and more accurate to say that something is gained by behaviour, which is to be seen as creative and intelligent, no longer as lifeless and mechanical, stripped of all 'mental qualities'.

(ii) Creative practice

The conclusion so far is that we create order by acting, and that language has meaning because it interweaves with this activity. Following a rule is a creative practice. It may seem, however, that there are distinctions being neglected here, for among human activities we distinguish those that are creative and inventive, from those that are repetitious and automatic. In this case, what is the sense in saying that all action according to a rule is a creative practice?

Actions according to a rule have meaning and purpose; though what this comes to in particular cases is not readily defined in advance. However, much of what we say and do no doubt happens without our needing to think about it; we, as it were, follow the rule blindly. In these cases, actions are largely predictable; the rule is 'already laid down', in that no alternatives occur to us. Even so, this does not mean that there is no intelligence in these actions; it is rather that not all of what we call intelligence is conscious, or has needed to remain conscious. There are creatures which cannot perform actions which to us are simple and automatic, such as counting from one to ten, and this is because, as we say, they are not sufficiently intelligent. Actions according to a rule may be dull and repetitious; as indeed meaningless and pointless behaviour may be dull and repetitious. On the other hand, for some activities, vigilance and flexibility are the rule. It could be said: insofar as there exist regularities in the world, we need not be concerned what to do next, but can simply proceed as before, while insofar as events follow no simple pattern, we must keep our eyes open. Regularities, however, must be found by us; it is up to individual men to decide whether the present situation is enough like previous ones to warrant continuing in the old way. And in some cases, if a man begins a new practice in place of the old, others may find this change difficult to assess. Maybe he does know that our aim can no longer be achieved by the old means, so we should take him seriously and try to follow; but perhaps he has changed the aim, and is doing something different altogether; or perhaps, the extreme case, others may judge that he has taken leave of his senses altogether. For it is true that not all changes in practice are creative; some lead to nothing.

The objection was: not all of what is called understanding is creative, so what sense is there in saying that understanding as such is a creative practice? This same problem, though inverted, can appear also as a dissatisfaction with the attempt to clarify the notions of meaning and understanding by using the term *rules*. For what exactly are the rules followed by the understanding, and which, for example, constitute the meanings of words? Can they be *formulated*? Certain rules for using words can be sketched or described, as in dictionaries. But such rules are at best a rough guide in the actual practice of making judgements, for they do not tell us what to say in particular situations. So it is also with the rules of chess, for example, which formulate constraints on the movement of pieces, but do not say what move is to be made in some particular state of the board, against a particular opponent. Our uses of words are generally not so straightforward that we can describe them easily or formulate them in definitions, and even if we can, the rules may change as we proceed. Considerations of this kind might lead us to say: *there are no rules at all*. Wittgenstein writes:

> 82. What do I call 'the rule by which he proceeds'?—The hypothesis that satisfactorily describes his use of words, which we observe; or the rule which he looks up when he uses signs; or the one which he gives us in reply if we ask him what his rule is?—But what if observation does not enable us to see any clear rule, and the question brings none to light?—For he did indeed give me a definition when I asked him what he understood by "N", but he was prepared to withdraw and alter it.—So how am I to determine the rule according to which he is playing? He does not know it himself.—Or, to ask a better question: What meaning is the expression "the rule by which he proceeds" supposed to have left to it here?

There is a question, then, whether the word 'rule' should be used at all in this philosophical context. Saying that to understand a word is to use it according to a rule seems to imply that the rule could be formulated, or at least that our use of words is relatively constant and predictable; but this is not always so. This objection is the converse to that made against describing understanding as creative, for this description seems to emphasise the other case, in which the use of language is complex and changing. These two objections together, indeed, would make the dictum 'following a rule is a creative practice', just paradoxical, since what is implied by the expression 'following a rule' is taken away by the word 'creative'.

The solution here is that neither the notion of rule nor the notion of creativity is being used in the ways presupposed by the objections. To say that judgement is a rule means that reality is ordered through time, and this implies that the understanding is active and creative. These assertions contradict the old theory of judgement, according to which the understanding only observes ready-made objects, which represent an order already given. When the senses of the terms are made clear, it is a tautology that action according to a rule is creative; it means to say that action which produces order through time brings order into being. In saying that the understanding creates rules, the old theory of judgement is being opposed at a high level of abstraction, and the distinction between more or less regular, and in this sense less or more creative, judgement is not yet to the point; it operates at a lower level. There is, however, a connection here, for, as we have noted, the idea that judgement passively reflects reality fosters the dogma that signs should be used strictly and according to definitions. The passage quoted above, §82, directed against the notion that we proceed according to rules, comes at the beginning of Wittgenstein's critique of normative logic.

When we try to express philosophical theses with words from ordinary language, we are liable to encounter difficulties of the kind described above; for words as ordinarily used tend to make distinctions in their range of application, but often in philosophy it is not the purpose to draw those distinctions. As soon as it was said, 'understanding is a creative practice', counter-examples abounded, cases of understanding which we do not ordinarily call 'creative'; and when we said 'to understand is to follow a rule', we were shown cases where there is no rule—that is, no simple rule which could be formulated. For a similar reason, there is danger in trying to clarify a philosophical thesis by giving examples. The claim, for example, that a proposition is distributed through time, is not meant to apply to some propositions rather than others, and consequently the giving of examples to clarify, or even to support the claim, is not only useless, but positively misleading. We might point, for example, to predictions, or to repeated uses of general terms, saying 'Here you see the proposition dependent on time'; but then someone will rightly produce other cases, such as mathematical propositions, which do not possess the superficial characteristics which made the examples given look plausible. In the same way it is no help, for example, to cite the truth-functions in support of the general claim that meaning is given by conditions of truth. One solution to these difficulties is that philosophy should rely on new terms to express its ideas. As, for instance, Frege and the young Wittgenstein used the term 'truth-conditions' for the meaning of a sentence, or as Wittgenstein in the *Investigations* introduced the term 'language-game', 'to bring into prominence the fact that the *speaking* of language is part of an activity, or of a form of life' (§23). However, for the reasons mentioned, the meaning of such terms can be explained only to a limited extent by reference to ordinary usage, or by giving examples. These technical terms derive their significance primarily from the whole philosophical framework in terms of which they were originally carefully defined. And the danger is that, partly because of their power, these terms will be detached from that framework and from their original function, so that in the absence of new definitions and explanations, they float more or less freely.

If theses in philosophy do not want to make practical distinctions, what is their purpose? Why write, for example, that judgement is made through time, or that understanding is a creative practice? Propositions of this kind hang together with one another, and with, for example, theoretical science. And also they stand opposed to propositions of equal generality, which are to be found in the history of philosophy.

The rule is formed by our saying on particular occasions: this judgement, or this action, is right or wrong, reasonable or unreasonable. There is no philosophical answer to the question why we speak and act as we do, neither in terms of regularities in the world, nor in terms of inner rational processes. And the answer to the question *when* we say an action or judgement is right rather than wrong, is open to view; we have only to look at our daily life. It is perhaps more difficult to find the right questions now, than to provide answers. The concept of following a rule may be approached in various ways, bringing out relationships with different concepts in philosophy, and with traditional interpretations of those concepts. We begin in the next section, with something remarkable and of great consequence, namely, the intimate connection between following a rule and doing what other men do.

2 COMMON JUDGEMENT (cf. c.§§198–242)

(i) Discourse

In his discussion of rules, from about §198 onwards, Wittgenstein begins to write of common human activity. For example: obeying a rule is a custom (§198); a rule cannot be obeyed privately (§202); the word 'agreement' and the word 'rule' are related to one another, they are cousins (§224).

Perhaps Wittgenstein is saying in these paragraphs that a man's practice accords with a rule insofar as he shares it with other people. As a philosophical claim, however, this can appear at first sight rather implausible. For how should we move from saying what following a rule is *not*—such as that it is not to obey the dictates of some table, nor to follow what has been laid down in some act of meaning, nor is it to be guided by an inner rational mechanism—to the positive claim that following a rule in some way essentially involves being in accord with other people? How can other people do what nothing else seems able to do, namely turn a practice into a rule (if this is indeed what they do)? And the initial puzzlement caused by these questions multiplies when we consider the history of philosophy. For in modern times the very concept of anyone else apart from the present thinking subject has been thought problematic; and if the concept was assumed, it was given little work to do (except perhaps in the theory of value, or in social theory, which would themselves be problematic, insofar as they conflicted with subjective metaphysics). And now it seems that Wittgenstein suddenly produces the concept of community out of thin air, and moreover, places it at the centre of philosophy, in the theory of judgement. The change that Wittgenstein made here is of such magnitude that it is difficult to follow. It took Wittgenstein a long time to reach his conclusion, and it is worthwhile here, I think, to consider briefly the path he took, which ended with the innovation of common judgement and practice. I have in mind the development through the *Blue Book* and *Brown Book*, to the *Investigations*.

In the early part of the *Blue Book*, Wittgenstein moves away from the idea that meaning is something immaterial associated with a sign. He wrote: 'But if we had to name anything which is the life of the sign, we should have to say that it was its *use*' (*Blue Book*, p. 4). The problem then arises what use is. More precisely, what makes the use of a sign ordered, and therefore meaningful, as opposed to something random? Wittgenstein goes on to consider this problem in terms of an analogy with measuring (op. cit. pp. 9–14). He discusses the question: why does an activity count as 'estimating length'? The conclusions reached, expressed in terms of meaning, may be summarised as follows: meaning is a rule, not an object; the rule is given in the *teaching* of the use of a sign; but this teaching interests us only insofar as it supplies us with a rule for subsequent use of the sign, symbolised in a table or chart; we then proceed in accord or in conflict with this symbolised rule.

Already in the *Brown Book*, however, Wittgenstein saw that there were difficulties for the last part of this account, insofar as tables, charts, etc. can be used in various ways. He supposed, however, that further schemes could be added to indicate how a table should be used. After giving examples, he wrote (21):

Schemes of this kind can be adjoined to our tables, as rules for reading them. Could not these rules again be explained by further rules? Certainly. On the other hand, is a rule incompletely explained if no rule for its usage has been given?

At the time I do not think that Wittgenstein saw clearly the answer to this question. The rule may be completely explained without giving a further rule, in the sense that someone may need no further rule in order to use the original (cf. *Investigations*, §86). But so far as the argument in the *Blue Book* is concerned, the rule *is* incompletely explained. For the idea was that the rule, i.e. the expression of the rule, singled out one method to be followed after the teaching process comes to an end; but this is just what it cannot do, since the expression of the rule can be used in various ways, each leading to different applications of the word whose use it is meant to guide. Certainly these different possibilities might not concern us, and we would perhaps just use the table in a natural way. But the question is, why are we thereby right? What constraints are imposed by the table? Thus we are left with the problem: what is the right way of using the expression of the rule? And this is equivalent to the problem we began with, and which the expression of the rule was meant to solve, namely, which is the right way of continuing to use a sign, going by what we have been taught? The table, or any other symbolisation of the rule, now serves no purpose.

Through the remainder of Part I of the *Brown Book* Wittgenstein continues with the question what it means to follow the expression of a rule, but the original problem is not fully solved in the course of this enquiry. Nor is it in Part II; but there, in section 5, Wittgenstein does dismiss the idea that the rule can be laid down in advance by an 'act of meaning', and also the idea that following a rule can be explained or justified in terms of reasons. The rule is not determined in advance; rather it is made in a continuing process. These conclusions anticipate the *Investigations*, but we do not find yet in the *Brown Book* the positive claim that following a rule is a custom. We are now, however, no distance from this claim; we have only to combine the assumption of the *Blue Book* with the conclusion of the *Brown Book*.

It was supposed that the right method for using signs is the one that we are taught. The trouble arose when the learning process comes to an end, for then what keeps us in line? No expression of a rule can do it, nor was the rule laid down by the intentions of our teacher, nor are we guided by an inner rational process. The rule cannot be grasped in any object, or by any act, and the practice of following the rule in the end cannot be justified by reason. But now what has to be said becomes clear: *the learning process does not come to an end*. We no longer invoke a radical change in the nature of what guides us, from being what others teach us, to being some table or chart, etc. It is communication with others that supplies the rule. For what is meant when we speak of learning how to use a word? It is being taught how to make judgements, what to call things, how to describe them, classify them together, and so on. And this process indeed does not come to an end. Continually men offer one another their judgements. This reciprocal 'learning and teaching' is communication. It is by comparing one's own beliefs and opinions with those of others, by agreeing, dissenting and discussing, that the rule is formed. Wittgenstein wrote in the *Blue Book* (p. 14): 'A rule, so far as it interests us, does not act at a distance'. This turns out to mean nothing less than that the rule is present always when we speak and act with one another; it is our discourse.

It appears, then, that what underlies the claim that following a rule is a common practice is the fact that men live in communities, and their communication rests in shared ways of acting and speaking; ways which children are shown as they are educated. This fact now belongs to logic. It is already presupposed in the first pages of the *Investigations*, where Wittgenstein describes how people (the shopper and the shopkeeper, the builder and his assistant) act together employing a common language. It is an innovation for logic to begin with the community, for previously it rested on different assumptions, ones which indeed made the concept of human community problematic, for example, the assumption of absolute being, given *a priori* and independently of human experience, or the assumption that what is immediately given is private, mental ideas.

(ii) Agreement (cf. §§ 241–2)

Let us consider further how logic should describe the agreement that men find with one another. Logic studies the proposition in its meaningful, true-or-false relation to the world; it is not concerned with whether particular propositions are true or false. Therefore the agreement that matters to logic is not agreement in judgement between two men, but rather their agreement on the meaning of the propositions they use. Men agree on the meaning of words insofar as they use them according to the same rule. Agreement in definition alone does not guarantee agreement in the rule; definition of one word by another may help to clarify how a word is being used, but it is the use itself which is the source of meaning. But since the rule is defined by the application of words, it seems to follow that agreement in meaning is agreement in the application of words, i.e. agreement which uses of words are right and which wrong; and this is nothing other than agreement in judgement. In this case, the status of logic is called into question; also communication is set in a queer light, insofar as it would be possible only between men who already agree!

The solution to this apparent paradox is that not all uses of a sign determine the meaning of the sign. Imagine a simple case: two men make a convention to call certain things by a certain name, and then they agree or disagree whether some other things are sufficiently like the original ones to warrant the same name. The original uses of the sign determine its meaning (they are, as it were, 'paradigm cases'), and they provide the basis for subsequent agreement or disagreement in judgement.

We make this distinction between uses of a sign, and in a variety of ways. Indeed the distinction is fundamental. It may be described abstractly in the following way. The concept of meaning refers to the medium of communication and description. This medium is naturally not all that there is; it joins men together, and men to their world. All of these factors appear in the use of signs. Holding the medium in common, men may confirm or oppose one another's judgement. And if men disagree, they may describe this disagreement either as differing beliefs about what the facts are, or as an opposition in their personal attitudes to agreed facts. Men experience the world differently, and therefore sharing a common language and common meaning does not entail sharing beliefs; these are different things.

But if the position were to be left like this, we would fail to bring out the similarity that there now is between agreement in meaning and agreement in judgement. The difference is only one of degree. This shows itself in various ways. For example, when two men share little or nothing of each other's judgement on a particular issue, it becomes doubtful whether they can communicate about it at all. And nor can radical disagreement of this kind necessarily be resolved by defining words in a mutually acceptable way; for there might not be a mutually acceptable way. One man may not *want* to proceed as the other does; he may not want to make the same connections, to classify such-and-such with such-and-such else, neither in his actions, nor with his words; and so on.

In general, therefore, we cannot expect to draw a rigid line between the uses of a sign which define its meaning, and those uses made on the basis of that meaning. In short, the concepts of method and result are interwoven. This is connected with the fact that Wittgenstein's attempt in the *Blue Book* to distinguish the process of learning the meaning of a word, or of explaining the meaning of a word, from subsequent use of the word, was in the end not successful. Also the opposition of the terms 'criterion' and 'symptom' in the *Blue Book* (p. 24-5) is another aspect of Wittgenstein's early attempt to distinguish sharply between the influence of meaning in guiding judgement, and the influence of, in this case, perceived regularities in nature. These terms pertain to the concept of evidence, and the dichotomy they were meant to mark was the swan-song of the old distinction between deduction and induction. No such dichotomy is found in the *Investigations* or in *On Certainty*, though the term 'criterion' is retained as a reminder that *not all* applications of a word are accidentally related to its meaning.

The point could be made also in this way: the medium does not relate two categories which can be grasped independently. Indeed there can be no medium between isolated terms, a so-called medium would rather be a third term, or else it would not exist at all. What we call 'meaning' cannot be grasped in isolation from the facts of the world, nor in isolation from inner life. Meaning is originally activity in the world; through this interaction we discover the facts, and in it we experience feeling. And so, when we distinguished meaning from beliefs about the world, and from attitudes men have, no rigid lines were in question. We begin with the whole, our practice and speech, and then make rough and flexible distinctions within it. This whole is made of agreement and disagreement; but insofar as there is communication, agreement predominates.

The constancy in men's judgement might be described by saying: 'men live in the same world, and therefore in general they will agree in their judgements'. But what is the logic of this truth?—If men live in the same world, they will be in different places, and will experience the world from those different points of view. Their experience will be relative to a point of view, and so too will be judgement based on experience. If men now compare their findings, what agreement could there be? There will be only differences. So it seems that if there is something common between men, it cannot be their experience; it must rather be an independent world. But how should men know of this world? The belief that the world in which men live exists independently of human experience would be faith. God who created the world, and then gave man a place within it, may assure men that this is indeed how things are. Without assurance of this kind, all that is given to an individual man is his own experience; and this he sees from no point of view, not from within at all. And what is seen is not the common world, and he is no longer a man, but 'subject'. The problem is: how can a man learn from experience that he lives in the same world as others?

A man must experience what others experience. But this will not be possible if he stays still; he must change his position, so as to share another's point of view. And in this case, experience and judgement are not a status, but rather a movement. The point of view from which a man experiences the world is a path. Insofar as men are different and experience differently, there will be disagreement among them. But agreement is possible if men share ways of acting, and hold in common the language in which the results of their activity are conveyed to one another. Shared activity and language affirm that we live in the same world; they overcome our differences, in them our paths cross. How do we know, for example, that a table is something common in men's experience? We say that it is; and we use the word 'table' in a way independent of the position from which it is viewed; and any man can eat from a table, or stub his toe on it; and so on.

The connection between the concepts 'agreement' and 'rule' may be brought out in the following way. A rule is created in the practice of distinguishing what accords from what conflicts with the rule, that is, in the practice of discerning right from wrong judgement. So far as a man is concerned, when he makes a judgement, he is right to do so. At the time, a man believes that he is following the rule. In this case, when will one man say of another that he is following the rule? The answer is clear: when he agrees with what the other is doing. Thus, so far as a man is concerned, the concepts of agreement and of following a rule are intertwined. In given circumstances, if the other's judgement is the same as one's own, then one believes the other to be following the rule. However, there are other possibilities related to this straightforward case. In order to suppose that the other is following a rule, it is not necessary that his judgement be the same as one's own; it is enough to see sense in what he is doing. The kind of his action may be different from one's own, and if it is the same kind, still there may be individual differences. In these circumstances, what needs to be acknowledged is that the other man, given his purposes and his experience, is right to act and speak as he does. To acknowledge someone else's point of view in this way is like acknowledging one's own. A man does what he thinks is right at the time; he is moved, we say, by feeling (emotion), reason, or by both. But if a man wants or needs to understand what others do, he may allow himself the inclination to behave differently; he may feel in himself movements and tendencies in other directions, which will therefore make sense to him just as his own practice does, even though they are not his own. Men learn to acknowledge each other's ways, by sharing them, in practice or in spirit. This acknowledgement is a form of correspondence between men, which ensures our ability to live together in the same world.

The agreement between men that is important to logic is agreement in ways of acting, and in the language based in those ways of acting. This is agreement at the foundation of communication and description; it is not simply the sharing of individual opinions about what is or is not the case. It is presupposed by what we call 'following a rule'. Unless there is constancy in action and use of language, between men and through time, there is no rule being followed, and therefore no rational action, and no description by means of language.

At §240, Wittgenstein writes that part of the framework on which the working of our language is based (for example, in giving descriptions), is that disputes do not break out over the question whether a rule has been obeyed or not. He then concludes his discussion of what it means to follow a rule, as follows:

241. 'So you are saying that human agreement decides what is true and what is false?'—It is what human beings *say* that is true and false; and they agree in the *language* they use. That is not agreement in opinions but in form of life.

242. If language is to be a means of communication there must be agreement not only in definitions but also (queer as this may sound) in judgements. This seems to abolish logic, but does not do so.—It is one thing to describe methods of measurement, and another to obtain and state results of measurement. But what we

call 'measuring' is partly determined by a certain constancy in results of measurement.

3 OUR CONCEPT OF TRUTH

(i) Harmony

'A judgement is true if it agrees with reality, otherwise it is false.' These words express a truth which will, under some interpretation, belong to any theory of judgement. Judgement is not inert; it tries to achieve a relation to something outside itself, a relation of agreement; if it succeeds it is true, otherwise it is false. But this is as yet little more than a philosophical truism; the problem is to define precisely the relation of agreement, and the two terms which it relates. One attempt to define truth is often called the 'correspondence theory'; it belongs with the philosophy described in Part I, and found its clearest expression in the *Tractatus*. According to this theory, the proposition is a combination of signs which matches or fails to match, that is, which truly or falsely represents, a combination of objects in reality, that is, a state of affairs. This correspondence theory presupposes that the proposition is a (complex) object. And this is the conception that has so far been rejected; rather, the proposition (or the meaning of a proposition) is a method. In this case, we need to ask, what account of truth belongs with this new conception of proposition, in place of the old correspondence theory?

In the *Tractatus*, Wittgenstein considers the problem how a state of affairs can be truly-or-falsely represented by a proposition. As we saw in Chapter 1, he came to the following conclusions (the first is discussed in section 2, the second and third in section 3):

A. What a proposition represents is a distribution of objects in space.
B. A proposition has something in common with what it represents; what is common is logical, in the nature of the proposition, and also natural, in the nature of objects.
C. A proposition is itself a distribution of objects (signs) in space, a picture of what it represents. The picture agrees with reality or fails to agree; it is correct or incorrect, true or false.

The *Tractatus* theory of meaning and truth is expressed by (C), and is entailed by the conjunction of (A) and (B); if the theory is to be rejected, then, one or both of (A) and (B) must be denied. Examination of the proof of (A) shows that it rests on the assumption that a proposition can be true or false. The true-or-false sign cannot represent just the existence of objects, for if this were so, the sign when false would signify no objects; and this is to say that it would stand in no relation at all to reality, and would not be a *sign* at all. The objects signified by a proposition must exist even if the proposition is false, that is, even if what the proposition represents does not exist. But this means that a proposition must represent a *relation* between objects, i.e. a distribution of objects in space. The import of thesis (B) is now simply this: it is indeed how things stand in reality that determines the truth or falsity of propositions; only two things of the *same kind* can accord or conflict, agree or disagree. Out of (A) and (B), then, it is (A) that must be the force behind (C). But the proof of it looks good. For how can it be denied that there are propositions which represent reality truly or falsely? This is no distance from the truism we began with: judgement reaches out to reality, and finds accord or conflict. But then let us consider what must be assumed in order to pass from this truism to (A). It is that judgement reaches out to *objects* (and their relations). So the axiom of the *Tractatus* theory of judgement becomes clear: it is that reality is *already given*, in the form of objects. The order in reality already exists, and the proposition must try to mirror it. All that thought can truly or falsely represent, the world that is all that is the case, is given at the beginning.

The correspondence theory of truth presupposes that the order in reality is given non-temporally. Here we may remark that theories of universals also affirm that order is given non-temporally, in this case being the unity of classes, and yet they preclude the spatial atomism asserted by (A), and hence the picture theory of meaning and correspondence theory of truth asserted by (C). The implication is that what represents the unity of a class is *not* true-or-false. This suggestion is borne out by the theories of universals: what signifies a class is an object of some kind (form, quality, abstract idea), but the object is not right or wrong; if it does signify a class, it does, and if it does not, it is irrelevant. That is to say, the *Tractatus* insistence on false but meaningful representation finds no hold here, and the proof of (A), the spatial ontology, is broken. Even so, it might be added, the analogue of thesis (B) remains valid, in that what represents the unity of a class was held (where possible) to be *like* the particulars in the class.

In abandoning the *Tractatus* account of the proposition, the conception of reality as a given status gives way to a conception of reality as process. If there is no given status for judgement to grasp, the question arises: what becomes of truth? We can safely say that truth is agreement of some kind with reality. And so, if reality is not a state but a process, and judgement too is a process (activity, or practice), it follows that the agreement between judgement and reality will not be a state of correspondence, but an agreement in movement. This agreement might be called 'harmony', or indeed 'correspondence', if we give this word a dynamic interpretation, and not a static one.

It may seem now that judgement represents not simply a distribution in space, but a distribution in space and time. This is partly correct, but also in several ways misleading. Firstly, it would be wrong to imply that what is represented already exists. While it is plausible (though now considered false) to construe spatial relations as already given, relations in time cannot be conceived in this way. What is represented is produced. The sequence of the *Tractatus* deduction is reversed; the proposition is not explained in terms of what it represents, rather it is through the means of representation, by means of a method, that we grasp what is represented. This leads on to the second error in the suggestion that judgements describe spatio-temporal relations, the implication that these alone are what is described. Rather, what is represented is as diverse as our methods. This means that the concept of reality belonging with the new logic cannot be precisely defined, or circumscribed in advance. It may be said in general terms that reality is what effects men; it includes those phenomena which men, together with any instruments they have made, are sensitive to. And examples can be given; tables and chairs are real, and other things involved in daily life. However, the boundaries of reality are flexible; they can be seen to change in certain ways, in individuals, and in social communities. We discover what is real by acting, by regular movement. In this movement we measure time, and come to know space (we see things from different places). All representation is made within space-time, and this is its special status. But what is represented depends on the activity which is the representation; for example, by using rods and clocks in certain ways we discover precise spatio-temporal relations, the more complex human eye in interaction with light registers colour, the whole human being in his dealings with others experiences emotion; and so on.

Representation is a moving order, not a static picture. This moving order is the human being. The human being as representation has something in common with reality, as did the old 'picture'. A human body is a body among others in the world, and with them it is in motion. The activity of a human body, that is to say, of a human being, is itself part of reality; and it is also logical, in that it constitutes judgement. Activity is the condition under which the representation of reality is possible. The picture theory of the proposition, and the later definition of meaning as use give alternative accounts of the *order* in judgement. The two systems of logic to which they belong are deeply opposed; for example, the general form of pictures is defined in advance, the general form of the use of signs is not. We cannot now define what representations are possible; men continually realise new possibilities.

The rules men follow in their activity and use of language are various, and there is no general form that can be defined. This means that what counts as being right or wrong, true or false, also cannot be specified in advance, but is different things in different cases. This is connected with the fact that predications of 'true' and 'false' to propositions conform with the rules:

It is true that p = p, and

It is false that p = not-p.

This analysis of 'true' and 'false' was originally given by Ramsey, who inferred from it that 'the problem is not as to the nature of truth and falsehood, but as to the nature of judgement or assertion' (1: p. 143).

Wittgenstein accepted Ramsey's analysis and apparently also the inference he drew from it. At the beginning of his discussion of rules, Wittgenstein criticises the notion of general propositional form postulated in the *Tractatus*, saying that our concept of proposition is to be defined rather by examples, which will include what may be called inductively defined series of propositions (§134, 135). He continues: 'At bottom, giving "This is how things are" as the general form of propositions is the same as giving the definition: a proposition is whatever can be true or false' (§136). But Wittgenstein then quotes Ramsey's analysis, and criticises the definition of proposition as whatever can be true or false, because it wrongly implies that we have a concept of true and false which could be used to determine what is and what is not a proposition. Rather, the concept 'true' belongs to our concept of propositions, as so to speak a constituent part of it, but does not 'fit' it, (see §136). Thus there is no theory of truth separable from the theory of judgement. And in accord with this the concepts 'true' and 'false' are not mentioned explicitly after these preliminary passages until the end of the discussion of rules (at §241); the concept of following a rule is fundamental, and already contains the concept of being right or wrong.

Wittgenstein writes at §241: 'It is what human beings *say* that is true and false'. What men say is no longer to be conceived as a collection of signs, or as any other kind of object, such as a mental idea, which in themselves are true or false. The meaning of what men say is found in human activity, in men's use of the signs. It is the agreement or disagreement of this activity with reality which guides what men assert or deny, and so also their predication of truth or falsity.

Activity and the judgement which accompanies it aim at truth. If a way of action agrees with reality, it can continue. Therefore it may be said, according to the new logic, that truth is what makes life possible. What this truth comes to, however, depends on the particular life-activity, and therefore on the particular aspect of reality, which is in question; and these are of many and various kinds. Truth is affirmation; error and falsity are denial. What is denied is that a man can continue in a certain way; and unless denial is overcome by affirmation, there is no movement, no activity, and no representation.

(ii) Relativity

In their thoughts, men represent to themselves the way things are in the world; they do so, for example, when they perceive, by eye, by ear, by touch, and so on. Philosophers have said that in sense-perception we are given ideas, they are impressions of reality on the mind, and they provide the materials for thinking. But in his *Tractatus*, Wittgenstein wanted to say: it is by means of language, by conventional symbolism, that we think, that is to say, make pictures of the world; and there was in this account apparently no place for perceptions as ideas. When we look at our language, however, we do not find pictures; the signs of language have meaning, not because they are images of what we find around us, but rather because we use them in our various activities. It is by thought and judgement that the world is measured. In the *Tractatus* this meant that the proposition, the picture made of signs, was laid against reality, and together they agreed or failed to agree; but the conclusion is now that insofar as the signs of language mark out the measuring rod, this rod cannot be a static form, it is rather human activity. It is the human being that is the measure.

Socrates says to Theaetetus:

> And it has turned out that these three doctrines coincide: the doctrine of Homer and Heracleitus and all their tribe that all things move like flowing streams; the doctrine of Protagoras, wisest of men, that Man is the measure of all things; and Theaetetus' conclusion that, on these grounds, it results that perception is knowledge. (*Theaetetus*, 160D–E)[1]

Socrates believed that these three doctrines were one, and this one view he rejected. Let us consider why he unified the doctrines, and what he has against them.

In saying that man is the measure of all things Protagoras meant, according to Socrates, that individual things are for me such as they appear to me, and are for you such as they appear to you; for example, when the same wind blows, it seems cold or warm to each of us. But in the case of warmth and everything of that kind, 'appears' denotes perceiving, so that perception, being always of that which is, cannot be false, and so is knowledge (151D–152C).

Thus we may say that perception is one form of knowledge, appropriate to the sense qualities, but there may be other forms of knowledge, in which appearance, though of what *is* for a man, and therefore knowledge, is not perception. But what other means of knowing does a man possess, apart from the organs of sense? Consider this question in the light of an objection which Socrates later raises to the view of Theaetetus, that knowledge is perception. We are able, he says, to grasp that what we perceive by the several senses has being, is one or several, like or unlike; but these truths cannot be known by means of the senses themselves, each of which is limited to its own sense qualities. But these are truths of the kind to which knowledge is directed, and therefore, Socrates infers, knowledge is not perception. The mind has knowledge not by means of bodily faculties, but by an instrument of its own, (184B–186E). But let us consider what the mind knows when it knows of being, number, identity and difference. If these qualities are already in sensation, and the mind abstracts them, then sensation is after all the foundation of knowledge, in that it supplies the objects and guarantees the possibility of knowledge. And if the qualities are not already in sensation, how can the mind by thinking find them there? It would have to be thought that produces them. And this might be done with language; for example, we say that there is a certain sensation in us, and we give the same name to a visual sensation as to a tactile one, and so on. And if the justification of this speech is not in sensation itself, it must arise from the activity to which the speech belongs; we react in certain ways to sensations, and sometimes in the same way to sensations of different modalities. In this case, thought is activity, and is expressed in language; but involved in activity is always perception.

We asked above what other means of knowledge a man possesses apart from perception. But this is not the right question. Knowledge comes from activity; and there are countless ways of acting (building, calculating, ritual, etc.) and these various sources of knowledge do not exist in addition to perception, rather perception underlies them all. For a man, or anything living, to find his way through the world, he needs at least contact with it, and this contact is made at the sense-receptors of the body. What a man does on this basis gives meaning to his contact with things, and determines what he finds. If perception alone cannot constitute knowledge, then to know is to make something from perception, it is an active process; but perception is itself part of this process (causally and logically).

If man is the measure of things, then knowledge makes use of perception by the senses, but is itself activity. The result of activity, or better, of inter-activity, is relative to the man who is acting; and when a man applies himself to things, what appears to him as the result is indeed there for him.

Socrates raises the problem: if a man is the measure of all things that are for him, how can one man be wiser than another? How can Protagoras claim the right to teach others, if each man's beliefs are all right and true, each man being the measure of his own wisdom? (161C–162E). But Socrates knows the answer Protagoras would give, and speaks for him:

> And as for wisdom and the wise man, I am very far from saying they do not exist. By a wise man I mean precisely a man who can change any one of us, when what is bad appears and is to him, and make what is good appear and be to him. (166D)

And as for the wise, my dear Socrates, so far from calling them frogs, I call them, when they have to do with the body, physicians, and when they have to do with plants, husbandmen. For I assert that husbandmen too, when plants are sickly and have depraved sensations, substitute for these sensations that are sound and healthy. (167B–C)

According to Protagoras, then, wisdom in a man is to produce what is good; for example, it is to help plants grow. And a man becomes wise, in a particular field of activity, by experience, or by training. For the measure is activity, and must be practised to become good; the measure must itself be cultivated.

Socrates goes on to observe that men look to the wisdom of others; for example, in moments of great danger, they look to someone who can take control of the situation. Having thus introduced a notion of wisdom close to or the same as Protagoras' own, Socrates then proposes the following definition: wisdom is true belief, and ignorance false belief (170–170B). This definition, we may remark, is related to the one Wittgenstein criticises at the beginning of the *Investigations*, which sums up the facts of human practice in which words have their meaning by saying: the meaning of a word is an object. These definitions, as we have already seen in the case of meaning, can have two uses; one is a harmless abbreviation, but the other is not harmless, for it conceals, and goes on to deny, those very facts about men and what they do, which are the origin of the concepts in question. Socrates is moving towards this second use of his definition of wisdom.

The definition of wisdom as true as opposed to false belief is designed to cause trouble for Protogoras, since, according to his doctrine, what a man believes to be so is so for him, and never is not so, and consequently there seems to be no place here for the concept of falsity. However, before we see how this argument strikes, let us consider more closely what it is made of. Socrates says to Theodorus:

When you have formed a judgement on some matter in your own mind and express an opinion about it to me, let us grant that, as Protagoras' theory says, it is true for you; but are we to understand that it is impossible for us, the rest of the company, to pronounce any judgement upon your judgement; or, if we can, that we always pronounce your opinion to be true? Do you not rather find thousands of opponents who set their opinion against yours on every occasion and hold that your judgement and belief are false?

To which Theodorus replies:

I should just think so, Socrates; thousands and tens of thousands, as Homer says; and they give me all the trouble in the world. (170D–E)

But if disagreement between men is the source of the concept of falsity, why should Protagoras' doctrine be unable to account for the concept? Socrates supposes that it cannot because he takes the doctrine to mean not only that what each man judges is true to himself, but also that it is true for everyone, so that there never could be conflict in opinion (170C–171C). But at most what Protagoras' doctrine implies is that everyone should affirm that a particular judgement is true for the man making it, and this is not the same as affirming the judgement itself. The deeper error, however, is that Socrates does not bring out an important consequence which follows if man is the measure of things, namely, that insofar as men are like one another, their measure is the same, and that it is on this basis that one man may affirm what another denies.

By supposing that Protagoras' doctrine excludes the possibility of disagreement between men, and therefore can include no notion of falsity, Socrates restricts the validity of the doctrine to measures of sense qualities (171D–E). The conclusion could also be expressed in this way: the doctrine is valid only for what is inner, or private. But, Socrates asserts, the doctrine does not apply in those cases where we know that not every man's judgement is true; for example, if a patient disagrees with his doctor about the future course of his illness, or if legislators dispute whether some law will be advantageous to the state (177C–179C). In this way Socrates demonstrates the possibility of truth and falsity, and hence of wisdom and ignorance, and so concludes that Protagoras' doctrine is invalid, or has at best very restricted validity.

Socrates takes the concept of falsity from human discourse, in which men disagree with one another, and from human experience through time, in which what men believe will come to be, sometimes turns out not to happen. But far from having no place for the concept of falsity so defined, Protagoras' doctrine entails it. If man is the measure of things, then insofar as men are alike, their measure is the same, and this ensures the possibility of their agreement or disagreement in opinion. And since men act through time, the measure is in time, so that judgement made at one time may accord or conflict with judgement made later.

Socrates' argument that Protagoras can give no account of falsity arises partly from a misinterpretation of his doctrine and a failure to bring out its possibilities; but the argument has also another source, an idea of falsity which indeed Protagoras would not allow. At the time two men disagree, one of them is wrong, or perhaps both are wrong; and if in the light of subsequent events, one man should change his mind, it is his earlier judgement which he says was wrong. So then it seems that if a man's judgement is false, it is false when it is made. But what is this falsity which can exist already when judgement is made? A man cannot believe that what he now judges to be so is not so (otherwise he would not make the judgement); but others may say now that he is wrong, and later he may come to think so himself. This is to say, so far as a man is concerned, falsity comes to be, through others, and through time. So the doctrine of Protagoras cannot explain how a judgement can be false at the time it is made. But what the doctrine cannot explain it was not asked to explain. If we dismiss the means by which we discover falsehood, as being inessential to the concept, and continue to press the question: 'how can assertion be false at the time?', then we have in mind the idea that falsity, and truth, are static relations which judgement bears to a reality which already is. It is this idea of falsity which ignores and then denies those facts concerning men's discourse and activity which enabled us to speak of falsity in the first place, and it is indeed something of which Protagoras' doctrine can give no account.

The concept of falsity as a relation existing already at the time of judgement implies a concept of being which is incompatible with the doctrine that man is the measure of things. Socrates himself has shown earlier in the dialogue that the unified doctrine of Theaetetus and Protagoras is in turn the same as the doctrine of Heracleitus, that all is becoming. This doctrine is described as follows:

It declares that nothing is *one* thing just by itself, nor can you rightly call it by some definite name, nor even say it is of any definite sort. On the contrary, if you call it 'large', it will be found to be also small; if 'heavy', to be also light; and so on all through, because nothing is *one* thing or *some* thing or of any definite sort.

All the things we are pleased to say 'are', really are in process of becoming, as a result of movement and change and of blending one with another. We are wrong to speak of them as 'being', for none of them ever is; they are always becoming. (152D–E)

If man is the measure of all things in perception, then everything is made of opposites, changing from one time to another; and opposition and contradiction exist also between men. But the connection between men and motion is not yet made clear.

Against the Heracleitan doctrine, Socrates raises the objection: if all things are in flux, it would be impossible to give names to things, for they would slip away from us even as we are speaking (182D). But to this the reply is: as men speak they too are in motion, or better, names have meaning because they are used in our activity— so there is no question that what moves and changes should evade our speech.

It is possible now to assess Socrates' criticisms against the three doctrines which he saw formed a unified philosophy. What happens in each case is that Socrates does not bring out fully what is implied, and confronts each doctrine with the opposite of one of the others; and by this method Socrates will indeed discover incoherence, for he has shown himself that the doctrines stand or fall together. Thus: perception is not knowledge because perception merely receives the sense qualities and is unable to make connections between them, or even to realise their existence. But the reply is that perception is part of a process, in which things become and order is made. Secondly, if man is the measure of things, these things can be at best private affairs, where disagreement is impossible. But this is not so, for men act and speak in similar ways, and therefore share their measures, and it is on this basis that they agree with or contradict one another. Thirdly, if man is the measure, no account of false judgement is possible. But what is inexplicable is rather that men should have a concept of falsity divorced from their methods of discovering error, in their discourse and in their experience through time, a concept which is impersonal and atemporal. And finally: if all things are in flux, how can we speak of things at all? Because speech belongs with our movement.

Socrates is able to refute the philosophy he has described because he does not fully accept it. However, it seems that he did accept the philosophy as valid in a limited domain. Socrates knew well the strength of the doctrine that motion produces what passes for being, that is, becoming, whereas rest is the cause of non-existence and destruction. This is so, he argues, for fire, and in the birth of living things, and in matters of the human body and human soul, and also in the rest of nature (153–153D). And as we have seen, Socrates does grant that in perception man is the measure of what becomes for him. Thus the doctrines of Heracleitus, Protagoras and Theaetetus are not rejected because they give a wrong account of nature and man, they are rejected because they can provide no stability for language, no objectivity for judgement, and no true objects of knowledge. In a word, it is not what the philosophers say that Socrates rejects, but nature itself.

Socrates, or best now to call him Plato, expresses his attitude to nature in the following way:

> Evils, Theodorus, can never be done away with, for the good must always have its contrary; nor have they any place in the divine world; but they must needs haunt this region of our mortal nature. That is why we should make all speed to take flight from this world to the other; and that means becoming like the divine so far as we can, and that again is to become righteous with the help of wisdom.
>
> (176–176B)

And in other dialogues,[2] Plato explains his alternative to natural philosophy in full: it is the theory of Forms, which are the true objects of knowledge and wisdom, outside of nature, time and change, and which are known not by what is earthly in man, but by the unnatural soul.

If a coherent philosophy of nature is to be possible, either the pre-Socratic view of nature, which Plato himself accepted, must be denied, or the Platonic standards for being and knowledge must be rejected. For nature, as conceived by the pre-Socratics, does not at all conform to the Platonic ideal. It is in these terms that we may consider the problems that arose in modern Western thought. The moderns made a philosophy of nature, but were guided by Platonic preconceptions. That is to say, nature itself was conceived as being, essentially unchanging and absolute, independent of man and his perception. The problem of becoming was then solved by postulating another substance, mind, to which was confined everything in flux and relative to man, including sense-perception. This solution, however, was at the expense of a coherent philosophy of man, for the connections between mind and absolute nature were themselves insolubly problematic. The modern conception of nature, and the consequent splitting of mind from nature was, I think it is right to say, wholly alien to pre-Socratic thought; as indeed it was to Plato's, except insofar as it followed logically from the conception of nature according to Platonic ideals.

Indeed several major themes in modern philosophy are already anticipated in the *Theaetetus*. Having dismissed the Protagorean doctrine, Socrates goes on to consider how false judgement can be possible, that is, how judgement can be a true-or-false representation of a given status. He states the paradox that false judgement must be of what is not, while still being of what is (188C–189B). This was the paradox which the *Tractatus* solved by the picture theory of meaning; it presupposes Platonic conceptions of '*is*' and '*is not*', and in the *Investigations* Wittgenstein calls it an illusion (§§95–6). Socrates then considers doctrines which came to be associated with empiricism, or with certain versions of empiricism, that perception is an impression on the mind, and that falsity is the misfitting of thought and perception (191C–195B). He also discusses the possibility that the basic constituents of nature are simple, indestructible elements (201D–202C). This statement of atomism, which anticipated modern philosophy and in particular the *Tractatus* ontology, Wittgenstein chose for criticism in the *Investigations* (§§46ff.) Thus the empiricist and materialist strands in modern thought are to be found in the *Theaetetus*, as well as a gesture towards what was to become the rationalist tradition, the postulate of absolute intelligible being, known by the divine.

The moderns applied Platonic conceptions to nature in a way which Plato himself did not envisage (except particularly in the *Timaeus*); they supposed that mathematical, geometrical form was to be found in nature itself. The concept of form is a fundamental one in philosophy. It refers to the order in things, as opposed to chaos; form is the object of knowledge and understanding, it is the origin of language. In Plato's thought, form was absolute and supernatural, but was responsible for such order as there is in nature; the forms ordered natural things into classes, or kinds. In modern thought, however, form became essentially geometrical, or spatial. Spatial form was in nature, but was conceived still as absolute, and therefore beyond human experience. It is this notion of spatial form which appears in the *Tractatus*: spatial form is the form of reality, and is also logical form, the condition under which the representation of reality by thought and language is possible. In Wittgenstein's later philosophy, the concept of form is radically changed, appearing there as the concept of *life-form* (see the *Investigations*, §§19, 23, 241, and p. 226). It is activity that produces order ('the rule'), and which is the origin of language. Life-form belongs to nature. In this respect it is like spatial form, and unlike Platonic form. But unlike both spatial form and Platonic form, form of life is movement, it is creation of order.

The main argument of this book is that Wittgenstein's early philosophy expressed the assumptions of the modern tradition, and that his later philosophy makes a radical break from that tradition. But it becomes clear at this point that the deeper the break becomes, the more it can be seen as a reaction against Platonic assumptions. In this way there are similarities between Wittgenstein's later philosophy and the pre-Socratic philosophy which Plato himself discredited. For example, there are connections between Wittgenstein's later account of language, meaning and truth, and the Protagorean doctrine that man is the measure of things. And in the *Fragments*, Heracleitus makes emphasis on what is common:

We should let ourselves be guided by what is common to all. Yet, although the Logos is common to all, most men live as if each of them had a private intelligence of his own.[3]

At the level of philosophical speculation familiar to the Ancients, there seems to be but a limited number of thoughts available to men. For example, either form (or 'order') is natural, known to men through their common humanity, or it is transcendental, to be known by the divine; and either form is in motion, or it is an absolute status. Rejection of one of these possibilities, or a combination of them, leads inevitably to the embracing of what remains; and conversely, affirmation of one is the denial of the other. For this reason it is inevitable that in affirming a way of understanding opposed to Plato's, Wittgenstein's philosophy makes contact with pre-Socratic thought; both point to what is human, to natural and social life.

There is, however, no question here of a 'return' to pre-Socratic consciousness. The *myth* is gone. It was broken in Plato by reason; it was replaced by religious faith for centuries; and in modern times rational experimental science became the predominant means of understanding. However science in theory, and in certain respects in practice, still followed the Platonic and religious way of looking beyond human experience, to the 'other world'. It is this initial tendency which is changing. During the last century or so science, through technology, has become increasingly integrated into culture, and so has come to be seen as an important and effective mode of human activity, among others. Reason and experience, joined with refined experiment, can now be applied to the problems of this world, to the problems of human life. A task of this kind is suggested by Wittgenstein's last work, *On Certainty*. In this work, reason and experience, conceived in modern epistemology as the two great supports of science, are examined rather in their relation to what is more fundamental, common human life. And by working through the meaning of doubt and confusion, Wittgenstein aims to define certainty, not for science alone, but for life itself. The enquiry uses the basis of the *Investigations*, going beyond this largely critical work, in a new direction for philosophy.

5 Being Human

I MAN'S PLACE

(i) Man as philosophical subject

Solipsism, according to which there is but one 'I', whose states are all that there is, or is known to be, is among the least comprehensible of metaphysical doctrines. Few philosophers have willingly subscribed to it, the young Wittgenstein being among them, but many have been led reluctantly towards it, as a consequence of other views that they held. Philosophers have been led towards solipsism because they defined the subject in a certain way, namely, as being outside reality, something transcendental. For in this case, the I can have no other subject (of the same status) as its object, and in turn cannot be object to any other subject. And if the subject relates to reality from the outside, it follows also that nothing in reality is closer to the subject than is anything else, and no part of reality is known by means of another part; everything stands at the same level of unmediated knowledge, and in this sense everything is the subject's own.

It may be felt, however, that men can themselves find sense in what the solipsist says, for example in the words 'the world is my idea'; for a man's experience between birth and death belongs to him, and is unique. Even so, solipsism means something different from what is true for a man, excluding as it does communication with others, and partial knowledge. It needs to be seen that the solipsistic I is not a human being; it is not a man among others on the Earth, with a particular place in space and time, who knows some things better than others, and some things not at all. This fact about solipsism removes some of the doctrine's initial paradox, for although it is discussed and held in the writings of men, it is not the man who can never meet his own kind and which is coordinate with the whole.

In the *Investigations*, in contrast with the *Tractatus*, Wittgenstein

mentions no transcendental subject. The subject-matter of the
investigations are people, what they do and what they say; in this
philosophy, it seems, there is no solipsism. But to this observation it
might be replied that perhaps Wittgenstein in his later works simply
stopped writing about solipsism and the subject which is transcendental, as though he lost interest in the issue, or found others more
pressing. However this is not to say, the reply continues, that the
egocentric predicament has in any sense been solved, or dissolved; it
is only that a philosophy concerned primarily with men will not
raise the problem—but it still remains, and could be brought out by
extending the scope of the philosophy. Such a view, however,
neglects the inter-dependence of different enquiries in philosophy; it
neglects particularly the coherence at which philosophy aims
between the conceptions of reality, judgement and knowledge, and
the nature of the thinking and knowing subject.

The dominant tradition in modern Western philosophy was
founded on assumptions which led inevitably, by logic and
psychologic, to solipsism. It was postulated that nature was
absolute. Absolute being, by definition, cannot be known by a
subject acting within nature, for action reveals being only in
relation to the act of knowing, not as it is in itself. Thus the human
being, limited by his body to a particular place and means of
perception, was not fitted to be subject. Rather, absolute nature was
fitted for the divine. And man, or rather the Cartesian ego, had
knowledge only by divine grace; or indeed, by divine intuition.
Faith declined, and with this decline in metaphysics there was need
for a new thinking and knowing subject, an ego transcending nature
itself. It was this ego which became the solipsistic self of the
Tractatus.

In his later work, Wittgenstein replaces the major assumptions of
the modern tradition, and therefore the supports of the concept of
transcendental subject collapse. Meaning, thinking and knowing
are grounded in activity, and consequently the world that is
represented and known is not already and independently given, but
comes into being with transactions. And so the thinking and
knowing subject is within the world, not coordinate with the whole,
not omniscient—but free to meet its own kind. A man is part of the
world; he acts in accord or conflict with it, and how he acts
determines what he finds, each man something unique. A man's
body is a body among others in space and time, which may be
touched and held by another man. More than this, a man may find,

in the movement of another, method like his own, so that the other is not only, as it were, object to him, but also subject. Practices and language are common; when men meet, for example, they grasp hands and greet one another (and this is the meeting of two subjects).

There is no solipsism here; men's paths cross. And the addition of a notion of transcendental subject to a philosophy like Wittgenstein's would be without justification or purpose. The role of subject (thinking, knowing, willing) is taken over now by men. The subject of philosophy has been brought down to earth. And if we were to speak here of the ladder by which it descends, it would be our common language. For it was Wittgenstein's study of language as the medium of thought which showed that the subject which is above the world has no language to express what it knows, and then that it is men living in the world who use language, who think and communicate, so that the subject outside has no place in philosophy. In the *Blue Book*, Wittgenstein stresses that the I of solipsism is not the human being (not, for example, L.W.), and observes that the words of solipsism spoken by a man (and there is nothing else that can say them) are merely a symbolism in which a certain person holds an exceptional place, a choice of notation which 'my fellow creatures' may fall in with (p. 66).

The self which concerns philosophy is now the human being. In this case, certain questions can be raised in philosophy which before were excluded from its *a priori* enquiries. They concern the processes and principles by which men come to be in the world, the nature of action; and so on. Enquiry into questions of this kind may at certain points make contact with Eastern thought, which has always held them in view. This contact is another aspect of the way that philosophy may now point away from the *a priori* systems of explanations and significances that can obscure life; away from the 'ever larger and more complicated structures' of Western thought which Wittgenstein referred to in the Foreword to his *Philosophical Remarks*.

(ii) Initiation

A woman gives birth to a child. Her care is the first order, outside the womb, that a baby knows. As a child grows he realises the potential of his body, he looks at what is around him, he crawls on the ground, then finds that chairs can be trusted to support his steps. Increasingly a child discovers and affirms regularities in his dealings with things: he plays with water and sees how it spills, he feels that fire burns, by wandering in streets or fields he discovers the relation of one place that interests him to another. What a child comes to know in his play and pastimes he learns to express in language; he makes up words with his friends, and takes part in the speech of his elders. Gradually a child is brought into the practices of adulthood. Young men and women learn, for example, to care for younger children in the family, to prepare or provide food, they find work, they discover the joy and tension of love between male and female. Life then has an aim in a way that it did not before. For a child plays and finds out many things, but he does not need to provide food or shelter or machinery or books, not for himself, and still less for others. But the youth must take on some of these tasks which maintain natural and social life, in all its diversity; no longer can it be whim or pleasure alone which guides activity, for these are not all that matters. But where is his own pleasure now? It seems elusive. But a man's action cannot be a one-sided affair, it is an intercourse between himself and the world, and in action both must be attended to; male and female realise this, men and women serve the world that they are born into.

Human beings are brought into nature and social community. But it may appear now that we are indeed subsumed within natural and social processes, so that our actions are simply part of them, governed by external forces and principles; and in this case we should have no freedom. This thought raises the problem of what is meant by action, and by freedom. Action, and therefore free action, exists only within what is ordered; in chaos there is simply movement, without motive or intelligence. But the introduction of a man into ordered reality is not the end of his freedom, it is the beginning. In acting we follow a rule; but following a rule is not a passive movement determined by what already exists, rather each step taken by a man is a production. And what a man does creates his place in the world. By playing and experimenting a child discovers his power, and when a child passes into manhood and takes part in work he at the same time assumes responsibility for his actions, and is identified with them. The 'subject' is defined by what lies within his power, or better, by what he really does; a definition of this kind naturally belongs to any philosophy of movement and change.

One form of determinism, which has had several expressions, denied not so much freedom, as action itself. For it seemed as though what we are inclined to call human action is rather part of a larger process which proceeded by independent laws and within which nothing new could appear; each field of enquiry could give its own account of this process and the laws that it obeyed (theology, mechanics, sociology). But there are no principles which we can grasp in isolation from our means of discovering them, that is, as prior to and independent of our activity. And this activity which is fundamental to our understanding is truly a bringing into being; the rule in action is not given in advance. Therefore nothing that a man discovers in the course of his life can take away his agency—every act affirms it.

Still, could not action be wholly determined by causes of some kind? But what are *causes*? The modern concept of causality arose to explain how one state of affairs gave way to another; and insofar as reality is no longer seen as static and fixed, that concept no longer applies. If change is continuous movement and transformation, not the succession of states of affairs, then understanding (or description) of one event makes reference to what has gone before and what will follow later. In change of this kind, it may be impossible to define *what* is the cause of *what*.

Further, insofar as action brings order into being, this order cannot be explained by reference only to the past; if, indeed, it can be 'explained' at all. This means, for example, that the regularities in action, such as recognition and memory, need have no causes in the nervous system, in the form of traces of past experience. On this possibility, that there may be psychological regularity to which no physiological regularity corresponds, Wittgenstein remarks: 'If this upsets our concept of causality then it is high time it was upset' (*Zettel*, §610).

Perhaps the issue is whether human action might be wholly predictable, if we knew enough of the principles which govern it. But the most sensitive measure of a man's activity in its fulness is another human being, and even such a measure as this will fail when the action of the other is too much unlike his own, when the other has different resources. It may happen, however, that a man's action is constrained and limited, by the way he is treated and by the language used to describe what he does, so that he is not allowed his inventiveness and individuality, and we are satisfied that he always behaves in the predictable way we have managed to formulate. But this does not show that a man is not free, only that others may deny him his freedom.

Activity is an order within nature. But we do not say that all natural movement, even if it is regular, is action. How, then, should action be defined? Action may be right or wrong; when a man acts he accords or conflicts with what is around him. But could we not also say that water conflicts with fire, in that one changes and may destroy the other? When a man is threatened, however, he runs or fights, and he cries out in pain if he is hurt. This is how animals react to conflict; and other living things struggle also in their own way to preserve their being and organisation. Yet among the animals it is to man alone that we apply the concept of action, and concepts related to it, rationality and freedom. What are the differences between human behaviour and behaviour of the lower animals which underlie the distinction we have in mind? It may be, for example, that one dog behaves much like another, at least so far as we are concerned, and for this reason we attribute the cause of a dog's behaviour to the nature of its species, rather than to the individual dog. There are perhaps also actions, or reactions, which are common to all men, or to all men of a given culture, and for these we may want to find causes within human nature, or within society, rather than in individuals. The question is where the authorship lies. The concept of individual action applies in cases where men act differently one from another. And it is by experiencing the diversity of the actions of others that a man can realise his own possibilities, between which he must choose. When a man acts in the way he has chosen, the reason for the action can be attributed to no nature other than his own. What a man does is self-caused, in this sense free, and his responsibility.

Thus action requires integrity and individuality, and implies that man is separated from the world in which he lives, not to be seen as simply part of nature and society. The relation between man and the world which goes by the name of action is therefore mysterious, for it presupposes both that man belongs in nature and society, and that he is and must remain separated from them. In this way action confines and offers freedom at the same time. And so there are always ways that we want to go, but lack the power; a man cannot enter a building if the door is closed, nor if the keeper bars his way.

Let us, then, consider what the wise mean when they say that we should pass over. The answer appeared to be clear within those metaphysics which described nature from the outside, for the self was transcendental, and there was no essential place for man. But what could the way be for the man within? How can he leave his daily life, which is the only reality that he knows? A man cannot avoid action; even the maintenance of the body is impossible without it, and the body will move whether he wills or not. Therefore action itself must provide the way. A man finds conflict continually with natural things, and disagreement with other men. But this trouble which action brings is possible only on the basis of correspondence between a man and the world, for without correspondence, even wrong action is impossible. All interaction between things presupposes qualities held in common, qualities which appear in different forms changing one into another; at different levels this truth appears in physics, in chemistry, in psychology, in logic. Conflict is possible on the basis of harmony. But this does not mean that conflict is only on the surface, as it were, an illusion. The pain which men feel in action is real; the worse the pain, the more a man is unable to act, and his contact with reality breaks down. Nor does the harmony lie beneath the surface; if it is difficult to see, this is because we dwell in the pain, and not in the reality which provides for life. So far as a man finds it possible to live, he is in enough agreement with reality.

Action relies on a balance between man and what surrounds him. Certain ways of acting, certain particular actions, preserve this balance. The man who knows this takes care not to run against forces which can destroy him, so far as it is within his power, and he does not go out of his way to disrupt the activity of other living creatures, including his fellow men. But it is not that action should be addressed to the self alone; for the balance on which a man's life depends was not made by him, rather he finds it out in his life, and a man needs to cultivate the order even where he is not directly involved.

Action of this kind may be described as inaction, for in seeking not to conflict, it becomes part of the order which is greater and which includes man. This inaction may be seen as guided not by the individual, but as falling under the same necessity as water in cycle between earth and the heavens. It may be also that the personal pain which does result from action, and the personal pleasure, is viewed with a certain indifference in the context of the whole.

Inaction can, however, be seen as affirmation not negation, in that it tries always to preserve what makes action possible. And affirmation also means that at times men must work against what they find, since there is destruction already in the world they are born into. Action implies both submission to the ways of the world, and the beginning of new ways. Men realise this in life, from birth to when action ceases altogether, and the body returns to its origin.

Some men may be persuaded, however, that with the aid of certain practices, all that they do in life is not to act, feeling neither pain nor personal pleasure. This seems to contradict all experience; but there is much that can be said on these matters. Otherwise, there is no escape from action until death, the final release. The limitations and conflicts can only be provisionally accepted and attempts made to find a way through. The attempts aim to change reality itself, and the more they draw on what is common, the more effective they will be.

2 MAN'S UNITY

(i) One language

According to the doctrine known as Cartesian dualism, man is a combination of two substances: material body, and mind. Descartes' distinction between matter and mind was deep and many-sided. Matter was extended in space, but mind was not. The mind was defined as the thinking substance, which doubted, willed, perceived, and so on. Mind and matter were distinguished also by the theory of knowledge, for the former was immediately and certainly known, while matter was not, and its existence could be doubted. A great support of this epistemological distinction was the postulate that matter in space existed absolutely, independent of our means of representation and knowledge; qualities which were subjective, or relative, belonged to the mind. The distinction between mind and matter was also the distinction between subject and object, for the subject is what thinks and knows, and matter in space was the object of thought and knowledge. Thus, by several kinds of consideration, the same conclusion followed: there are two substances, ontologically distinct and therefore independent of one another. This dualism brought many problems in its wake, each being an aspect of the intractable difficulty how two substances so different as mind and matter could have any relation to one another. There was the problem of knowledge: how could the subject, confined to its own ideas, know that these ideas really did correspond to material things outside the mind? Another problem arose in the account of thinking, for how could non-spatial immaterial ideas of perception be representations of spatial arrangements of matter? A further aspect of the same difficulty was the problem of volition, the problem how immaterial mental events, acts of will, or emotions, could exert influence on a massy body. These problems were chronic, and in large part the mainstream of philosophy following Descartes was addressed to their solution. The simplest kind of solution, proposed in various forms of idealism and materialism, was to deny the existence of one or other of the two substances; other attempts to restore unity were more subtle, in that they questioned the dichotomy between mind and matter.

Wittgenstein begins his *Philosophical Investigations* with a conception of language which is deeply opposed to the assumptions of the Cartesian tradition. Words have meaning because they are used by men in their activity. In this case, it is no longer possible to regard thought as divorced from human action. It is by thinking that we find the order in reality. The conventional signs of language may be used to signify this order; this is how they have meaning, and are not just noises, or marks on paper. The concept of thinking is thus not identical with the concept of using a language (though indeed in certain circumstances they may coincide), nevertheless what underlies the two concepts is the same, namely, the concept of order (or form). The Cartesian assumption is that the order in reality is perceived from the outside; reality makes impressions on the mind. But now the argument is that order is found by acting in the world. At §202, Wittgenstein draws the conclusion that activity is the ground of the concepts of intellect: 'And hence also "obeying a rule" is a practice'. Thus the same philosophical revolution which changes the concept of language and meaning, at the same time overthrows Cartesian dualism, the idea that thought is independent of the body. The Cartesian assertion that thought and reality are radically different was already rejected in the *Tractatus*, according to which both have common spatial form. The further step now taken is that this form is no longer static and timeless; it is a form of movement, the activity of the whole human being.

This kind of consideration shows that dualism in its original Cartesian form is no longer tenable in the context of Wittgenstein's later philosophy. The fact is, however, that much of what is now known as dualist thought, whether in philosophy, science or daily life, has left the original Cartesian form far behind. People who would now take for granted that, for example, they know of the existence of the material world, that they communicate with one another in a common language, might still be inclined to affirm that a man is a combination of two kinds of process, mental and physical. This possibility is connected with an exegetical problem: if dualism has indeed been refuted by the early §200's of the *Investigations*, what then is the point of the argument beginning at §243, the so-called 'private-language argument', which has generally been taken to be an attack on dualism? I suggest that there is what may be called a mild form of dualism, 'mild' in that it tries to exist alongside non-Cartesian assumptions and convictions of the kind expressed in Wittgenstein's later philosophy of language; this mild dualism is what the private-language argument is directed against, and the conclusions which follow the argument are Wittgenstein's new alternative to these remains of dualist conceptions.

Let us begin by saying, then, that human activity is the origin of meaning and understanding. Is it possible, nevertheless, that man is a mixture of two substances, one mental, the other physical? The first problem is to define 'mental' in contrast to 'physical'; for in particular we cannot define mental processes as thinking or understanding, since these are grounded in practice, and practice is not independent of the physical body. So the mental events would have to be non-intellectual ones, such as sensations, feelings and moods. But it should be seen that already doubt hangs over this move, for Descartes included in his notion of thinking feeling and sensation, as well as belief, understanding, and so on. That is to say, he did not split off man's non-intellectual faculties from his intellectual ones, and we should expect this same integrity in Wittgenstein's philosophy of man. But even if this objection is ignored, still so far we have given only a list of mental events; how are they to be defined in contrast to physical ones?

Suppose I am pricked by a pin, I see the pin enter my hand, but I also feel a pain; so there are two events occurring here. One difference between them is that anyone can see my hand being pricked, but I alone feel the pain that is caused. Or in perception, light comes from an object onto the retina of a man's eye, electrical impulses travel from there along the optic nerve to the cortex of the brain, and then, as it were suddenly, there appears a visual image of the perceived object, something wholly different from the accompanying activity in the nervous system, experienced by the one man alone. Such stories as these can appear utterly convincing in their proof that there are two kinds of events known to us, private and inner mental events, and public physical events. But let us ask how these two kinds of event are in fact known to us. One temptation is to say that physical events can be observed by the outer senses, and mental ones by the inner sense. This reliance on observation, however, is inappropriate in dualist terms. For the so-called 'outer' visual field and its contents are as much inner, private and mental as pain. Introspection of the contents of consciousness cannot reveal what is outer. And in this case we are obliged to acknowledge the problem whether anything other than introspection of the contents of consciousness is possible, whether the existence of the public physical realm can be known at all. The problem is familiar, and it is not raised in the hope of finding an unfamiliar answer, perhaps framed in the terms of Wittgenstein's later philosophy. The problem is raised to show how quickly and forcefully the mild version of dualism transforms into the stronger Cartesian one, with all the difficulties that implies. We intended, however, to keep certainty in the external public world, certainly not only in belief but in the concept itself; so we retreat from the stronger position, and leave ourselves in a muddle.

Let us stand firmly in the common world. From this point of view, what do we know about the private, inner world? We can infer what a man is feeling from his behaviour. But how should it be supposed that what is inferred in this way is *independent* of behaviour? Whence the idea of *another* process behind what men do? To this it may be replied that the inference is made from what the other man tells me is going on in him; he uses certain self-descriptions which are apparently independent of his mode of behaving. So it seems to be language which shows the existence of mental processes behind behaviour. And it would be language also that teaches me in my own case what introspection cannot discern; for I use two languages. One describes what is physical, including my own body, and is shared equally with other men; the other language I have authority over, for it describes my inner experience.

The step from this line of thought to dualism in short and plausible. It would be supposed that even if facts about our use of language seem essential to the definitions of the mental and physical, still they can hardly be what is fundamental. What is fundamental is that there are two kinds of process, which then naturally are described in different ways. The fact that, for example,

I cannot speak of feeling your pain, while we can speak of us both perceiving the same tree, only reflects the great difference there is between a sensation and a tree—the one is mental and private, the other material and public.

It is possible to justify in this way a form of dualism apparently compatible with non-Cartesian conceptions of meaning and understanding such as are found in Wittgenstein's later philosophy. We have seen signs already, however, that dualism of this kind is misconceived. Particularly, it reaches out forcefully to the original Cartesian system, restrained only by obscurity, and by realisation that the consequences are now intolerable. But the conspicuous mistake appears at the last step: it is assumed that words with different uses stand for different kinds of reality. This assumption is not necessarily justified within the context of the new logic, and particularly, in the case of dualism, it leads to incoherence. The incoherence in the mild version of dualism can be brought out in various ways.

Having sketched a frame of reference, let us now consider the private-language argument. At the beginning of the argument, it is assumed for the time being that there are mental and physical processes, and that the former are private. The possibility to be raised is whether, in this case, a man could use a language for describing his own private mental processes, a language which, in referring to what he alone is acquainted with, would make no sense to anybody else. At §243 Wittgenstein mentions several ways a man could use words for his own purposes, and then asks:

> But could we also imagine a language in which a person could write down or give vocal expression to his inner experiences—his feelings, moods, and the rest—for his private use?—Well, can't we do so in our ordinary language?—But that is not what I mean. The individual words of this language are to refer to what can only be known to the person speaking; to his immediate private sensations. So another person cannot understand the language.

Wittgenstein makes it clear that this private language is not our ordinary language for describing inner experiences, which includes words such as 'pain' and 'sensation'; he says 'that is not what I mean'. The private language makes sense only to the man whose experiences it refers to, but ordinary language has a common use between men. Wittgenstein anticipates the account of our language of sensations that he will work towards; one consequence of the account is naturally that this language is used by us all. To the question how names become connected to sensations, Wittgenstein replies, §244:

> Here is one possibility: words are connected with the primitive, the natural, expressions of the sensation and used in their place.

This raises the question in what sense sensations are private. Between §246 and §255, Wittgenstein considers the proposition that sensations are private, and other related propositions, and argues that they are grammatical propositions, masquerading as empirical ones. It is partly this masquerade which, I have suggested, underlies the mild form of dualism against which the private-language argument is directed. We shall return later to Wittgenstein's arguments against what he considers to be misconstructions of language, as well as to his positive account of our language of sensations, but for the moment let us remain uncritically with the view that sensations are private, inner events behind their bodily expressions at most only causally connected with them.

At §256 Wittgenstein returns to the problem of the private language. The words of this language would not refer to sensations as ordinary words do, that is, they would not be used on the basis of the natural expressions of sensation. Rather the words would be simply and directly associated with sensations. This possibility envisaged by dualism is considered in §258; Wittgenstein asks us to imagine that he wants to keep a diary about the recurrence of a certain sensation, so he associates with it the sign 'S' and writes this sign in a calendar for every day on which he has the sensation. He then considers how the meaning of this sign 'S' is established:

> Well, that is done precisely by the concentrating of my attention; for in this way I impress on myself the connexion between the sign and the sensation.—But "I impress it on myself" can only mean: this process brings it about that I remember the connexion *right* in the future. But in the present case I have no criterion of correctness. One would like to say: whatever is going to seem right to me is right. And that only means that here we can't talk about 'right'.

The argument seems to be: if there is no bodily expression

connected with the use of the sign 'S', then the use of the sign is neither right nor wrong. In this sense the sign is not being used according to any rule, and is therefore not a *sign* at all, but merely a random mark with no meaning. Following §258 up to §269 Wittgenstein illustrates in various ways his contention that subjective or private attempts to name something, to establish or follow a rule would be, as it were, empty gestures, in fact achieving nothing of the kind. If this is correct, the imagined private language turns out to be an impossibility; such a language would be no language at all. Wittgenstein concludes at §269:

> Let us remember that there are certain criteria in a man's behaviour for the fact that he does not understand a word: that it means nothing to him, that he can do nothing with it. And criteria for his 'thinking he understands', attaching some meaning to the word, but not the right one. And, lastly, criteria for his understanding the word right. In the second case one might speak of a subjective understanding. And sounds which no one else understands but which I '*appear to understand*' might be called a "private language".

If private language is an impossibility, any language for describing inner experience (including ordinary language) must be related to the natural bodily expressions of experience. Wittgenstein continues at §270:

> Let us now imagine a use for the entry of the sign 'S' in my diary. I discover that whenever I have a particular sensation a manometer shews that my blood-pressure rises. So I shall be able to say that my blood-pressure is rising without using any apparatus. This is a useful result. And now it seems quite indifferent whether I have recognized the sensation *right* or not. Let us suppose I regularly identify it wrong, it does not matter in the least. And that alone shews that the hypothesis that I make a mistake is mere show.

In this case, there is no further process behind and independent of the bodily expression of sensation; in other words, dualism is false.

Now I have hurried over three stages in this argument against dualism: firstly the proof of the impossibility of private language, secondly the assessment of what exactly this proof concludes, and thirdly, the implications of this conclusion for dualism. But now that we have an overview, let us turn to the details, particularly in the light of powerful objections which have been raised to the private-language argument.

A dualist concerned to defend the possibility of private naming of sensations might reply to the remarks in §258: 'Of course I could distinguish right from wrong uses of the sign "S", for I can recollect those sensations which I have previously called "S", and see whether a sensation I now have is like or unlike them'. But at §265, Wittgenstein rejects this possibility of subjective justification by memory, saying that 'justification consists in appealing to something independent'.

Ayer has replied to such a move, however, that unless there is something that one is allowed to recognise, no test can ever be completed, and there will be no justification for the use of any sign at all (2: p. 256). Further, if there is something that I can recognise, why should it not be a private event as much as a public one? (op. cit., p. 257). Bennett has reinforced Ayer's point, arguing in particular that other people's reports cannot be taken as an 'independent check' on memory, since like any other happening in the objective realm, they must be assessed by me for relevance (1: p. 212). These objections are very powerful. Apparently the fact that bodily states are physical and public gives them no privileged epistemological status, and if this is so, Wittgenstein's argument comes to grief.

Indeed these objections point in the opposite direction to Wittgenstein's conclusions. Far from external things being the primary checks on memory, it would seem that the epistemological priority is the other way round, so that the evidence of the senses underlies recognition of external things, including the speech reports of others. We are led towards familiar empiricist presuppositions. It would be necessary then to distinguish outer from inner experience; if not in the patently problematic Cartesian way, perhaps characteristic empiricist or Kantian solutions are in order (on these see respectively Ayer, op. cit., p. 261, and Bennett, op. cit., pp. 206ff.). The objections raised by Ayer and Bennett are indeed so powerful that their appropriateness as defences of private language can be questioned. For the possibility of private language is not being envisaged, if I am right, in the context of Cartesian or neo-Cartesian assumptions, but rather in terms of the radically different conceptions which belong to Wittgenstein's new philosophy of language. Particularly, the issue raised is not whether a Cartesian (or Kantian) ego can use or make 'ideas' or 'concepts' in isolation from others of its kind (and since it will necessarily always be isolated, the answer to this question is likely to be positive); the issue is rather whether *a human being can speak a language of his own*. Wittgenstein introduces the problem by asking at §243 whether we can imagine a language in which a person could write down or give vocal expression to his inner experiences for his private use. Cartesian or Kantian egos do not write down or give vocal expression to anything.

The importance of this can be brought out, for example, by considering Bennett's continuation of his argument that the speech of others has no special status so far as 'I' am concerned. He writes:

> The picture of communication as the insertion of propositions into other people's minds, although always wrong, is especially harmful at our present level of epistemological grass-roots. We should replace it by the cold maxim: what people say is just a special case of what objects do. (op. cit., p. 213)

But so far as the possibility of private *language* is concerned, this is wrong. What other people say has a special place in my assessment of my judgement, because I too am a person, and my judgement is what *I say*. In communication with others their judgement comes into direct accord or conflict with my own (though certainly this has nothing to do with inserting propositions into minds, but rather with men speaking the same language). Bennett is right, of course, to resist this conclusion from an empiricist standpoint, according to which men's use of language is indeed just a special case of what objects do; but such a view effectively denies the new conception of meaning and judgement, and belongs with a quite different conception, of an empiricist kind. And this empiricist opposition to Wittgenstein's philosophy is correctly addressed to the first page or two of the *Investigations*, not to the argument against private language. The appeal to 'epistemological grass-roots', moreover, cannot settle the issue. The basis of epistemology is no deeper than the basis of logic; what is fundamental is the same for both in any philosophy, including empiricism and Wittgenstein's philosophy. And the basis of the new logic is that men act in the world, communicating by means of language. In brief, then, the private language argument is not directed against the solipsism of some metaphysical ego, a concept already made superfluous by the preceding parts of the *Investigations*; it concerns rather the subjectivity of man.

But what, then, is the argument against one man using a language no-one else can understand? Even if the empiricist tendency to begin with what is private and inner is rejected, still the point pressed by Ayer remains: why is the memory of private events on which private language would be based any less reliable than memory of public events? The reply here, I think, is that it is misleading to represent the private-language argument as a scepticism about memory, still less as scepticism about the memory of 'private events'. Suppose a man is saying numbers out loud, and claims that he is expanding an arithmetical formula. Failing to find a method in his enumeration, we ask him what makes the number he just said the right one at that point. He replies: 'Well, I remember all the numbers I've said so far, they were all correct, and now I'm just going on in the same way'. Of course we might protest by questioning his memory, for how does he know that he has correctly remembered all the numbers he has said so far? But this scepticism about the man's memory is not strictly to the point, which is rather: in what sense is what he (correctly) remembers saying earlier right rather than wrong? And this is not a question about memory at all, but about whether he is following a rule; it is the same question we started with.

One interpretation of Wittgenstein's argument between §258 and §269 would be this: if a man used a sign not connected in any regular way to his behaviour or the condition of his body, then he would not be following any rule in the use of the sign, it would indeed not be a sign, and in particular not 'the description of an inner event'. And a particular use of the sign cannot be justified by reference to earlier uses, not because they might in some way be misremembered, but because they themselves still stand in need of justification. The main thrust of the private-language argument is against private or subjective following of a rule; several possibilities come under this head, such as private naming, and perhaps private remembering; but in this latter case the argument is that subjective or private memory is an impossibility, not the 'memory of what is private'.

Under this interpretation, however, the argument seems weaker still! For why cannot one man do on his own what he can do when other people are involved? It seems and is absurd to say that before I can name or remember something, other people have to be there.

But of course the claim is not that other people must be present, it is rather that if they are, they must be able to follow what I am doing. Still, the support of this claim is unclear. The question remains: if I can follow a rule by myself in matters which others could share, why should I not be able to do so when the rule concerns events with which I alone am acquainted? (And of course the reply at this stage cannot be that there are no such private events.)

Wittgenstein's objection to the private use of the sign 'S' is that there is no distinction between using it correctly and seeming to use it correctly. But can we not imagine criteria which would serve to make this distinction? We may suppose, for example, that the present recollection of an earlier sensation is a faded version of it, so that it is a matter of fact—observable by the inner eye— whether a present sensation is like or unlike a present recollection of an earlier sensation. Perhaps there would be a basis here for distinguishing correct from incorrect uses of signs; but it would seem now that the real bearers of 'truth' and 'falsity' are sensations and faded mental images, which match or fail to match one another; the use of linguistic signs is so far irrelevant. In other words, we have argued our way back into the old theory of judgement. It is once more apparent that attempts to defend the possibility of private language draw on traditional philosophical conceptions which Wittgenstein has already abandoned.

'But the fact is that I can tell whether a sensation I now have is the same as one I had yesterday, or last year for that matter, and this recognition could determine my private use of a sign.' But then what would decide whether two sensations are sufficiently alike to warrant application of the same sign? Perhaps it just strikes you that they are similar enough, but there is no independent check whether you are right or wrong. No; practice according to a rule, for example in the use of a sign, cannot be explained in terms of perceiving regularities, for both stand or fall together.

This argument, however, is a familiar one; and its familiarity raises the question whether the position here for private sensations is any worse than for public physical objects. In using the word 'chair' for example, we go by what strikes us as the same for our purposes, and if this is to count as following a rule, why not also in the case of one man who is describing his own private sensations? Admittedly it will not be possible for him to compare his use of signs with other people's, but still his use of signs could lead him to certain expectations which turn out right or wrong, and this is the same as with descriptions of public objects. For example, I notice that whenever I have sensation S there follows soon after another kind of sensation which I call 'T', and so reliable is this connection that I turn it into a rule for using the sign 'S': if I call a sensation 'S' and then find that it is not followed by T, then I say that it must have been a sensation like S but was not in fact S—so although it seemed to me right, I was in fact wrong to use the sign 'S'. Rules for using such signs may be imagined as complicated as you please. And now, the dualist will say, all these sensations and their inter-connections may be conceived to be independent of the body and behaviour, and the language based on them will therefore be private, intelligible only to the man whose sensations are described.

Is there anything incoherent about this private language? Its only curious feature seems to be: just that it is private! Failing to find a valid argument that private rules and private language are impossible, some commentators have thought that the best conclusion that can be rescued from the private language argument is a weaker one, namely, that any language which is to be used for the communication of inner experience must be based on bodily conditions and behaviour, so that others can follow and use the rules of description.[1] This weak interpretation of the argument finds some support in Wittgenstein's previous discussion of rules. If the claim that following a rule is a custom, a common practice, is intended to define the essence of following a rule, then clearly it would exclude private rules and therefore private language. But a possibility which the text perhaps leaves open is that common practice is necessary only insofar as the rules and language in the practice are common and used for communication. The concluding paragraph §242 does, after all, say: if language is to be used for communication, there must be agreement in judgements.

The weaker conclusion by itself perhaps admits the legitimacy of dualism, albeit as a doctrine inexpressible by a public language. The signs of a private language could not contain words such as 'sensation', 'experience', and so on, and the dualist would reach the point where in order to say what he wants to say, that there are *really* private events and processes, he has to make an inarticulate sound (cf. §261). Even so, perhaps he could make many inarticulate sounds, a whole language of them, which he could say demonstrated the truth of his contention. This is the possibility admitted in the absence of the strong conclusion that a man cannot follow a private rule. It is likely, then, that Wittgenstein wanted to establish this strong conclusion. Indeed already at §202 he writes that a rule cannot be obeyed privately, otherwise thinking one was obeying a rule would be the same thing as obeying it. And this is the argument which reappears in more detail at §258: it is not just that the speaker of the private language follows no rule which others can follow— which is vacuously true according to the definition of 'private language'—it is that he is following no rule at all, because there is no distinction between what seems right and what is right. But we have still to find the proof of this.

In arguing earlier for the possibility of a private language, it was assumed that the actual participation of others is not required in order that a man be able to follow a rule. If this assumption is false, however, then indeed private language as defined in §243 would be impossible. For the claim that there cannot be a language which in principle only one man can understand, would follow from the proposition that there cannot be a language which *in fact* is understood by just one man. This kind of proof has been offered by several defenders of the private language argument.[2] It is rather implausible, however, to suppose that without the active partici- pation of more than one person, there can be no language. As Ayer has argued (2), we can imagine Robinson Crusoe using signs for describing and recording before, just as well as after, the arrival of Man Friday. It may be that he would use signs randomly, just as he pleased; but equally, he might be guided by experience in a rational way. Indeed the point to be made here is already apparent in social life, for others are not so preoccupied with us that they attend to our every action and judgement, guiding us or passing opinion. Each individual is responsible for using language as he sees fit. And if others do think that what I say is wrong, still that gives me no distinction between 'seems' and 'is', but only between 'seems to me' and 'seems to them'.

The private language argument turns on the difference between following a rule and merely thinking that one is following a rule. But when we turn back to Wittgenstein's earlier discussion of rules for an account of this difference, we find something remarkable and curious: in an important sense there is no difference at all! This is one effect of the passages which say: 'I cannot justify the way I am inclined to proceed, in the end I can only say: this is simply what I do' (e.g. §§217, 219)'. What distinction can I make, then, between what seems to me right and what is right? It is tempting but wrong to say here that I know I am right if I agree with the others.

Agreement may be evidence that I am right, but it is no guarantee, for we may all turn out in the light of subsequent events to be wrong. Conversely, disagreement does not show that I am wrong. Nevertheless, it is clear that the argument against private language requires that common practice has a critical role.

Wittgenstein rejects many accounts of what it means to follow a rule, for example in terms of using tables (§201 and elsewhere), or in terms of listening to an inner voice (§232). Now what exactly cannot such accounts explain? Presumably they could explain how a man goes his way, believing he is right. And it is no objection that they could not provide justification for a way of proceeding, for neither can we produce justification in the normal case, when it is granted that we are following a rule. No; what alone those rejected accounts cannot guarantee is just this: that we are able to follow the man's procedure. (On this point see particularly §§232 and 237.) Therefore it may be concluded that nothing short of a man's practice being like ours makes his practice the following of a rule. But this does not mean that agreement turns 'seems' into 'is'. Rather: if there is agreement between myself and another, then what seems right to me is the same as what seems right to him, and so far as I am concerned for the time being, what seems right to me *is* right.

Let us return now to the private language we imagined. How is it different from gibberish? To us, after all, it is gibberish. But it might be replied: yes of course, but to the man speaking it makes sense. In this case, what is said here depends on our point of view.

Suppose we were to grant that the private language is a language. Then what would we say is *not* a language? Presumably any use of signs whatever would count, whether orderly or chaotic so far as we were concerned. And we might characterise a random use of signs which constituted a language in this way: whatever seems to the speaker right is right. But this whole supposition is a nonsense; it breaks down the distinction between following a rule and not following a rule, and it does away with the concept of language altogether. The point is this: we must be able to find order in the use of signs, we must be able to feel and judge whether the use of a sign is correct or not, for only then can we say: 'it seems to him right, and it is', or, 'it seems to him right, but mistakenly'.

The concept of sharing language enters into the judgement whether a man's use of signs is rule-governed and therefore a language, not because a man cannot follow a rule without others there to share it, but because if the judgement is made at all, it is made by other men, and on the basis of whether they can follow and share the man's practice. Thus what we called the weak version of the private language argument is at root the same as the strong version. 'A rule cannot be followed privately' comes to the same as: no-one will say that a practice which they cannot follow or take part in, which makes no sense to them, is following a rule. If language is to be used for communication, its signs must be used in ways we all can follow; but the apparent qualification here is really no qualification for us, since our judgement that a use of signs does indeed constitute a language is based on our ability to follow and take part in the practice, that is, primarily on the possibility of communication.

Earlier the conclusion of the private language argument was summarised by saying that a private language is impossible; but it is apparent now that this is too simple. What Wittgenstein actually says in §269 is: sounds which no-one else understands but which I *'appear to understand'* might be called a 'private language'. We, the onlookers, have no grounds for saying that the man speaking is understanding anything, because we can find no rule (no rhyme or reason) in what he says. Nevertheless, he may give the appearance of understanding something. There are various cases here. The incomprehensible signs might be used by a man who *usually* communicates with us rationally. Further, he may show the characteristics of understanding, such as deliberation, thoughtfulness, and so on. In certain circumstances we might even suppose that the man speaking this strange tongue is alive and sensitive to processes which we are unaware of. This supposition, however, is an extension of the normal case, for what we imagine hidden is sensitivity and movement of the whole man who speaks the language, not something independent of him.

We have seen that there are two major ways in which the concept of a private language can be made to appear plausible. Firstly it may be supposed that the language belongs to a 'metaphysical self', particularly a Cartesian or Kantian ego. Against this I have suggested that the private-language argument concerns human beings, and is not intended to refute the whole tradition of ego-centricity and solipsism.[3] Of course the conclusion of the private-language argument is incompatible with that tradition, but to say this is misleading, because the position against which the argument is directed is itself already opposed to it. The egocentric predicament really was a predicament for the ego, not for human beings;

but the speaker of the private language is a man, among others.

The other way of defending the notion of private language is to imagine that a man could have an elaborate system of signs for describing experiences which are independent of the body, signs incomprehensible to anyone but himself. But then everyone but himself would be inclined to say that this sign system was *not* a language.

It can be seen that the two objections raised to these two described possibilities of private language both rest on the same point, that judgement is made by human beings. The underlying premise appears at §241 of the *Investigations*, just prior to the private-language argument: it is what human beings say that is true and false. This means that judgement, reason and so forth belong to men already within the world, in particular not to an ego which in some way infers or constructs the natural world, including men. It means also that there are no propositions true or false independently of what men say, so that particularly, whether a private language really is a language cannot be answered except relative to someone making the judgement; it is not an *abstract* question. Thus it becomes clear that the refutation of dualism is at root the same as the refutation of solipsism. This is to be expected, since the Cartesian cogito was outside the world, independent of the body and nature, and therefore isolated, and this idea already contains what is essential to solipsism. Dualism and solipsism are both refuted if the 'I' is part of the world, and able to meet others of its kind.

The conception of judgement which belongs with the concept of a self outside the world is one of passive representation, passive because the self, being outside, cannot act in the world. This conception was made perspicuous in the *Tractatus*: a proposition is a picture of the world. A proposition has logical form in common with reality, and its signs mark out this form. Considering now the account of language in the *Investigations*, we can say that if signs be taken away from judgement, what remains is activity. The form in common between judgement and reality is the living human being. Human activity accords or conflicts with reality; it is ordered movement.

A man's judgement leads him *to do* certain things; in this action he finds accord or discord, confirmation or disconfirmation of his beliefs. Whether other men agree or disagree with his judgement does not yet determine its truth or falsity, so far as he is concerned;

agreement does not show him that what seems to him right is right, still less does disagreement show him that he is wrong.

The accord or conflict which guides judgement is found in real action, not in observation and expectation of immaterial events, of the kind envisaged earlier when postulating a private language. In such a process there is not yet defined a sense in which 'judgement agrees or conflicts with reality'. And even if a definition could be found, still it would not demonstrate the possibility of a private language, which is to be spoken by a human being, not thought by an observer in some sense in or behind the man.

Signs must be used in accord with bodily conditions and behaviour not because memory of bodily events is more reliable than memory of 'mental events', nor because the body is 'material' or 'outer' in the old dualistic meanings of those terms, but because it is in relation to what men do, their responses and their activity, that their use of signs constitutes judgement. Thus the conclusion of the private language argument can be made to follow swiftly, in one step, from the first pages of the *Investigations*: words have meaning in human activity, therefore, words whose use is linked with activity in no regular way are apparent nonsense. Essentially the same conclusion can be reached, as we have seen, by various routes, but this short one is, I think, explicitly part of the 'private language argument' as Wittgenstein presents it. For in §269, quoted above, reference is made to 'certain criteria in a man's behaviour' for his understanding or attaching meaning to words he uses; and in terms of behavioural criteria for understanding and meaning, the 'private language' is clearly problematic, since it is defined so as not to satisfy them.

In conclusion, then, language is shared between men, interwoven with their common activity. It is wrong to suppose that there are or could be languages which each man used, incomprehensibly to others, and that these would describe mental processes independent of action and behaviour. The only language that we have, the common one, is capable of conveying our inner experience. This inner experience depends on the body, its reactions and spontaneous movement. It is not a private reality; for there is no 'private order', any more than there is private language to express it.

(ii) 'Inner' and 'outer'

The language that we use to describe inner experience is common between us. The implications of this for dualism, however, need further clarification. Let us begin by considering the possibility that words whose use is based on bodily conditions and behaviour may nevertheless describe private mental processes occurring parallel to the material ones. For example, a child learns the meaning of the word 'toothache' in connection with his swollen mouth, perhaps his crying, and can use the word to tell others the degree and place of his pain; but although the word is used for communication on the basis of bodily symptoms, perhaps the child comes to realise that it refers to something with which he alone is acquainted. The question is raised: is the assumption made at §243 correct, that if words refer to immediate private sensations, no-one but the speaker could understand them?

The following argument seems plausible: rules for using a word define its meaning, but in general, a word does not only have meaning, it also has a reference, an object or event which it stands for, and so, even if we do grant that words must be used according to commonly agreed rules, that is, that they have public meaning, still this leaves open the status of the references of words, which may, particularly, be private objects as well as public ones. The suggestion is, then, that inner reports do refer to private events, even though used on the basis of shared behavioural criteria.[4]

Wittgenstein considers this suggestion explicitly at §293, the well-known 'beetle in the box' passage. He imagines everyone has his own box, which no-one else can see into, with something inside which we call a 'beetle'; but this expression, he says, would not be the name of a thing. The thing in the box has no place in the language-game at all. He continues:

That it to say: if we construe the grammar of the expression of sensation on the model of 'object and designation' the object drops out of consideration as irrelevant.

According to the model of sense and reference, a statement containing reference to an object may be meaningful if the object does not exist, for the referring expression may still have sense, but it fails to be true; it is false, or perhaps neither true nor false. Applying this model to inner reports, the possibility arises that the attribution to oneself or to another of, say, pain, which has meaning because correctly used in accord with the natural bodily manifestations of pain, may nevertheless fail to be true, in case the private object referred to does not exist. But it is just this possibility of error which, according to §293, does not exist. Essentially the same point is made at §271:

'Imagine a person whose memory could not retain *what* the word "pain" meant—so that he constantly called different things by that name—but nevertheless used the word in a way fitting in with the usual symptoms and presuppositions of pain'—in short he uses it as we all do. Here I should like to say: a wheel that can be turned though nothing else moves with it, is not part of the mechanism.

Only the behavioural criteria matter to the use of words like 'pain'; therefore there is no 'inner object'.

The simplest objection to this argument is just to deny it; perhaps with indignation, bearing in mind certain familiar epistemological problems. For the claim that inner reports do have a private reference of course straightforwardly implies that *not* only behavioural criteria do matter to their use. In this case, if a man did forget what the word 'pain' meant, and so called different things by that name, then his reports would just be wrong! The behavioural criteria may determine the correct use of inner descriptions, that is, their meaning, but the argument is precisely that they do not settle the issue of truth or falsity. In this case there would indeed be a problem how we know that each of us refers to the same thing with words like 'pain', 'sensation of red', etc. Indeed how should I know that other people refer to anything at all with such words? Perhaps other people, to follow this line of thought, are just machines going through the motions.

This whole idea, however, is wrong so far as it draws on the theory that the meaning of a word is an object, and it is incoherent insofar as it tries to combine that theory with the conception that meaning is given by use.

If we suppose that the word 'pain' refers to a private object (event or quality), then we must admit the possibility that someone who is showing all the signs of pain could nevertheless legitimately say, in the absence of the 'inner object': 'I have no pain'. (It is true that some people do not feel pain with injury that normally does cause pain, but in these cases the body itself does not react in the normal way.) The converse possibility must also be admitted, that a man who appears quite at ease, with no sign of suffering, could truly say: 'I now have that feeling which occurs when I have a terrible sore tooth, when my mouth swells and I am groaning, the feeling which I refer to by the word "pain"'. Envisaging these possibilities, however, is incompatible with supposing that the meaning of the word 'pain' is determined by its normal use in accord with the natural causes and expressions of suffering, for they postulate cases in which the word could be regularly used wholly independently of those causes and expressions. Of course those cases do make sense if we have in mind a different account of the meaning of the word 'pain', namely, that its meaning is a correlation with its alleged private reference, made necessarily in one's own case. But this conception of meaning, which properly belongs with and supports the idea of a 'private object', leads back to the possibility of private language, which has already been rejected. And the attempt to find a midway position, which grants that the meaning of inner reports is determined by their common use but retains the idea of private reference leads, we have seen, to contradiction.

Sceptical doubt concerning 'other minds' is also shown to be baseless by these considerations. Someone who is injured and showing signs of suffering is correctly seen as being in pain. The ascription of pain to another on the basis of the natural expressions of pain may in certain circumstances be wrong, but these circumstances involve counter-evidence again concerning the man's reactions and behaviour—for instance, we may imagine that once left on his own he shows signs of relief, and abruptly stops his moaning. The 'correct' uses of a proposition that determine its meaning are not to be radically distinguished from its 'true' uses; truth is not correspondence with a reality which can be separated from the circumstances that guide our judgement.

We described at the beginning of this section a version of dualism milder than the original Cartesian form. According to this dualism, a man is a combination of body and mind, but this is not meant to imply characteristic Cartesian (or neo-Cartesian) doctrines, such as the identification of concepts with images in the mind, nor is it meant to raise Cartesian problems, such as the problem of knowledge of the external world. On the contrary, the assertion that there are two substances, body and mind, is meant to be consistent with apparent commonplaces of the kind Wittgenstein assumes at the beginning of the *Investigations*, that there is a human community in the (external) world, that men use language in their various activities, that we learn the meaning of words by having their use explained to us. But the intended fit here is a poor one; this mild dualism is incoherent. The incoherence shows up in various ways, but particularly in its grasp of language and meaning. Beginning with the common world, the existence of a private, inner world behind a man's activity can apparently be inferred from his reports of mood, sensation, etc. But if there is such an inner reality, it could in principle be described by a language intelligible only to the one man whose reality it was. So far as concerns his fellow men, however, his use of signs would be no language; they could not from their position find any meaning in the signs whatsoever. Thus the weak conception of dualism implies an extreme possibility incompatible with assumptions about language and meaning of the kind Wittgenstein makes, and it contradicts itself by attempting to rest on just those assumptions. The argument then proceeds against a dualist claim made weaker still, being obliged to include explicitly stronger non-Cartesian assumptions: it is granted that the meaning of inner reports is common between men, determined by their use according to bodily conditions and behaviour, but (and this is the last ditch) it is claimed that such reports nevertheless have a private, inner reference. The distinction between meaning and reference, however, cannot bear this kind of weight in logic and epistemology; either the correlation between word and the object of reference is the source of meaning, in which case this dualist view collapses back into the previous one, or reference is to be conceived in accord with the new conception of meaning, as being defined by a method of using signs. And in this latter case, what we find is that our method of using inner reports excludes there being any inner reference. This conclusion that there is no 'inner object' described by psychological predicates signifies the end of dualism, or better, the end of the end. It is the conclusion which properly belongs with the account of language and meaning proposed early in the *Investigations*, and it points further towards a new kind of distinction between 'inner' and 'outer'—but the issues here are exceedingly difficult to grasp.

It might be thought that the argument so far already creates exegetical problems. At the beginning of the *Investigations*, Wittgenstein argues that words such as 'slab' have meaning not because they are correlated with objects, but because men use them in their activities. But now in later passages of the book, it appears to be argued that sensation-words in particular do not stand for objects, presumably as opposed to words like 'manometer', 'tooth', etc. As if no words stand for objects, but some words stand for objects less than others!

At the beginning of the *Investigations*, Wittgenstein mentions several legitimate senses in which words can be said to stand for objects; for example, to say that a word stands for an object might mean just that it has meaning, that it belongs to language (§13). But it is one particular interpretation of the dictum that is singled out as radically mistaken, namely, the one which denies that use in human activity is the origin of meaning, by claiming instead that meaning simply reflects independently given objects and their order. However, within the new conception of meaning, it will still be correct to affirm that at least some words stand for objects, and not just in a trivial sense. For of course there are objects—slabs, chairs, mountains, etc.—and they are represented in language. But this representation can no longer be regarded as a simple and undefined 'correlation'; it has to be rethought. We know that the word 'chair' derives meaning from its use in our activity, and therefore to say that the word stands for an object is to say something about that use. And whatever it is about the use of words like 'chair' which we express by saying that they stand for objects, we can expect to find absent from the use of words like 'pain'. And this will define the sense of the assertion: 'pain' is not the name of an object (or inner object).

We tried to mark the difference between physical and psychological predicates by saying that they represented two kinds of reality. But the force behind this is the old conception of language, which assumes that it is only by 'representing reality' that words have meaning. Once this conception is rejected, the relation between meaning and ontology becomes less straightforward, and less familiar. The use of language is to teach us what, if anything, is represented. 'Inner' and 'outer' will be distinguished by means of different methods of using signs in activity. Ontology will follow on, but the first problem is to clarify grammar.

The connection between self-report of pain and bodily causes and symptoms is not a rigid one. A man can claim to have pain, and we should believe him, in the absence of obvious causes or symptoms. Nevertheless, if someone does find that a pain persists with no obvious physical cause, perhaps also with no physical symptoms, or perhaps with some incapacity, he is likely to believe that there is a hidden cause, and perhaps he will seek examination by a physician. The physician too will suppose there is a physical cause. But if after thorough examination no organic basis is found, the case will probably be considered a strange one by all concerned. It might be reasoned that there is an organic basis, but present instruments and methods are not sensitive to it. If the belief that there is an organic basis for the pain is abandoned, however, then some question-mark settles over the pain. It would likely be foolish or cruel to say to the man 'Stop complaining, you are in no pain at all' (though within reason men can respond as they please). Alternatively, the doubt settles not over the pain as such, but over the whole man including his pain. Why is he honestly saying that he is in pain? This problem may involve consideration of the man's work and social life; to whom does he complain, and what follows his complaint? The suffering complained of may indeed have no cause in the body, but it may be caused by the man's life; and the cry of pain may be the only available expression, the only way left to call for help; or again, it may be the best way to become treated as an invalid.

If a man reports pain with clear bodily causes and symptoms, we take his word. Cases where this connection breaks down are the exception, and either it is assumed that physical causes are hidden, or in some way the man and his pain are regarded in an unusual light. However, now it must be stressed that these exceptions are themselves essential to our concept of pain. If they were not permitted, then a report of pain would mean 'There is something visibly wrong with my body'. And this proposition is quite unlike reports of pain as we now have them, for it is not incorrigible, and should be based on examination of one's own body. The limited value of such a proposition compared with pain reports is conspicuous, though not yet philosophically defined; it would limit self-report to what is visible to anyone, making no use of the special and unique access a man has to his own condition.

The grammar of inner reports implies that a man is the authority on his own experience. Because in general inner reports are connected with certain bodily conditions and behaviour, they have a common use and common implications. But a man does not need to base an inner report on examination of his body or his behaviour, and he is not contradicted if in a particular case the usual conditions are apparently not fulfilled. The speaker's authority also appears in another feature of the use of inner reports. We identify the sufferer of a pain, for example, as the man whose body is injured and who says he is in pain, and we do not say that two men can have the same pain. For otherwise it would presumably be possible, if one man claimed to feel pain, for another to contradict him, or to negotiate with him how severe the pain was.

It can be seen that some of these features of inner reports are exactly what is emphasised by the dualist. The dualist notes particularly that a man can truly report pain even though there is no apparent damage to his body, and he naturally takes this to mean that pain reports do not describe the body, but rather an immaterial reality. Further, the dualist will continue, this reality is known for certain, since a man cannot mistake it in himself, and it is private, for no other man can share it. The strength of dualism is that it stresses the cases in which reports of inner experience are unrelated to the body. But it cannot do justice to the rule that in general the relation must hold. At best the dualist can postulate a causal link between mental and physical processes, but causal connections can be imagined to break down entirely. Conversely, the strength of behaviourism is that it stresses the general rule, but its weakness is that it has no account of the exceptions, which are equally essential to the use of inner reports. Without the possibility of exceptions, there is no authority, no special place assigned to the speaker. Indeed, this authority cannot be explained by dualism either. If reports of pain, say, described an inner process, then they could be false even when made in accord with the normal symptoms and presuppositions of pain; but exactly this possibility of error, and the possibility of doubt which would accompany it, is not envisaged in our use of the statement 'I am in pain'. As has already been argued, the grammar of the word 'pain' shows that it describes no 'inner process' (on this see also §288).

Valid though this argument may seem to be, however, one is tempted to say that its conclusion is certainly obscure, or else obviously wrong. One resistance to the proposal that there is no 'inner reality' comes straightforwardly from introspection. In introspection we are aware of sensations and feelings and their reality is manifest; it is absurd to say that in some sense, or in any sense, these experiences are not there! But of course sensation, feeling and the rest are not being denied; the claim rather concerns the grammar of the 'inner' language, compared with the grammar of the 'outer'. However this claim too runs up against a thought-experiment. Suppose I am asked to describe the variable felt effect of a stimulus on my hand, and I describe the feeling as starting, stopping, growing more or less intense, and so on. Compare this with a case in which I am asked to describe, say, the movement and brightness of a light-point on a screen before me. What I do in these two cases seems to be just the same. I describe my inner feeling just as I describe the physical phenomenon, and there seems to be no radical difference in the 'kind of description' involved, which makes what I do in the case of the physical object 'describing a process', but what I do in the case of the sensation, 'describing nothing'. The antidote here is only to say: there may be no difference at the time in what happens in these two cases (and that there is not, is of course important), but the differences come out in their whole contexts, as soon as questions of justification, application, and comparison of results from different observers, are raised. It is the significance of the whole context to what happens at the time which is hard to grasp, for we seem disposed to imagine and believe that meaning and reality can be grasped in an instant. This belief fosters dualism, and then returns to cause it trouble. Seeing a radical difference between reports of inner experience and descriptions of the common world, but not content to accept these differences for what they are, the dualist mentality seeks to explain them by postulating two realities. But having rejected as irrelevant what happens through time, the dualist never can find two realities in his experience, which indeed is all the same, and therefore he must postulate that the outer reality lies beyond.

Judgement is made by men using signs in their activity; insofar as men share activity and their use of signs, their judgement may be compared one with another. A man makes a judgement, but others may disagree with him, and in the course of subsequent events, he may change his mind. We have forms of words, however, for assertions which cannot be contradicted or altered. They are used to express what seems at the time to be so to a man. Any judgement can be prefaced by the words 'It seems to me that . . .'. A special category is that of perceptual judgements. The claim 'I see a table' can be contradicted by others, and subsequent checks may prove the speaker wrong. But the claim 'I seem to see a table' has a different use; by expressing just what the speaker wants to say is so at the time, it stands firm regardless of what others want to say, and regardless of what may happen later. Reports of sensation, feeling, etc. are a different though connected category, and not a uniform one. They are related particularly to the condition and behaviour of the speaker. Reports of pain, for example, in some respects and circumstances are akin to descriptions of injury, in others to the natural reactions of an injured man, his crying out, his appeals for assistance and for comfort. They are expressions of a man's condition, not as it appears to anyone, but as it appears to the man himself.

Expressions of inner experience are, as it were, the limiting case of judgement. The use of propositions can commit the speaker to less and less concerning what is available to others and through time. The *authority* of the speaker is established when judgement is reduced to vanishing point. But these 'inner reports' are the extreme end of a spectrum of judgements, and this ensures their common use and meaning.

It should be remarked here that according to the Cartesian view also there is no judgement made about inner experience, for the mind was itself taken to be the medium of judgement. And this in turn is why the mind is certainly known. For suppose something in the mind were to be represented, say a perception by a faded image, then the representation could be wrong, and presumably false judgement could in principle be made by means of it. The impossibility of error and doubt relies on the inner life not being described. And so any conception of language which supposes that description alone is its function will be unable to comprehend inner reports. Wittgenstein sees that in certain circumstances they are like descriptions of different kinds, but the expressions of sensation and emotion can also be quite unlike descriptions, being akin to men's natural responses to life, for example, to a cry (see §244, and Part II, ix).

Descartes saw also that inner experience, the mind, was in time but not in space. This truth reappears, for the concept of space is now connected with perception and judgement from different positions in space-time, and what we call 'inner experience' is exactly what is observed from one point of view only. But this is not yet the right way of expression: inner experience is not observed from one point of view, rather it is the observation itself, it is the one point. Thus it can be said that the inner is the outer seen from one point of view, and in this sense, that inner and outer are identical. The outer world of natural forces and growth which is distinguished from the inner world of perception, colour, feeling and belief, is not *another* world. A man experiences one world, which is as he finds it to be. Inner and outer coincide in a man, for the time being; they are distinguished through time, by comparing experiences. Then what we can find in common is outer reality, the remainder is what is inner. And the inner does not exist in this sense: as my perception becomes less and less answerable to what can be seen from another point of view, judgement and reality itself disappears.

The Cartesian problem of knowledge of the external world, and the connected egocentric predicament, both expressed a failure to find and make work a distinction between inner and outer. One aspect of the original Cartesian problem was that subject and object were defined as separate substances, with no common element. In Wittgenstein's philosophy, notwithstanding certain analogies to the Cartesian view, this one great difference is implicit, that there is no longer a dichotomy between subject and object, since activity is the activity of subject in the objective world.

But it might be said that the problem of knowledge cannot be so quickly solved even by an epistemology of action, since there remains the problem how reality is to be known as it is in itself, independent of active relation to it. Indeed something like this thought did underlie the Cartesian problem. It was supposed that the sense-receptors of the body interacted with other material bodies, but the product of this interaction, experience, was seen as something wholly different, in retrospect absurdly different, namely immaterial perception. Perception was relative to interaction, and so could not belong with the independent material world. Thus the human body was no longer regarded as the instrument and agent of knowing, but was rather just another material body to be known by an immaterial ego. The insight that interaction is the source of knowledge can be preserved, therefore, only if interaction is taken to be fundamental. Subjective experience and the objective reality which it knows must both be defined with reference to activity, not as separate categories, in which case knowledge would be insolubly problematic, and activity after all quite irrelevant.

Human beings know, or believe they know, that the world exists independently of them. But this fact is not taken in at a glance. A child takes years to define himself, and to discover the independent world.[5] At first the child seems to perceive no difference between his own body and other things; later, he still fails to distinguish what in perception is due to himself and his position, and what is due to the object perceived. A child also learns in stages to define himself among other people; he finds that there are others like himself, that they have will and power too, which can conflict with his own; and so on. Gradually the child learns to separate out from action, perception and social life, his own self from what is independent.

It may be objected that the way knowledge develops makes no

difference to the *fact* which we come to know, that the world is independent of us. For it is not that 'independent' here means anything less than it seems to. Exactly what we find out is that nature does not depend on man, for example that men did not make the sun. But in this case, where is the non-Cartesian proposition? The Cartesian problem did not arise from the assertion of what is obvious, that human beings do not produce nature, nor from the assertion which under a natural interpretation is equally obvious, that nature exists independently of human perception and knowledge. It is not these propositions which we should have to take issue with in some odd way. On the contrary, they belong with the concept of action, or interaction. Action is ordered movement, and already implies that a man cannot do whatever he pleases. In action we find out that things are independent of us; they stop us, for example, or move us with greater power. What a child learns indeed is how to *act*, and this is how he finds out the meaning of 'independent'. The essential supposition of the modern tradition, however, was that nature is something wholly different from, and therefore beyond, human methods of representation and knowledge. But this is to be denied, since those methods are ways of interacting, and are themselves included within nature.

The problem of knowledge did not arise for the human body: the human body is a body among others, and is in contact with them. The 'I' that could doubt the existence of nature was not itself part of that world, but was an immaterial ego. The Cartesian problem is therefore solved if the 'I' is identified with the human body, that is to say, with the whole human being. And indeed, since what speaks is always the man, how should this identity be denied?

Action distinguishes the living body from other objects which are independent of it; this is so for man, and for other living creatures. But how should men go beyond the concept of self as a living creature, and beyond the concept of reality as what is given to action? Men learn not only how to act, they have language too. In language we fasten names to constancies in action which are common to us. But there is also a different use of language, interwoven not with shared activity, but with the behaviour of each individual. And each individual has authority over language of this kind, authority which rests, moreover, on a certain independence between assertion and deed. It is language, therefore, which makes the possibility of separating subject from object. For in language we apparently describe two realities: the outer reality which is independent of us, and a private inner world. The inner world must be immaterial, since it cannot be identified with the body. And under certain presuppositions, it may seem that outer reality, fixed and held static by names, cannot be identified with the flux known to action.

The philosophers of nature in the Renaissance believed that their mathematical, geometrical symbols represented ideal and absolute entities, and because of success in prediction and experiment, they supposed that this language corresponded to nature. It was thus language, or men's conception of it, which led to the postulate of absolute nature, wholly distinct and independent from the flux and relativity of human experience. But the Cartesian—or the modern—predicament seems in this way to be the extremity of a dualist thought which is already implicit in daily language. For signs seem to find objects and order in reality despite the movement of action, and it is language which carries on its surface the misleading analogy between descriptions of the common world and reports of the inner life, so that there seems to be an inner world, a shadow of the real one.

We can see now from another direction the opposition between dualist thought and the account of language proposed in the *Investigations*. For according to this account, the origin of meaning is human activity, and what language signifies cannot be grasped independently of this origin. 'Outer' and 'inner' are alike inseparable from action. Words may be used to affirm what is the case, to signify and describe objects of various kinds. But these objects are what we find by ordered activity; and they are as we find them to be, they are not hidden above or behind our experience. A man may use words also to express just what appears so to him, to express his inner life, but in this case the words do not describe a reality, a private one separate from what is common. There is no private reality in which a man is confined, nor one which accompanies action in the common world. Dualism, whether in extreme or weaker forms, is untenable.

If dualism is mistaken, it will perhaps be thought to follow that man is body alone, and that the doctrine of materialism is true, since body is matter. This reasoning, however, can be taken no longer at face value. Dualism and its two off-springs, materialism and idealism, traded off each other's weaknesses. Matter, stripped of all life and intelligence, was no basis for a whole philosophy of man, which needed to postulate mind. Philosophy based on mind found knowledge of matter problematic, or even superfluous. On the other hand mind, the impotent ethereal correlate of material processes, was irrelevant to natural philosophy, and was seen as irrelevant also to the scientific study of man. But in their opposition, dualism, materialism and idealism had much in common, namely, the concepts which they each denied or affirmed; to reject what is fundamental to any one of these doctrines is to reject the others as well.

To say that what is essential to materialism is its denial of mind does not yet define a positive doctrine. Particularly, the simple denial of mind so far fails to comprehend and resolve the problems which made necessary the postulate of mind in addition to matter. As a positive doctrine, materialism asserts that matter is all that exists. But what is *matter*? It is clear that the definitions of seventeenth-century science are no longer adequate, and have been much transformed in the present century. Perhaps 'matter' should be defined as whatever is to be found by physics. At the foundation of contemporary physics, however, it is affirmed that what is observed depends on our methods of measurement. Insofar as this is so, there is no longer justification for the view that physics is the unique access to what exists. Physics discovers what is suited to its instruments and procedures; by other means other things are discovered. These 'other means' include many and various forms of life. What is 'outer'—reality—is no longer stripped of all qualities which are relative to men. The inner life is a measure of the richness and diversity of reality, and becomes real when it is common to all.

The implication of the arguments given in this chapter is that man is a unity, one living being. But this being is not 'material' in the sense of the philosophy and science from the seventeenth to nineteenth centuries. Rather, the human being acts, speaks, is conscious, shows intelligence, perceives, feels, is afraid, hopes; and so on. To correct the old picture, one might say now that the body is matter, but in such organisation that it is alive. And to emphasise the purposeful nature of life, and the correspondence between human beings, one might say that we are guided by a spirit common to all. But there is a problem of language here. The words 'matter' and 'spirit' retain their old connotations, worlds apart, each denying the validity of the other. We need new concepts to reaffirm the unity.

The problem of the unity of man re-appears now in another form. Action is the foundation, but it is not one whole; it is diverse, and cannot be circumscribed. Unity cannot be achieved, however, by denying our humanity, as if by ascending higher; this is to pass over what we do have in common. Nor can diversity be resolved by force; to arrest action is to suppress and distort reality, and is no improvement. Unity is to be found in the face of differences, opposition, and ignorance; it is hard to imagine and to achieve, and awaits the right attempts.

Notes

CHAPTER I

1. The argument used above which draws on the non-arbitrary nature of truth does not appear at all, so far as I can see, in the *Tractatus*. It may be beneath the surface where the picture theory first appears in the *Notebooks*, pp. 6ff. The argument was suggested to me by the *Cratylus*, in which Plato is led partly by it to the tentative conclusion that words must *sound like* what they represent, or at least, that they must have done so originally; characteristically, Plato was concerned with spoken language, not with written. Plato, unlike the young Wittgenstein, had trouble accepting the conclusion to which he was led.
2. This example of analysis is given in the *Investigations*, §60. I believe it shows what Wittgenstein had in mind in the *Tractatus*, but the main points made in this subsection do not depend on this being so.
3. I believe that this is the bare structure of the celebrated argument given by Hume in his *Enquiry* (2: IV). What Hume says needs to be justified by induction—hence introducing circularity—is not the conclusion of a particular inductive inference, but is a proposition which, together with the original evidence, entails the conclusion. An example of such a proposition would be that the future will be like the past.
4. In the Hermetic Philosophy, the Macrocosm is represented by the circle, and the Microcosm by the axial point, the symbol for both thus being⊙
5. For discussion of the concept of operation and of the symbolic notation see Anscombe (1: chs. 8 and 10) and Kenny (1: ch. 5, pp. 85ff.)
6. The *Tractatus* accounts of symbolism in relation to the doctrine of showing have received much attention in the literature. For example, Professor Anscombe discusses formal concepts and tautologies (1: chs. 9 and 13), Kenny discusses logical syntax, tautologies and identity (1: ch. 3), and Pears, tautologies (1: ch. 4).

CHAPTER 2

1. Following Koyré, I use the term 'modern science' for the science of the seventeenth and eighteenth centuries which lasted until the present century, i.e. the period, roughly, between Galileo and Einstein (Koyré, 2: p. 89n). The following discussion of some assumptions of modern science is essential to the aims of this book, but is necessarily brief. For interpretation of this philosophically and historically complex topic I have relied particularly on the following: E. A. Burtt (1), E. J. Dijksterhuis (1), M. Jammer (1) and A. Koyré (3, 4, 5). I should like to record a special debt to Burtt's study, for the idea

which forms the basis of this chapter, that the major themes and problems in modern philosophy were closely tied to the assumptions of modern physical science.

2. The works by Dijksterhuis, Jammer, and Koyré (3, 5) cited in the preceding note contain discussion of Aristotelian physics and references to primary material (mainly the *Physics*).

3. That is, superstition is nothing other than the belief in the causal nexus. Pears and McGuiness' translation has been changed to secure this meaning, in accordance with Wittgenstein's note to Ogden of 1922 (*Letters to C. K. Ogden*, p. 31).

4. The problem of primary and secondary qualities is a complex one. Primary material includes Descartes (1: Second Meditation) and Locke, J. (1: II, VIII). Burtt (1) provides excellent commentary.

5. Similarities and differences between Cartesian dualism and earlier forms are discussed by Burtt (1: pp. 113ff.) and by Copleston (1: pp. 120ff.).

6. A fuller analysis of Locke's doctrine of abstract ideas and of Berkeley's criticisms is given by Craig (1).

7. Stenius has argued, however, that the 'objects' of the *Tractatus* include properties as well as spatial particulars (1: V, 1). Textual evidence against this view has been adduced by Copi (1: 4).

8. On this subject of the influence of late-nineteenth-century physics on Wittgenstein it is also interesting that, as Toulmin has observed (1: p. 66), the notion of 'logical space' originates in Boltzmann's thermodynamics.

9. This is sometimes known as Russell's 'principle of acquaintance'; see, for example, Russell (1: p. 60).

10. On this analysis (by whatever name) see, for example, Russell (2, 3), Schlick (1) and Ayer (1).

11. On philosophical behaviourism see, for example, Carnap (3). On statements about the past see, for example, Ayer (1: pp. 101–2, also Introduction to 2nd ed., p. 19). Carnap conceived the whole reductionist programme in grand manner in his (1), and tried to show how various kinds of analysis would proceed.

12. On the verification principle see, for example, Schlick (2) and Ayer (1). On the criterion of meaning see, for example, Ayer (1: including Introduction to 2nd ed.); and for an historical survey of its progress, Hempel (1). On the elimination of metaphysics see, for example, Carnap (2), Ayer (1: I); and on positivist attitudes to ethics and theology, Ayer (1: VI).

13. Discussion of Hume's philosophy and of Kant's is beyond the scope of this book. References are Hume (1, 2), and Kant (1).

14. See, for example, Russell (4) and Ayer (1: VII).

15. See, for example, Ayer (1: VII) and Carnap (1: 63–6).

16. This difference between the *Tractatus* and the Kantian philosophy is stressed here because of its importance to the general theme of the present work. In other respects there are strong similarities, discussed, for example, by Pears (1: Introduction) and by Stenius (1: XI). Wittgenstein is known to have been impressed by Schopenhauer's work in his youth, and several commentators have pointed to connections between Schopenhauer's transcendental idealism and Wittgenstein's solipsism; for example, Anscombe (1: pp. 12, 168) and Hacker (1: pp. 58ff.).

17. Ryle gives a penetrating, and an amusing, description of the tendency to define mind by what it is not (1: p. 20). On the status of numbers, see Frege (1: II, 21–6, 61). On what goodness is not, see Moore (1), on the so-called 'naturalistic fallacy'.

CHAPTER 3

1. Einstein (1). Nearly all that follows concerning relativity theory can be found in Einstein's masterful popular exposition (2). I am indebted to Bernstein's little book on Einstein (1), which helped me to see the philosophy in the theory.
2. It may be noted also that Heisenberg later found in Einstein's proposition— that the theory decides what we can observe—the inspiration which led him to the Uncertainty Principle (Heisenberg, 1: pp. 77ff.) The idea expressed by the proposition is one fundamental to twentieth-century philosophy and physics.
3. In Newtonian mechanics it did not matter that the velocity of light was additive, and so varied between frames of reference. The crisis arose rather in electrodynamics, during the nineteenth century, culminating in the realisation that Maxwell's equations presupposed the invariance of the speed of light. Einstein's solution was to construct a new mechanics on the basis of this invariance.
4. The sense in which space and time form a continuum in Special Theory was clarified by Minkowski's four-dimensional pseudo-Euclidean geometry. See Minkowski (1), or Einstein (2: ch. XVII and App. II).
5. Sections referred to throughout Part II are in the *Philosophical Investigations* unless otherwise stated. Where possible I have indicated the sections of the *Investigations* to which a particular section or subsection is intended to be relevant, following the title of that section or subsection.

CHAPTER 4

1. Translated by F. M. Cornford (Cornford, 1). All textual references in this sub-section are to the *Theaetetus* unless otherwise stated. Cornford's translation is used for direct quotations, and indirect quotations in general conform to its terminology.
2. See, for example, the *Meno*, *Phaedo* and *Sophist*.
3. Diels Fragment 2, translated by P. Wheelwright (Wheelwright, 1).

CHAPTER 5

1. Bennett (1: pp. 213–14) and Strawson (1: pp. 42–9) distinguish strong and weak versions of the private-language argument roughly along these lines, and reject the former, while granting the latter.
2. See, for example, Rhees (1); also Malcolm (1: pp. 73–4).
3. In this respect I disagree with the interpretation given by several defenders of the private-language argument, e.g. Kenny (1: pp. 16–17) and Hacker

(1: pp. 201, 217ff.) Attempts to refute egocentricity and solipsism by means of the argument are in my view as misconceived as the (equally forceful) attempts to do the converse, which have been discussed.

4. For arguments of this kind see, for example, Locke, D. (1: pp. 93 ff.); cf. also Blackburn (1).

5. I am indebted to Piaget's work for the line of thought in this paragraph, for example his (1).

Bibliographical References

A. *Wittgenstein's works cited in the text (in order of composition)*

'Notes on Logic' (September 1913), repr. in *Notebooks 1914–16*, pp. 93–106.
Notebooks 1914–16, ed. G. H. von Wright and G. E. M. Anscombe, trans. by G. E. M. Anscombe (Oxford: Blackwell, 1961).
Tractatus Logico-Philosophicus, trans. by D. F. Pears and B. F. McGuiness (London: Routledge & Kegan Paul, 1961).
Letters to C. K. Ogden, ed. G. H. von Wright (Oxford: Blackwell; London and Boston: Routledge & Kegan Paul, 1973).
'Some Remarks on Logical Form', *Proceedings of the Aristotelian Society*, supp. vol. ix (1929), 162–71.
Philosophical Remarks, ed. R. Rhees, trans. by R. Hargreaves and R. White (Oxford: Blackwell, 1975).
Philosophical Grammar, ed. R. Rhees, trans. by A. Kenny (Oxford: Blackwell, 1974).
The Blue and Brown Books (Oxford: Blackwell, 1958).
Philosophical Investigations, ed. G. E. M. Anscombe and R. Rhees, trans. by G. E. M. Anscombe (Oxford: Blackwell, 1953).
Zettel, ed. G. E. M. Anscombe and G. H. von Wright, trans. by G. E. M. Anscombe (Oxford: Blackwell, 1967).
On Certainty, ed. G. E. M. Anscombe and G. H. von Wright, trans. by D. Paul and G. E. M. Anscombe (Oxford: Blackwell, 1969).
Vermischte Bemerkungen, ed. G. H. von Wright (Frankfurt a.M.: Suhrkamp, 1977). (Remarks from the period 1914 to 1951).

B. *Other works cited*

Anscombe, G. E. M., (1) *An Introduction to Wittgenstein's Tractatus* (London: Hutchinson, 1959).
Ayer, A. J., (1) *Language, Truth and Logic* (London: Gollancz, 1936). 2nd ed., revised (1946).

Ayer, A. J., (2) 'Can there be a Private Language?', *Proceedings of the Aristotelian Society*, supp. vol. xxviii (1954), 63–76. Reprinted in *Wittgenstein*, ed. G. Pitcher (London: Macmillan, 1968). Page references to this volume.

Bennett, J., (1) *Kant's Analytic* (Cambridge: Cambridge University Press, 1966).

Berkeley, G., (1) *The Principles of Human Knowledge* (1710), in *The Works of George Berkeley*, ed. A. A. Luce and T. E. Jessop, vol. ii (London: Thomas Nelson & Sons, 1949).

—— (2) *De Motu* (1721), in A. A. Luce and T. E. Jessop (ed.), op. cit., vol. iv (1951).

Bernstein, J., (1) *Einstein* (London: Collins/Fontana, 1973).

Blackburn, S. W., (1) 'How to Refer to Private Experience', *Proceedings of the Aristotelian Society*, lxxv (1974–5), 201–13.

Burtt, E. A., (1) *The Metaphysical Foundations of Modern Physical Science*, 2nd ed. (London: Routledge & Kegan Paul, 1932).

Carnap, R., (1) *Der Logische Aufbau der Welt* (Berlin: 1928). English translation by R. A. George, *The Logical Structure of the World* (London: Routledge & Kegan Paul, 1967).

—— (2) 'The Elimination of Metaphysics through Logical Analysis of Language', in *Logical Positivism*, ed. A. J. Ayer (Glencoe, Illinois: Free Press, 1959). Original article appeared in *Erkenntnis*, vol. ii (1932).

—— (3) 'Psychology in Physical Language', in *Logical Positivism*, ed. A. J. Ayer (Glencoe, Illinois: Free Press, 1959). Original article appeared in *Erkenntnis*, vol. iii (1932–3).

Copi, I. M., (1) 'Objects, Properties and Relations in the "Tractatus"', *Mind*, lxvii (1958), 145–65.

Copleston, F., (1) *A History of Philosophy*, vol. iv (London: Burns & Oates, 1960).

Cornford, F. M., (1) *Plato's Theory of Knowledge* (London: Routledge & Kegan Paul, 1935).

Craig, E. J., (1) 'Berkeley's Attack on Abstract Ideas', *Philosophical Review*, 77 (1968), 425–37.

Descartes, R., (1) *Meditations on First Philosophy* (1641); quotations from and references to *The Philosophical Works of Descartes*, trans. by E. S. Haldane and G. R. T. Ross, vol. i (Cambridge: Cambridge University Press, 1911, repr. 1967).

Dietrich, R-A., (1) *Sprache und Wirklichkeit in Wittgensteins Tractatus* (Tübingen: Niemeyer, 1973).

Dijksterhuis, E. J., (1) *The Mechanization of the World Picture*, trans.

by C. Dikshoorn (Oxford: Oxford University Press, 1961).

Einstein, A., (1) 'Zur Elektrodynamik bewegter Körper', *Annalen der Physik*, 1905. Reprinted in *The Principle of Relativity*, a collection of papers by Lorentz, Einstein, Minkowski and Weyl, trans. by W. Perrett and G. B. Jeffery, with notes by A. Sommerfeld (New York: Dover, 1952).

—— (2) *Relativity*, trans. by R. W. Lawson (London: Methuen, 1920; University Paperback, 1960).

—— (3) 'Autobiographical Notes', in *Albert Einstein: Philosopher–Scientist*, vol. i, ed. P. A. Schlipp, Library of Living Philosophers, vol. vii (La Salle, Illinois: Open Court, 1949).

Frege, G., (1) *Die Grundlagen der Arithmetik* (Breslau: 1884). Parallel text edition with English translation by J. L. Austin, *The Foundations of Arithmetic*, 2nd ed. (Oxford: Blackwell, 1953).

—— (2) *Grundgesetze der Arithmetik*, vol. i (Jena: 1893), vol. ii (Jena: 1903). §56 of vol. ii is included in *Translations from the Philosophical Writings of Gottlob Frege*, ed. P. Geach and M. Black, 2nd ed. (Oxford: Blackwell, 1960).

—— (3) 'The Thought: A Logical Enquiry'. English translation by A. M. and Marcelle Quinton in *Mind*, lxv (1956), 289–311. Original article appeared in *Beiträge zur Philosophie des Deutschen Idealismus*, i (1918–19), 30–53.

Galileo, G., (1) *Dialogue on the Great World Systems* (1632), in the Salusbury translation (1661) revised by G. de Santillana (Chicago: Chicago University Press, 1953).

Griffin, J., (1) *Wittgenstein's Logical Atomism* (Oxford: Oxford University Press, 1964).

Hacker, P. M. S., (1) *Insight and Illusion. Wittgenstein on Philosophy and the Metaphysics of Experience* (Oxford: Oxford University Press, 1972).

Heisenberg, W., (1) *Physics and Beyond: Encounters and Conversations*, trans. by A. J. Pomerans (London: George Allen & Unwin, 1971).

Hempel, C., (1) 'Problems and Changes in the Empiricist Criterion of Meaning', *Revue Internationale de Philosophie*, 4 (1950), 41–63.

Herz, H., (1) *Die Prinzipien der Mechanik. In neuem Zusammenhange dargestellt* (Leipzig: 1894). English translation by D. E. Jones and J. T. Walley, *The Principles of Mechanics, presented in a new form*, (New York: Dover, 1956).

Hume, D., (1) *A Treatise of Human Nature* (1739). References to L. A. Selby-Bigge's edition (Oxford: Oxford University Press, 1888).

Hume, D., (2) *An Enquiry Concerning Human Understanding* (1777). References to L. A. Selby-Bigge's edition, 2nd ed. (Oxford: Oxford University Press, 1902).

Jammer, M., (1) *Concepts of Space. The History of Theories of Space in Physics*, 2nd ed. (Cambridge, Mass.: Harvard University Press, 1969).

Kant, I., (1) *Kritik der reinen Vernunft* (Riga: 1781; rev. ed. 1787).

Kenny, A., (1) *Wittgenstein* (London: Allen Lane/The Penguin Press, 1973).

Koyré, A., (1) 'Galileo 'and the Scientific Revolution of the Seventeenth Century', *The Philosophical Review*, 52 (1943), 333–48. Reprinted in (5) below, page references to this volume.

—— (2) 'An Experiment in Measurement', Lecture, American Philosophical Society, 14 November 1952; published in *Proceedings of the American Philosophical Society*, 97 (1953), 222–37. Reprinted in (5) below, page references to this volume.

—— (3) *From the Closed World to the Infinite Universe* (Baltimore: Johns Hopkins Press, 1957).

—— (4) *Newtonian Studies* (London: Chapman & Hall, 1965).

—— (5) *Metaphysics and Measurement: Essays in the Scientific Revolution* (London: Chapman & Hall, 1968).

Locke, D., (1) *Myself and Others. A Study in Our Knowledge of Minds* (Oxford: Oxford University Press, 1968).

Locke, J., (1) *An Essay Concerning Human Understanding* (1690), ed. P. H. Nidditch (Oxford: Oxford University Press, 1975).

Mach, E., (1) *Die Mechanik in ihrer Entwicklung, historisch-kritisch dargestellt* (Leipzig: 1883). English translation by T. J. McCormack, *The Science of Mechanics: A Critical and Historical Account of its Development* (Lasalle, Illinois: Open Court, 1942).

Malcolm, N., (1) 'Wittgenstein's *Philosophical Investigations*', *Philosophical Review*, 63 (1954), 530–59. Revised version in N. Malcolm, *Knowledge and Certainty: Essays and Lectures* (Englewood Cliffs, N.J.: Prentice-Hall, 1963). Reprinted in *Wittgenstein*, ed. G. Pitcher (London: Macmillan, 1968). Page references to this volume.

McGuire, J. E., (1) 'Force, Active Principles and Newton's Invisible Realm', *Ambix*, 15 (1968), 154–208.

Minkowski, H., (1) 'Space and Time' (1908), in *The Principle of Relativity*, a collection of papers by Lorentz, Einstein, Minkowski and Weyl, trans. by W. Perrett and G. B. Jeffery, with notes by A. Sommerfeld (New York: Dover, 1952). Reprinted in *Problems of Space and Time*, ed. J. J. C. Smart (New York: Macmillan, 1964).

Moore, G. E., (1) *Principia Ethica* (Cambridge: Cambridge University Press, 1903).

Newton, I., (1) *The Mathematical Principles of Natural Philosophy* (1687), in the Motte translation revised by F. Cajori (Berkeley: University of California Press, 1960).

—— (2) *Opticks, Or a Treatise of the Reflections, Refractions, Inflections, and Colours of Light* (2nd ed. 1717). Quotations from the Dover edition (New York: 1952).

Pears, D., (1) *Wittgenstein* (London: Collins/Fontana, 1971).

Piaget, J., (1) *La construction du réel chez l'enfant* (Neuchâtel and Paris: 1950). English translation by Margaret Cook: *The Child's Construction of Reality* (London: Routledge & Kegan Paul, 1955).

Ramsey, F. P., (1) 'Facts and Propositions', *Proceedings of the Aristotelian Society*, supp. vol. vii (1927), 153–70. Reprinted in F. P. Ramsey, *The Foundations of Mathematics and other logical essays*, ed. R. B. Braithwaite (London: Routledge & Kegan Paul, 1931). Page reference to this volume.

Rhees, R., (1) 'Can there be a private language?', *Proceedings of the Aristotelian Society*, supp. vol. xxviii (1954), 77–94. Reprinted in *Wittgenstein*, ed. G. Pitcher (London: Macmillan, 1968).

Russell, B., (1) *The Problems of Philosophy* (Oxford: Oxford University Press, 1912; 2nd ed. 1967).

—— (2) *Our Knowledge of the External World* (Chicago: Open Court, 1914).

—— (3) 'On the Relation of Sense-data to Physics', *Scientia*, no. 4 (1914). Reprinted in *Mysticism and Logic*, B. Russell (London: George Allen & Unwin, 1917).

—— (4) *The Analysis of Mind* (London: George Allen & Unwin, 1921).

—— (5) *My Philosophical Development* (London: George Allen & Unwin, 1959).

Ryle, G., (1) *The Concept of Mind* (London: Hutchinson, 1949).

Schlick, M., (1) 'Positivism and Realism', in *Logical Positivism*, ed. A. J. Ayer (Glencoe, Illinois: Free Press, 1959). Original article appeared in *Erkenntnis*, vol. iii (1932–3).

—— (2) 'Meaning and Verification', *Philosophical Review*, 45 (1936). Reprinted in *Readings in Philosophical Analysis*, ed.

H. Feigl and W. Sellars (New York: Appleton-Century-Crofts, 1949).

Stenius, E., (1) *Wittgenstein's Tractatus: A Critical Exposition of its Main Lines of Thought* (Oxford: Blackwell, 1960).

Strawson, P. F., (1) 'Review of Wittgenstein's *Philosophical Investigations*', *Mind*, lxiii (1954), 70–99. Reprinted in *Wittgenstein*, ed. G. Pitcher (London: Macmillan, 1968). Page references to this volume.

Toulmin, S., (1) 'Ludwig Wittgenstein', *Encounter* (London), vol. xxxii (January 1969), 58–71.

Westfall, R. S., (1) *Force in Newton's Physics* (London: Macdonald; New York: American Elsevier, 1971).

Wheelwright, P., (1) *Heracleitus* (New York: Atheneum, 1963).

Index of Names

Index of Subjects